A stronomically, Black Holes are have imploded, shrinking in u⌐ so tightly compressed, and their gravitational forces so overwhelmingly strong, that not even light can escape them; hence the name. Theoretical physics states that Black Holes are doorways to parallel universes, alternate realities, and higher dimensions, and making contact with one in our daily lives can often feel like that, as if we have been uprooted from the everyday reality of the Light World and thrust into an alien environment, an Underworld which, although ominous and threatening, can also be the repository of vast riches and the wealth of the knowledge of the subconscious.

Astrologically, Black Holes promote change and transition. Highly mercurial and quixotic, with a power base that makes Pluto seem infantile and a capriciousness which makes Uranus' disruptions pale in comparison, Black Holes represent the *volte face*, the sudden, swift, complete reversal of the status quo, when conditions change in the twinkling of an eye to ones wholly unrecognizable from what went before. Returning to the way things were becomes impossible; in essence, you have changed universes—you can't go home again.

Panta Rei Press is an imprint of Crossroad Press Publishing

Copyright © 2015 by Alex Miller
Cover illustration by Dave Dodd
Design by Aaron Rosenberg
ISBN 978-1-941408-43-8

First edition

# THE BLACK HOLE BOOK

## BY ALEX MILLER

# DEDICATION

*For Joseph Campbell, who opened my Eyes*
*For Alan Watts, who opened my Mind*
*and for John, who opened my Soul*

*A Word to the Reader:*
*You have this book for a reason.*
*An aspect of yourself which guides*
*and informs your growth and development*
*has placed it in your hands consciously.*
*Honor that.*

# CONTENTS

# FOREWORD

Why Black Holes? Well, for one thing, in the words of the old adage, "because they're there." And like everything else in the universe, they are a part of us, as we are of them.

Light, in its varying forms of radiant energy, permeates our existence. We are physical beings born of the etheric matrix which comprises the energetic universe; the molecules and atoms that compose our bodies were formed billions of years ago in the hydrogen furnaces of stars long dead, self-destructive supernovas which spewed the building blocks of carbon-based life forms into the cosmos.

Matter is simply light vibrating at a slower rate, radiant energy trapped into the illusion of solidity. Vast intergalactic voids permeate the spaces between the nuclei and electrons of the molecules in our bodies, like so many mini solar systems; as much material substance as there is, there is infinitely more space. In this we see astrology's basic credo, "As above, so below." The void of space is mirrored within ourselves, and in that space, we find the Black Holes.

We may not see them, but they exist, and have a verifiable effect on our world and our lives. Powerful, enigmatic, transformational and inescapable, Black Holes (and other Deep Space anomalies such as Quasars, Pulsars and Masers) are the latest piece in the puzzle of creation which astrologers for millennia have attempted to reassemble into a picture portraying the whole of existence, striving for a fuller understanding of the cosmos and our place within it.

My own journey with these points began more than twenty years ago, when in 1989 I was handed a copy of Llewellyn's *Spiritual, Metaphysical & New Trends in Modern Astrology*, a collection of essays edited by Joan McEvers, which included a chapter by Philip Sedgwick entitled "Galactic Astrology." Those twenty-five pages opened a whole new world for me, one I want to share with you in this book. At the time, unbeknownst to me, my progressed Sun was transiting over the event horizon, or orb of influence, of the reality-warping Black Hole at 6 Virgo, and had just conjoined a Pulsar at 3 Virgo, an anomaly informational in nature which provides insights and expands consciousness. The timing was right.

I followed this introduction with Sedgwick's full length work, *The Astrology of Deep Space*, and began my own researches using the points he listed, chronicling the manifestations these Deep Space behemoths evoked, and working with them in my own life and the charts of clients across the globe.  By 1993 I had begun writing and publishing in this field, in print outlets such as "Welcome To Planet Earth" and "The Mountain Astrologer," and later online for Maya del Mar's "Daykeeper Journal." Drawing on astrophysics theory and the works of leaders in the field such as Stephen Hawking, Kip Thorne and Michio Kaku (a selected bibliography appears at the end of this book), and correlating that to my own experience and observations of the world around me, I developed a broader under-standing of how these points interact with, inform, and transform our reality.

It is that perspective I wish to communicate in *The Black Hole Book*. We'll begin with a brief overview, followed by detailed inter-pretive material you can apply to your own life, to better under-stand the ways Black Holes impact you personally. Later sections of the book will provide practical examples of their effects from mun-dane events and the biographies of well-known individuals, as well as in-depth explorations of the astrophysical theories of Black Holes and the astrological usage which stems from them. We'll also dis-cuss mythologies the world over which resonate to these energies, and provide metaphors for our experience of them.

I still concentrate my work on the original points I began my research with two decades ago, and those will be the focus of this book. However, many more have been discovered since, and that process of scientific discovery is ongoing, and will likely never end. The interested reader will find some of these additional points in the appendix, although, of necessity, this list will always be incom-plete. As scientific knowledge grows, our understanding of these points will no doubt alter, but what the Black Hole represents, the metaphors it conjures in the collective consciousness—of isolation, dislocation, transformation, overwhelming and inescapable power, and access to the creative force of the unknown, the limitless potential of the unmanifest—these will remain constant, and continue to resonate in the human experience. It is my profound hope that this Black Hole primer may guide you as you embark upon your own exploration of the mysteries of the universe, and your Deep Space connection to it.

# AN INTRODUCTION
# TO BLACK HOLES

Astronomically, Black Holes are the remnants of stars which have imploded, shrinking in upon themselves until they are so tightly compressed, and their gravitational forces so overwhelmingly strong, that not even light can escape them; hence the name. When a star of sufficient mass ages, and begins to exhaust its fuel, it cannot support the weight of its own circumference, and collapses in upon itself. Sometimes the star explodes in a dramatic supernova, spewing gases and elements many light years into space; at others the compression continues to a virtual pinpoint which still retains all the mass of the original star, and the Black Hole is born, a gravity well which is essentially cut off from this universe, where the ordinary laws of physics do not apply. These exist both within our galaxy and outside it, but only suns with a mass at least three times that of our own have enough gravitational force to become Black Holes at the end of their life cycle. Some are relatively small, but these deep space anomalies can also come in the supermassive variety, cosmic behemoths which power spiral galaxies such as the Milky Way, their insatiable maws slowly but inexorably sucking in the associated stars, causing the galaxy to rotate, like water coiling down a drain.

Astrologically, Black Holes promote change and transition, and can be difficult to work with. Highly mercurial, with a power base that makes Pluto seem infantile, Black Holes represent the *volte face*, the sudden, swift, complete reversal of the status quo, when conditions change in the twinkling of an eye to ones wholly unrecognizable from what went before, and returning to the way things were becomes impossible. In essence, you have changed universes; you can't go home again. Many of these manifestations will seem negative, particularly to humans, who typically don't like change, but the high drama they evoke can often elicit rags-to-riches stories, such as *Harry Potter* author JK Rowling (with Sun conjunct a Black Hole), or even rags-to-riches-back-to-rags stories like investment banker/fraud Bernard Madoff (with Sun in square). Wherever you see dramatic turnarounds or improbable happenings, positive or negative, Black Hole energy is there.

Black Holes act as liminal guardians, portals between realties. As such they govern stages of maturation, both physical, such as birth, puberty and death; and socio-cultural, such as losing one's virginity, marriage, the birth of a child, the death of a parent, and divorce or loss of a spouse. But it is not just in these life-altering moments that Black Hole energies can be seen. They are active even on a daily level, any time we act to change our reality, for example, by leaving one environment for another, or deciding when to go to sleep or when to wake. At a basic level, they may be connected to the very process of choice and change itself, enabling us to choose from between opposing alternatives and then enact these choices.

Theoretical physics states that Black Holes are doorways to parallel universes, alternate realities, and higher dimensions, and making contact with one in our daily lives can often feel like that, as if we have been uprooted from the everyday reality of the Light World and thrust into an alien environment, an Underworld which, although ominous and threatening, can also be the repository of vast riches and the wealth of the knowledge of the subconscious. The Black Hole zone is one of unlimited creativity, encompassing as it does all potential realities, allowing the native who is well connected to envision, not just the way things are, but the ways they might become. Two such tapped-in individuals are Albert Einstein, whose theory of relativity forever altered our scientific perspective, and Thomas Edison, whose nearly 1000 US patents bespeak his tremendous inventiveness; both men had Sun in square to Black Holes.

Black Holes are sources of energy drain, requiring more of our focus and attention than we would often like, and they come in many forms—health crises, parenting issues, relatives or friends needing emotional support, financial troubles—depending upon the celestial body to which they are contacted, and the affairs that body governs. They can also act as sources of energy attraction, repositories of incredible reserves of power; some folks seem to have the knack of tapping these energies, others merely contribute

to them. Singer Michael Jackson (Sun conjunct a Black Hole), arguably the world's first global superstar, and Princess Diana (Sun in
semi-square), the "People's Princess," both epitomize the type who
absorb the energies, attentions and projections of millions of their
fellow citizens, becoming almost quasi-divine in the crucible of
their fans' adulation.

Black Holes tend to extremes, and are often active at times when
record-setting or precedent-breaking events occur. They can produce manifestations which are polar opposites, a seemingly con-
tradictory pattern of providing both the best and the worst of any
given situation, and predicting in advance which way the cosmic
cat will jump is virtually impossible. On March 12, 1992, with Venus
exactly conjoined the Black Hole at 28 Aquarius, two high profile
relationship shifts were announced: Tammy Faye Bakker had filed
for divorce from jailbird televangelist hubby Jim; and longtime,
notorious bachelor Warren Beatty, aged 55, had finally married,
to Annette Bening, both dramatic changes in relationship status
evoked by Venus' deep space contact.

Any celestial body contacted by a Black Hole is susceptible to its
influence; in the natal chart, these conditions will form a lifelong pattern, providing manifestations at appropriate developmental levels
as the individual ages and matures, allowing the native to adapt to
their effects over time and essentially form a working relationship
with these energies, however lopsided. In the transit sky, planetary
interaction with Black Holes provokes random, often shocking or
extreme, sometimes one-of-a-kind manifestations, watershed events
which are life-altering for those involved, and which reverberate far
beyond their origins. The 9/11 attacks, the start of the Iraq War, the
massive Indian Ocean Tsunami of 2004, and Hurricane Katrina's
New Orleans landfall all occurred with Sun conjoined or in hard
aspect to Black Holes, to name just a few from recent memory.

Relative size and distance have no effect on astrological interpretation; no added weight is given to Venus' proximity to earth,
nor to Jupiter's vastness, and Pluto's recent demotion by astronomers to minor planet status has not altered its psychic impact one
whit. Similarly, the almost incomprehensible distances between us
and these deep space anomalies has no bearing upon their effectiveness. Their position in the Tropical Zodiac is computed just as with

Fixed Stars which lie above or below the ecliptic, and they "transit" at the same rate, shifting one degree approximately every 72 years. Moreso than any other recent scientific theory, except perhaps for relativity in the early decades of the last century, Black Holes have captured the imagination of the general population and entered the cultural lingo with a startling impact. Seen as a metaphor for alienation, disempowerment, waste and dissociation, Black Holes have emerged as a powerful image of our times.

Several major themes emerge in the lives of those whom the Black Hole touches, although the ways these manifest are as unique and individual as the lives they affect. Predominantly, these involve changeability; personal magnetism/repulsion; extreme instability/unpredictability; unique perspective; attraction of unparalleled, singular, often bizarre experiences; energy absorption, transmutation, or depletion; and a greater than typical impact on one's environment or peers.

"Interdimensionality" is a term I'll use to encapsulate the quality of changeability or differentiation with which Black Hole natives grapple, no matter which area of their lives it affects, and this is best illustrated by using the example of the Black Hole Sun individual, as central to one's being and thus reverberating throughout the entirety of the native's life. This quality is an adaptive mechanism which enables these individuals to blend into their surroundings, chameleon-like, and assume traits or characteristics enhancing their image or facilitating their interactions with their current audience. This "all things to all people" quality effectively splinters the native's primary reality into many sharply defined alternate realities, depending on the circumstances they encounter, in each of which they appear and act differently. To some extent we all do this, it's termed "compartmentalization," but for the Black Hole native these divisions and the manifestations they evoke, culled from the infinity of nonphysical parallel universes, alternate dimensions, and potential realms which open out from the tear in spacetime which the Black Hole creates, can be especially dramatic and extreme.

This quality is more useful for some than others. Actors notably benefit from Black Hole contacts in adapting to various roles, and making them believable. Meryl Streep, with Sun squared a Black Hole, and Albert Finney, with Sun conjoined, are acknowledged masters of this ability to become the parts they play. Heath Ledger, with Sun opposed a Black Hole, was cut from the same cloth but tragically lacked the internal mechanism to separate himself from the character, and ultimately succumbed to this inability to extricate himself from the parallel reality of his performance. Examples of actors who embody the star power they convey, adapting the role to themselves rather than themselves to the role, include Elizabeth Taylor, John Wayne, Joan Crawford and Cary Grant, all with Sun opposed a Black Hole. Elizabeth Taylor, in particular, also personifies the disruptive, extreme manifestations which can constellate about Black Hole Sun personalities, with her eight marriages and highly public divorces, dramatic weight fluctuations, and several severe illnesses bringing her to the brink of death, only to rally via the recuperative powers for which Black Hole Sun is often noted.

Although they often prefer to operate behind the scenes, Black Hole Sun natives are noted as magnetic and compelling, both attracting and repelling others, but always feeding on their energies, which are directed towards them almost against our will. Often seen dramatically differently by various audiences, these individuals can be deified by one group and demonized by another, to the extent that finding common ground between these disparate views, or persons who are neutral in their opinion of them, is virtually impossible. They tend to absorb others' energies, reflecting back whatever is expected of them by their audience, and can prove highly catalytic players on the world stage, galvanizing both support and opposition, and turning whatever they touch topsy-turvy, creating an up-is-down, black-is-white alternate reality wholly different from what pertained previously.

Such is surely the case with George W. Bush, born 7:26 AM CDT 6 July 1946 in New Haven, CT, whose Sun at 13 Cancer is in exact square to the Black Hole at 13 Libra which conjoins the nation's 14 Libra Saturn, symbol of the presidency. Love him or hate him, it's hard to find anyone neutral, and the amount of energy expended in decrying or defending him and his record for the eight years he spent in the White House has been truly astounding. The Black Hole's tendency to invert reality and go to extremes, flipping current conditions to their opposite pole, is well in evidence in his political career. Bush inherited a vital economy with a federal budget

surplus of $236 billion and transformed it into a devastated econ-
omy with a federal budget deficit of $407 billion, nearly doubling
the national debt in the process, from $5.6 trillion to $10.1 trillion.
He found a nation at peace and left it with two wars, adding torture
and abuse to official governmental policy and illegally wiretapping
thousands of US citizens, while scanning their emails and monitoring their library selections. He polarized the American electorate to an unprecedented extent and changed the international face
of America for a generation. All these are hallmarks of Black Hole
interaction, reversing the status quo and birthing a radically different reality, while extracting the maximum amount of energy from
any given situation.

In addition to the Sun, Bush's Ascendant, Midheaven, Mercury,
Mars, Jupiter, Saturn, Uranus, Neptune, and Pluto are all conjoined
or in hard aspect to Black Holes, exact or within a degree of orb. As
such, his biography well illustrates the varying types of manifestations to be gleaned from interaction with these deep space power-
houses, and we'll be returning to him periodically throughout this
introduction.

Other Black Hole Sun natives are more unalloyedly admired or
reviled. Michael Jackson, with Sun exactly conjoined a Black Hole,
is another fine example of a truly creative, uniquely individualistic
presence, a music icon idolized by millions worldwide, whose personal life became so bizarre and alien as to make him extremely
unsympathetic and incomprehensible to millions of others. His
physical transformation over decades (an all too real manifestation
of the Black Hole's "black is white" quality of bizarre upheaval), the
allegations of child sexual abuse, the eccentric masks worn in public and his extreme reclusiveness, the unusual procreative methods
by which he acquired his children, as well as the fantasy theme
park he called home, all speak to the Black Hole Sun's inability to
conform to common standards and behavioral norms. And yet he
was an artistic phenomenon, creator of the best-selling album ever,
1982's "Thriller," an enormous influence on pop culture and music,
fashion, dance and music video, an artist always noted for being on
the cutting edge creatively and technologically. Not content with
the fame and power of his own success, the King of Pop's Black
Hole Sun reached out to ally itself with the dynasty of the first pop

King, Elvis Presley, in marriage to his daughter Lisa Marie, and incorporated into its insatiable grasp the Beatles catalog, one of the few groups whose net worth rivaled Jackson's.

The outpouring of global emotion at Jackson's death was reminiscent of the excess of grief accompanying the fatal car accident which took the life of Diana, Princess of Wales, when literally tens of thousands of people left floral memorials to her at her Kensington Palace home, and a crowd of more than 1 million clogged the streets of London to view the funeral cortege. An estimated 750 million people had viewed her wedding in 1981; more than 2.5 billion watched her funeral in 1997, the single largest global audience ever, and a tremendous testament to the Black Hole's power to mesmerize and attract. With Sun in semisquare to a Black Hole, Diana's biography portrays the typical Black Hole quality of extreme duality, with a position of public prominence, virtually universal adulation, and a seemingly fairy tale existence which hid a dark underbelly of raw emotion, despair and depression. Eventually the two sides of Diana conflicted to such an extent that she could not refrain from making her woes public, precipitating the break in her marriage and exposing both the callousness of those around her and her own emotional fragility. But to millions across the planet, the "People's Princess" was a shining example of power and position channeled for the service of others, her face one of the most recognizable globally.

Two examples of Black Hole Sun individuals who wore an outer mask radically different from the true essence they concealed are serial killers Jeffrey Dahmer, with Sun opposed a Black Hole, and Ted Bundy, with Sun conjunct. Both used the charm and persuasion of which Black Hole Sun is capable to lure their victims, Dahmer claiming at least 17 and Bundy more than 30, all these lives subsumed by the insatiable appetites of the Black Hole, as literally depicted by the cannibalism practiced by Dahmer.

Con men have also found an ally in the Black Hole Sun's ability to dissemble and temporarily step into another persona; Frank Abagnale, whose life story was portrayed by Leonardo DiCaprio in 2002's *"Catch Me If You Can"*, was adaptive enough to convincingly impersonate an airline pilot, a chief resident pediatrician, a lawyer, and a university teaching assistant over the course of his career.

With his Sun opposed a Black Hole, Abagnale also well illustrates this deep space anomaly's ability to genuinely remake itself, as opposed to simply donning yet another disguise—after a decade on the run and a five year prison stint, Abagnale went straight, using his former expertise to found a security consulting company, and now lectures for the FBI, a complete reversal of life path typical of Black Hole energies.

Black Hole Sun individuals are also often found on the cutting edge of their disciplines. Pablo Picasso and Jackson Pollock, both with Sun square a Black Hole, and Salvador Dali, with Sun in semi-square, exemplify famed artists who challenged the world to adapt to their own unique perspectives, which were initially impugned but eventually understood for the creative genius they embodied. Elvis Presley, with Sun conjunct a Black Hole, and Madonna, with Sun in square, depict musical icons and trend-setters with astounding popularity and cultural impact, both pioneers in their own way.

Authors JRR Tolkien, with Sun in square to a Black Hole, and JK Rowling, with Sun conjoined, typify writers whose literary output has captivated millions of readers worldwide, crafting fantasy worlds which have been very successfully adapted to the wide screen, netting their creators, or their heirs, billions, all fodder for the Black Hole. Rowling's personal story of transformation from single mother on welfare to multi-millionaire in a span of less than five years has all the hallmarks of the Black Hole's ability to dramatically alter our reality in previously inconceivable ways, while Tolkien's work speaks to the enduring, entrenched quality of Black Hole Sun individuals' contributions, which continue to resonate long after their creators' deaths.

Black Hole Mercury often experiences difficulties with communicating, being subject to misinterpretation, misrepresentation, and outright deception, perpetrated by the native or directed toward her. It is as if their message is confined within the gravitational grip of the Black Hole, and cannot penetrate to the world at large. But often these individuals are visionary thinkers, able to develop unique, creative solutions to problems that have dogged others for years; the difficulty can be in getting others to listen, understand, and accept the truths they have to impart.

George W. Bush's 9 Leo Mercury is exactly conjoined a Black

Hole, and makes a good example of the potential problems that can arise, especially when the person afflicted with this aspect just happens to be president of the United States. Probably the most obvious manifestation of this energy on a personal level is Bush's speaking style, rife with malapropisms, misplaced syntax, invented words, massacred grammar and punctuated with a seemingly endless stream of "ums" and "uhs." Black Hole Mercury can be extremely persuasive and often enjoys superb rhetorical gifts, as witness FDR, Adolf Hitler and Winston Churchill, all of whom shared this placement. This is one type; the other is more akin to retrograde Mercury, where the native simply thinks, processes data, and expresses himself differently from the norm (Churchill was a mix of both types— a brilliant orator, he also stuttered). Some have diagnosed Bush as possibly dyslexic, which would square well with his "Gentleman's C" academic record and the distorting qualities of the Black Hole.

Playing fast and loose with the truth is a common Black Hole Mercury issue, one which has been laid at the feet of the Bush administration on more than one occasion. Black Hole Mercury tends toward a form of lying which is particularly insidious, in that the native who owns one often does not think of what he is doing as lying. Rather, he is expressing reality as he sees it, from the altered perspective of his confines within the Black Hole, and the parallel realities that opens him to. This may or may not be based on objective facts in the real world we all inhabit, but regardless, it is what the native experiences as reality.

Sometimes this unique perspective leads to breakthroughs in understanding from which we can all benefit; at others, it leaves the native hopelessly isolated and out of touch with his peers. Massaging or cherry-picking data to conform to a preconceived worldview or support an already decided-upon policy comes naturally to this type, who excels at denying inconvenient facts and revisioning and repackaging conflicting information until it becomes recycled as a supporting argument. This pattern of twisting data and intelligence to fit policy goals can be traced throughout the entire Bush administration, whether it be the flawed intelligence about WMD which led us into Iraq, the purposeful downplaying of the true costs of the Medicare drug benefit, or the imminence of the fiscal crisis in social security, to promote its agenda of privatization.

Many noted authors have Black Hole Mercury—James Michener, famed for his ability to recreate historic periods with great detail and accuracy, bringing these lost eras back to life, has Mercury conjoined; Ernest Hemingway, with a Leo Mercury in square to a Black Hole, captured all the drama and romance of war, strife and struggle, and was one of the most popular authors of his day. Sir Arthur Conan Doyle, creator of the world's most famous fictional detective, Sherlock Holmes, and Agatha Christie, the most popular and prolific mystery writer of the twentieth century, also shared Black Hole Mercury, Doyle's in opposition, Christie's conjunct. Dramatists Eugene O'Neill and Tennessee Williams, both with Mercury opposed a Black Hole, captured all the angst and social turmoil of their generations, and altered the path of American theater, granting it enhanced international respect and prestige.

Educators, too, can be influenced by Black Hole Mercury. Annie Sullivan, the brilliant governess who opened the reality of language and communication to deaf and blind Helen Keller, had Mercury conjunct a Black Hole; her famed pupil shared that aspect, a moving testimony both to Black Hole Mercury's ability to limit or distort our senses, and to the resilience of these natives, capable of rising above their limitations. Louis Braille, creator of the alphabet for the blind, also had Mercury conjoined a Black Hole.

Black Hole Venus often manifests as turmoil or instability in romance and intimacy, as well as affecting other traditional Venusian arenas such as fashion and art, beauty, creative expression and personal finances. Establishing firm foundations in love or finance can be difficult with this placement, though for the native who perseveres, it's possible to find one's soul mate, or reap windfall profits, though typically there are quite a few frogs to be kissed on the path to true love, and often unexpected expenditures equal or exceed even the largest incomes. Michael Jackson, whose net worth peaked at approximately $2 billion at the height of his career, died more than $400 million in debt; his natal Venus was in exact square to a Black Hole, and contributed greatly to his financial success in the creativity he displayed, while simultaneously compromising his reputation in his alleged romantic attraction for underage boys.

Elizabeth Taylor, Ingrid Bergman, and Sophia Loren, all with Venus in square to a Black Hole, have all been considered among

the most beautiful women in the world, icons of feminine pulchri-
tude and grace; Taylor's eight marriages and eight divorces also
speak to Black Hole Venus' difficulties in forming stable relationships. Fashion icons such as Gianni Versace, Oscar de la Renta and
Ralph Lauren (all with Venus opposed a Black Hole), and super-
models such as Tyra Banks, Kate Moss, Cindy Crawford, Heidi
Klum (all with Venus opposed), Naomi Campbell (Venus in square)
and Christie Brinkley (Venus conjoined) are all vivid examples
of Black Hole Venus' role in successful fashion careers, where the
Black Hole's natural ability to present an image or remake appear-
ances is an obvious asset. Multi-billionaires Warren Buffett (Venus
opposed a Black Hole), Bill Gates (Venus in semisquare) and Michael
Bloomberg (Venus in square) illustrate the enhanced ability of Black
Hole Venus to attract massive amounts of wealth. Conversely, the
Great Wall Street Crash of 24 October 1929 saw Venus forming a
T-Square with two Black Holes, and the current severe economic
downturn which gained critical mass on 15 September 2008 showed
Venus in exact square to a Black Hole; both periods signaled a rapid
and devastating erosion or depletion of wealth, consistent with the
Black Hole's tendency to take without mercy, giving nothing in
return.

   Black Hole Mars evokes bizarre or extreme manifestations constellating about Mars issues, such as anger or aggression, death,
sex, sports and athletics, military service and war. It manifests as
world-class athletes such as seven-time Tour de France winner
Lance Armstrong (Mars conjunct a Black Hole) and record-setting
Olympic swimmer Michael Phelps (Mars in square); military leaders such as Dwight Eisenhower (Mars in square), architect of victory in World War II, and William Westmoreland (Mars in square),
architect of defeat in Vietnam; sexpots such as Marilyn Monroe
(Mars in square) and Madonna (Mars conjunct); bestial serial killers such as John Wayne Gacy (Mars in square) and mass murderer
Adolf Hitler (Mars conjunct), responsible for millions of deaths.

   George W. Bush's natal Mars at 9 Virgo is exactly conjoined
a Black Hole, and this is another area of his life where its effects
can be clearly seen. Bush's experience of Black Hole Mars began
early—when he was seven, his little sister Robin, aged three, died
of leukemia. This was the boy's first brush with death, and must

have been traumatic and confusing in the extreme, but the way his parents dealt with it has likely left lasting scars. Basically, George Sr and Barbara ignored the event—there was no funeral service for their daughter, and the day after her passing, the bereaved parents went golfing. In essence, Bush's Black Hole Mars had absorbed Robin, leaving no trace. This total lack of normal human response to this tragedy may have seriously warped Bush's psyche on the issue of death. Within a few years, he was gleefully stuffing lighted firecrackers into live frogs, tossing them in the air, and watching them explode; there were other incidents with wild and domestic animals, involving BB guns. This type of behavior is common in the youths of persons who would later become serial killers, and although Bush has never personally killed anyone, he has left an official trail of blood that rivals many.

Black Hole Mars followed him to the governorship of Texas, where in his six years there he approved the execution of 152 men and women, an average of one every two weeks, more than any other governor in Texas history. The wars in Afghanistan and Iraq have added immeasurably to that tally, with more than 4500 American servicemen and women killed, and perhaps as many as 100,000 Iraqis. The financial drain on the US treasury for these wars has been of truly Black Hole proportions, with expenses of $2.3 billion per week and more than $830 billion already invested; total costs, including health care for wounded veterans, estimated to exceed $2 trillion. But there are not just these more tangible costs to be considered: the Iraq War has generated an immense amount of emotional energy, both in opposition and support. The first war ever to be globally protested even before it began, it became one of the primary rift factors in the American electorate, and led to the torture, humiliation and sexual abuse perpetrated at Abu Ghraib and Guantanamo.

Bush's Vietnam military service is well documented elsewhere, and this is not the place to recount it. Suffice to say that his original acceptance and preferment to the Texas National Guard, catapulted ahead of other better-qualified but less well-connected candidates, as well as his mysterious and never explained disappearance a year before his duty ended, both qualify as Black Hole Mars manifestations *par excellence.*

Black Holes and other deep space anomalies form a vital part of the celestial fabric of our lives, the cosmic warp and woof underpinning the more obvious manifestations of the planets and asteroids of our own system. In the examples of well-known celebrities cited above, and in George W. Bush's life story in particular, we've seen illustrated the types of energies evoked by Black Hole activation, and the manifestations they elicit. Most of us are fortunate enough to be gifted or afflicted with less numerous deep space contacts, but their effects are still to be noted daily, in our personal lives and the great events of the wider world we inhabit.

With the stark quality of a lightning flash, Black Holes as metaphor illuminate, and perhaps, define, the culture of our times, a culture bearing a veneer of Judeo-Christian good and evil; a culture that is resistant to change unless change is forced by a "greater power," a culture that consumes without reflection and devours without remorse; a culture that produces less and less self-sufficient individuals, individuals whose daily lives can be disrupted, spun slowly out of existence by conglomorate beasts and tyrannical governments; a culture where union (spiritual, sexual, or otherwise) feels like a descent into a Black Hole. All this and more.

For astrologers, the challenge then is to mine the metaphor. Whether or not the scientific cosmology of a universe with a Black Hole at its center is to be believed, the corresponding metaphor, the image of a transformational force, invisible, yet powerful beyond belief, has emerged and cannot be ignored. Our very existence in this time calls for interpretation, introspection and reflection on the meaning of Black Holes. What better place to start than with the impact of Black Holes on chart and consciousness?

Turn the page and step carefully, ever so carefully across the event horizon.

# GALACTIC POINTS

Galactic Points comprise several classes of Deep Space astrophysical anomalies which are invisible to the naked eye, among them Black Holes, Quasars, Pulsars and Masers. Along with the visible Fixed Stars which have long been part of the astrological repertoire, Galactic Points provide a superstructure of energy underpinning and reinforcing the infrastructure of energies in our system which we commonly reference as planets and asteroids. In fact, just as the personal planets can be seen to have their reflections, or "higher octaves," in the social planets and the transpersonal planets, so, too, does this progression continue into an even higher order of the music of the spheres, the octave which includes Galactic Points.

Just as the Trans-Saturnian planets of our own system are invisible to the naked eye, but no less significant in their effects, so, too, do Galactic Points have at least as great an impact on the human psyche as their visible stellar cousins. And just like these Fixed Stars, Galactic Points transit extremely slowly (a rough guide for measuring their movement would be one minute of zodiacal longitude per year, or sixty years per degree), providing constant points of reference for successive generations, and an underlying framework upon which the planets' dances attain a new meaning. For in addition to their interaction with each other, the celestials in our system trigger the activation of complex deep space energy shields and patterns created by these Galactic Points, and provide us with a link to energies which are always there in potential, but for a connection to which, until recently, we could not hope to aspire. Essentially, if the planets and asteroids of our system can be taken to represent manifestations of the archetypal field, Galactics provide access to the ideal forms which lie behind even the archetypes, and which are, to us, a faceless and unchanging energy.

But what are galactics? Much more will be said of their structure and effects, both in the birthchart and in mundane events, but in brief, Black Holes act as interlocutors, providing avenues of mediation into parallel universes, evoking dramatic reversals of the status quo, conveying requests, and occasionally, if strongly contacted in the chart, supplying answers. Quasars, also known as "white holes," more commonly provide the avenues for the manifestation of our requests, and are indicative of lasting, pervasive change, while Pulsars provide information and Masers act as high voltage energy transducers, supplying the energies needed for transformation to occur.

The importance and potential of this field should not be underestimated. Galactics may provide answers to the questions regarding how we manifest reality into the physical, how we create the circumstances of our lives and attract people and events to us to further our growth or acknowledge and reinforce our psychological life scripts, as well as how we enact change and transformation. The mysteries of manifestation lie within their grasp, and an understanding of their basic principles is an understanding of our own role as the co-creators of our individual realities.

Black Holes on an astrological level represent the principle of transubstantiation, which is a literally alchemical process necessary for true change to occur and manifest itself in the physical. Where Pluto mutates the structure from a cellular level, in a molecule-specific, cancerous type of way, his higher octave the Black Holes are the guardians of the fluctuations in the quantum process, where matter is first generated from pure energy.

Black Holes depict areas of susceptibility to dramatic, intense, sometimes violent and usually unsuspected shifts in the status quo reality, shifts which may or may not be permanent in the physical but which always leave their mark in rite-of-passage-type situations which change the individual's perceptions forever.

They further show points of energy influx, or energy drain, in a chart and life, and aspects to them indicate what areas of life are being sapped. [For example, a Sixth House Mars aspecting a Second House Black Hole may find that a loss (BH) in earnings (2) or a drain (BH) in personal finances (2) is a direct result of health issues (6) or anger (Mars) expressed at work (6). Diet (6) and exercise (Mars) routines may suffer, leading to further low esteem issues (2).]

The cycle can be considered to be almost endless, especially if the Black Hole is linked by aspect to a Quasar, which could indicate where the energy which is drained from the psyche rebounds into the chart. [To expand upon the illustration above, if the Second House Black Hole further aspects an Eleventh House Quasar, then feelings of low self esteem (2) may prove a catalyst to activity with a twelve-step or self-help group (11), or friends (11) may lend us money to get us through the financial (2) crunch (BH).] Quasar contacts in themselves show points where we are challenged to manifest our purest essence, our most uniquely personal and yet intensely archetypal activation (more, incarnation) of the planetary energy involved.

Quasars promote visibility, success and achievement, the attaining of goals, and coming to prominence or public notice and attention. Financial affluence being a leading indicator of what our society deems success, we can see Quasars showing prominently in the charts of individuals who head that parade. Bill Gates, the world's richest man, has Sun exactly conjoined a Quasar, and Warren Buffet, second richest, has Sun opposed. New York Mayor Michael Bloomberg, the richest man in politics, has Sun conjoined a Quasar, and Tiger Woods, the first pro athlete to amass more than a billion dollars, has Sun exactly opposed a Quasar. America's richest celebrity is Oprah Winfrey, eighth richest woman in the country, with Sun sextile a Quasar, and Madonna, the richest female singer, has Sun opposed. Michael Jackson, the highest earning male solo artist of all time, had Sun opposed a Quasar, and *Harry Potter* author JK Rowling, the richest writer in the world, has Sun in trine.

Pulsars provide points where information enters the system. Usually this is "felt" energy, "body knowledge," being in some sense packets or "quanta" of information which enter pick-a-back upon the elementary particles, quarks and leptons, etc., which modern science sees as the origin of matter. Very often, however, there is actual intellectual knowledge or experience which is imparted to us in some conventional manner, but which we "know" has special relevance for us. In these instances look to the types of persons or situations/interactions which are typical of the House positing the aspected Pulsar. [In the case of Pulsar contacts with celestials, the information can be a two way street; this same Mars in aspect to a Twelfth House Pulsar may find that fortune tellers (12) or hospital workers (also 12) both give him valid information concerning his sex life (Mars), or that after he works out (Mars) his dreams (12) are more vivid and charged with useful images or actual information.]

Pulsars being informational in nature, and often evoking news-worthy events, it's not surprising that they also show prominently in the charts of news personalities. CBS news anchors Walter Cronkite, with Sun conjunct a Pulsar, and Dan Rather, with Sun in square, top the list, which also includes ABC anchors David Brinkley, who had Sun sextile a Pulsar, and Diane Sawyer, with Sun also in square. NBC anchor Brian Williams has Sun opposed a Pulsar, as does perennial favorite Barbara Walters.

Masers are least understood at this time, and should be seen as points of high voltage intensity, "cosmic cattle prods." They seem to have Black Hole affinities in that they act as psychic catalytic energy converters, but without the apparently random or unpredicted nature of Black Hole manifestations. Rather, current conditions are likely to pertain, but become exacerbated, and more highly charged in their effects. [Mars in aspect to a Maser might undergo a rhythmic cycle of comparatively low-stress sexual relationships increasing to moments of peak stress which coincide with a breakdown in the system, beginning the cycle again either from a higher plateau with the same individual or a similar plateau with a new partner.]

Maser energy evokes controversy, volatility and disruption. Some examples of Maser-afflicted individuals who have become controversial for their actions are investment banker Bernard Madoff, who perpetrated the single largest financial fraud ever by an individual, and has both Sun and Venus (ruling money and finances) conjoined Masers; President Bill Clinton, noted for extramarital shenanigans in the Oval Office, has Sun in square and Mars trine a Maser; and controversial Fox News commentator Bill O'Reilly has Mercury (news, opinion) in sextile to a Maser.

Physiologically, Black Holes are involved with the ingestion and storage of energy, Quasars with its dissemination, distribution and elimination, Pulsars with information processing in the neural/nervous system and Masers with cellular processes such as meiosis and mitosis, cellular splitting or replification.

Current Positions of Galactic Points Discussed in This Book, circa 2010

(BH = Black Hole, M = Maser, P = Pulsar, Q = Quasar)
P 3 Aries
Q 10 Aries
BH 24 Aries
BH 27 Aries
Q 5 Taurus
M 8 Taurus
BH 16 Taurus
BH 24 Taurus
M 28 Taurus
M 7 Gemini
P 22 Gemini
P 24 Gemini
Q 26 Gemini
BH 4 Cancer
Q 8 Cancer
BH 28 Cancer
P 2 Leo
BH 3 Leo
BH 9 Leo
M 14 Leo
P 3 Virgo
BH 7 Virgo
BH 9 Virgo
P 18 Virgo
BH 1 Libra
Q 5 Libra
P 7 Libra
BH 13 Libra
Q 15 Libra
BH 29 Libra
Q 5 Scorpio
BH 7 Scorpio
P 15 Scorpio

Q 28 Scorpio
BH 4 Sagittarius
BH 4 Sagittarius
BH 5 Sagittarius
P 6 Sagittarius
BH 10 Sagittarius
BH 18 Sagittarius
BH 19 Sagittarius
P 24 Sagittarius
BH 26 Sagittarius (Galactic Center)
P 28 Sagittarius
BH 5 Capricorn
BH 19 Capricorn
P 27 Capricorn
P 29 Capricorn
P 9 Aquarius
P 10 Aquarius
BH 12 Aquarius
BH 13 Aquarius
P 16 Aquarius
Q 25 Aquarius
BH 28 Aquarius
Q 6 Pisces
BH 28 Pisces

# SECTION I:
# BLACK HOLES IN NATAL
# INTERPRETATION

# BLACK HOLE SUN

In general, Black Hole Sun individuals are magnetic, forceful and attractive, able to pull others into their orbits almost effortlessly, for good or ill, bringing them into contact with the right people at the right time; but they are also changeable and liable to reverse themselves without warning. Gifted with an inherent ability to adapt to situations and reflect what others expect of them, they fit well into a wide variety of circumstances and situations, though none of these may reflect their true essence or desires. Chameleon-like, they change to suit their surroundings, and often prefer to work behind the scenes, pulling strings and manipulating events from off-stage. Outwardly changeable and capricious, the Black Hole Sun native can also be very determined and driven, refusing to accept defeat, and has the ability to shift events in their favor in a dramatic and unexpected fashion, changing imminent capitulation into stunning success. The native has a greater than usual ability to affect events, and can be pivotal in transforming the current status quo into a different reality altogether.

Difficult to penetrate or clearly know, perhaps even to themselves, they can be deceptive or artful, but in the main are simply adaptive individuals who usually "remake" themselves several times over the course of the lifetime, sometimes in subtle ways, more often dramatically. Black Hole Sun natives are masters of disguise and projection, and can usually point to specific periods in their lives when one or other aspect of their personas was dominant, causing them to express themselves differently. These individuals have the ability to remake themselves completely, from the ground up, or from the inside out, as it were, and may do so frequently.

Black Hole Sun natives have the unusual combination of resilience and adaptability, able to conform to any situation or circumstance. They can appear to be all things to all people, and if they wish to expend the energy, can slip comfortably into any setting. They may tend to conform to others' expectations, or at any rate, to appear to do so, allowing each interlocutor to see a different facet of themselves or receive whatever impression they most desire of the native. This is not deception per se, but rather a natural coping mechanism which the Black Hole uses to extract the maximum energy from any given situation, allowing the native to blend in or stand out by turns, depending on the desired effect. There is a tendency to compartmentalize the life, so that others whom they come into contact with in different circumstances, will each perceive the native quite differently, and these separate selves may not mesh very well, leaving the native feeling divided and out of focus. Feeling comfortable with compartmentalization may be the key to success in this regard; if the native can keep all these personas separate, and deal with each significant other severally, it may be possible to maintain the delicate balance required to sustain them. This ability to live different lives, as it were, can be a very enriching experience, allowing these natives to garner much from the varied perspectives via which they interact.

The Black Hole lends a quality of uncertainty, a changing, shifting ground of being which seeks to put itself in accord with its environment, or else to alter that reality completely, remaking it in its own image. Creative and insightful, these individuals may be difficult to pin down or anticipate, and some may see this as lack of conviction or fickleness, though in reality it stems from the Black Hole Sun's need to conform to changing circumstance. But they can adhere to an agenda or belief very stubbornly, overcoming seemingly insurmountable odds to attain their desires. Black Hole Sun can be very disruptive; stability is rare, as conditions change rapidly and the effect may feel like standing on sinking sand, with no firm foundation. This fast-paced change and the dramatic reversals which often accompany it can become the norm for the individual, eventually causing little comment. These sudden upsets may seem to be arising from others, a situation where the native feels at the mercy of events outside oneself or beyond one's control, but these incidents are manifestations of an inner turmoil and restlessness which is endemic of Black Hole energies.

Black Hole Sun natives have the ability to warp time to some extent, and may often find themselves "lost" in reverie or so focused on the task at hand that they seem abstracted from the field of time. Hours can pass without any awareness of the length of time or its passage; similarly, minutes can seem like hours, with time appearing to slow or stand still. Some natives find that they have an effect upon plant life, causing accelerated growth exceeding the usual term.

Creative and gifted with a unique perspective, they can be effective problem solvers and often act as agents or catalysts for others in crisis or transition. Black Hole Sun natives may often feel themselves so different from others that they seem cut off from them; alienation can be an issue for these individuals, particularly if they find themselves in an environment which is not supportive of their differences.

There is an attraction for power and a desire to wield it. Secretive and mysterious, many Black Hole Sun natives often prefer to work behind the scenes, manipulating circumstances indirectly and using others as their agents rather than outwardly showing their power, but when they do step out of the shadows, they can be truly formidable. They may shun the spotlight, but enjoy being at the center of things nonetheless.

Black Holes act as centers of energy attraction or energy drain, and the native may be seen by others in either of these capacities, or both in turn. There are vast reserves of energy, but it may be difficult for the native to consciously access this, as the Black Hole does not readily disgorge its repast. The energy will be there in a pinch, however, as the Black Hole is also loathe to lose its host, and will do what it can to preserve this conduit for draining energy from this reality into its own. Of a generally sound constitution, the native has a tendency to hold back and conserve energies unless pressed to expend them. There may be issues with excess weight with this placement, as fat is the body's mechanism for storing energy until it is required.

The native may have interactions with alternate dimensions or parallel realities; it is difficult, if not impossible, to determine to what extent these experiences are "real" and to what extent they proceed from the native's own psyche, as expressions of powers felt but not completely perceived or understood.

In the case of the Sun exactly conjoined the singularity, or center, of a Black Hole, the two become one to an even greater extent than would two celestials of this system, which each have their own flavor or distinct characteristics. The Black Hole, however, does not have a distinct character per se, but rather acts as a modifier of whatever energy it encounters. And in the case of the conjunction, the Sun is so caught within its power that the two become inseparable; there is nowhere for the Sun to turn to escape the Black Hole's embrace.

The Sun opposed a Black Hole indicates one who is subject to others' expectations and projections more than usual. Although these natives are able to pull others into their orbit as needed, for purposes of education or progression, there is less control of the situation than occurs with a conjunction, and less movement or crisis than occurs with a square. Rather than feeding off the energies of others, it is others who tend to feed off them. The opinions and perspectives of others can assume an inordinate importance, becoming formative and constricting, preventing these individuals from expressing who they truly are, or achieving full development. Nevertheless it should be remembered that it is the native who attracts these experiences for the purpose of soul growth, although once manifested, they may take on a life of their own, with ramifications not at all to the native's liking, or according to plan. The more exact the aspect, the more crisp and laser-like the manifestation, with little or no "wiggle room."

The square to the Black Hole affords more freedom of action and promotes growth through conflict, but it may be more difficult to see its effects, which are not as stark as the opposition. Conflict can be the key to activating Black Hole energies in square, and these natives may often feel themselves to be trapped within the horns of a dilemma, having to choose between two or more apparently unpalatable alternatives. There may be a strong sense of instability, of the ground giving way beneath them, or of being trapped in quicksand by circumstances from which it is not easy to extricate themselves. They may feel as if carried along willy-nilly by a tide of events beyond their control. The square allows the native to reach out to others in a manner which is more of one's own volition, as compared to the oppositional aspects which are seemingly thrust upon one willy-nilly, at the behest of others. Yet paradoxically, with square aspects the native is much more at the vagaries of chance and the whim of the Black Hole, leading to a more chaotic atmosphere. This ability to pick and choose where our energies are directed and to whom may require some effort to bring under conscious control. Not as strong as a solar conjunction with a Black Hole, the square aspect nevertheless evokes a great deal of energy and magnetism, albeit the results are often skewed or different from what the native intended.

Trines and sextiles from Black Holes to the Sun are probably the most useful, but also among the most capricious. While the manifestations they evoke are usually viewed as positive, they are sporadic and highly unpredictable, and often have a window of opportunity which is very short-lived. Sextiles are less effective than trines—sextiles will provide opportunities to change or enhance reality; trines will present altered realities in a sort of *fait accompli*— use it or lose it. Sextiles can be so subtle in their manifestation that it is sometimes only after the fact that the native recognizes that an opportunity was presented, and the short shelf life of these options often means flabbergasted disappointment or disgruntlement follows in their wake. With trines, the benefit is obvious, but as always with Black Holes, beware the price—what looks good up front may have unpleasant ramifications down the line. Black Holes in sextile to the Sun require our active awareness of the possibilities being proffered; those in trine merely require our acceptance and participation in the alternatives they present.

Black Holes in inconjunct aspect to the Sun can be very powerful, but tend to respond more incrementally than other aspects. That is, while the incidents they evoke may be typically startling or stunning, the changes they bring about will more likely tweak the native's overall reality rather than transform it, appearing as ancillary rather than central to the native's development. Over time, however, these seemingly minor, if abrupt, changes can add up to major transitional patterns. How many tweaks are there in a full-fledged reality revolution? This will vary from person to person, depending on the overall tenor of the chart.

The Sun tied to multiple Black Holes indicates one whose energies are pulled in a multitude of directions. The native tends to "fragment," trying to be all things to all people, and ultimately satisfying none, until learning the lesson that being true to oneself first is the best way to be of service to others. Subject to sudden whims and changes of direction, both on a daily level and as regards overall life path, the native whose Sun is distracted by peripheral Black Holes may find it difficult to center oneself or move steadily towards goals.

# BLACK HOLE MOON

The Moon linked with Black Hole energies has a variety of manifestations. Primarily domestic environments will be affected, with the likelihood of frequent moves, not always at the native's behest. These may occur suddenly, with little or no warning, and could extend to changes in domestic environment not specifically related to moving, such as changing roommates. The Moon tied to a Black Hole indicates that there is a great deal of energy put into the domestic sphere, where the atmosphere may be tumultuous and fast-paced or hectic.

Much energy and attention can be spent on the physical structure of the home itself, which may require constant upkeep or maintenance, draining resources. There may be frequent need for repair or other issues which consistently bring the native's focus and energies back to the domestic sphere. Recurring issues are common, and the same themes will continue to emerge until lessons are learned and fully incorporated into the native's psyche.

Home life can be unstable and subject to sudden or unexpected shifts and changes. A large amount of time and focus may be expended in the home, which the native views as a retreat, a private space in which to retire from the stress of the world, a safe haven which is often dark or cavernous in some respect, the ring-pass-not within which the native creates a private reality, one separated from the outside world by the Black Hole's event horizon, which prevents others from seeing the reality within. Others may feel mystified as to what actually occurs in the native's domestic life, as there can be an air of secrecy and a strong need for privacy. The native may spend a great deal of time and energy working on the home space to create just the atmosphere or appearance desired, and may be somewhat reluctant to share that with others. There may be a tendency to redecorate or shift the positions of furniture or the function of particular rooms frequently, remaking the environment on a regular basis. There is a strong potential for owning more than one home simultaneously with this placement.

Emotions, too, are in flux, with the native running the gamut from A to Z in the twinkling of an eye. Emotions can be volatile and intense, but generally do not last for long, the native moving rapidly through emotional states, which can be extremely unsettled, especially in youth. The positive reward of this is a tendency not to brood, as emotional states can be so fleeting that the next has begun to emerge almost before the last has registered. The down side is that others may see the native as fickle or lacking emotional substance, a will-o-the-wisp who is carried on a tide of feeling so intense that they are wary of being swept away themselves.

Rarely does the Moon/Black Hole native become fixated on any particular emotional state. They are able to throw off even intensely strong emotions comparatively easily; not, perhaps, with a shrug, but often without permanent emotional damage from even the most devastating events. While they have the native's attention, however, the grip of the current emotion can seem overwhelming, albeit transitory. Emotions may seem larger than life, and can become hugely important to the native, with little reference to the overall importance in the native's life of the actual event evoking the emotion. That is to say, trivial matters may set off emotional conflict just as easily as significant ones. Impossible to predict, the native may react in one way to a certain stimulus at one time, and completely differently to that same stimulus the next time it is encountered.

Although overall health may be consistent and untroublesome, there is the likelihood of at least one dramatic, life-altering health crisis in the course of the life, taking the form of a confrontation with accident or disease which redirects the native's energies and focus. Health crises can erupt unexpectedly; careful monitoring of general health parameters is encouraged to keep these to a minimum. Many Black Hole Moon natives tend toward chronic, non-life-threatening, low level sickness, which feeds the Black Hole's need for attention and focus, and may be debilitating or wearing. Often these are stress related.

Black Hole Moon tends toward those conditions which require

high maintenance, as a way of funneling energy into the anomaly; whatever creates the most opportunity for draining resources is the preferred target of the Black Hole. There is more percentage for the Black Hole in ongoing complaints, which drain energy on a regular basis, although it may enjoy the high drama of a crisis moment on occasion as well. The overall constitution is generally good, and there is a great deal of energy available for healing in the reserves of the Black Hole, if the native can access it. Black Hole Moon natives can cling tenaciously to life, even with major illness, and are often able to throw off even serious health problems which would devastate others. There is a very strong likelihood of mis-diagnosis, and second opinions are essential with this placement.

There may be issues with appearance, with these natives frequently changing their image, which may alter radically at various times throughout the life. There may be a strong desire to alter the physical appearance, remake one's image, or adjust one's presentation in matters such as wardrobe or hairstyle, and perhaps extending to cosmetic surgery in more extreme cases. These natives may be obsessed with image to the degree that others consider them frivolous or vain.

The body is naturally amorphous, and the native gains and loses weight comparatively easily; fluctuation is common, and maintaining a consistent weight may be difficult. Body issues can become a problem, as can eating disorders which focus on nutritional issues, such as anorexia or bulimia. The native may be a "yo-yo" dieter, rapidly gaining and losing weight in turn, and there can be an attraction for the latest fad diet of the moment. Nurturance of self or others may be erratic or fraught with complications. The body may be prone to self-sabotage, as in developing allergies or difficulty absorbing nutrients or processing foods properly.

There may be issues with early childhood experience or the Mother, who may have been seen as in some way unapproachable, vacant or absent; or else as manipulative, dominating, devouring and controlling. This placement can also manifest as actual separation for the mother at an early stage, via death or divorce. Black Hole Moon natives often feel isolated or emotionally distant from their mothers; alternately, some Black Hole Moon children feel smothered or overprotected. These patterns may continue into the next generation with the native's own children and parenting skills, with these individuals either repeating or consciously rejecting the ways in which they were raised.

Natives with this combination are apt to experience one aspect of this duality in their childhood, and exhibit the other in their relation with their own children. Thus, if they saw their mother as controlling, they may bring too light a touch to their own parenting duties; or if they failed to make contact with their mothers in youth, they may be overly involved in their children's lives, unable to let go when appropriate, and may have issues with allowing their own progeny to grow into independent individuals separate from themselves.

Early childhood trauma, as in abuse, is common for Black Hole Moon natives, and these experiences may have been repressed. The native may experience difficulty in pregnancy, either in conception or carrying to term, and can feel very ambivalent or uncomfortable about parenthood, fearing to recreate what is seen as the mistakes of one's own parents.

There is also the potential for the mother to become a source of energy drain for the native, particularly later in life. Another manifestation of the Black Hole Moon can be the parent-becoming-child syndrome, where a positive early relationship with the mother becomes one of overburdening responsibility when that parent ages and the child is called upon to provide or care for her. The energy and pathos which remained unexpressed in youth becomes the central focus of the relationship in old age.

The incidence of a Moon in exact aspect to a Black Hole is comparatively rare; as the Moon spends barely two hours per degree, its precise contact with the singularity is swift and transitory. The effect is to greatly increase the pull the Black Hole has on Moon issues, even moreso than a 'normal' celestial in exact aspect, and certainly moreso than even a Moon which is merely within orb of the anomaly.

Conjunctions are the most intense aspect, granting little freedom for the Moon to avoid the Black Hole's grip. However, within this limited freedom, there is wide latitude for expression and manifestation of the effects, and over time, as the native "grows into" the combination, a greater ability to work within the Black Hole's confines emerges. In many ways the conjunction, although all-consuming, is the easiest contact to manage, once the native learns the rules of the game. There is the least amount of external influence or impingement, granting the individual a sort of internal mastery which may help to direct the Black Hole's manifestations over more productive, or pleasing, lines.

With the opposition aspect, it is others who intrude most strongly into the native's reality, making the altered conditions appear to be coming from "out there," perceived as beyond the native's conscious control. In actuality, the Black Hole Moon native magnetizes these individuals and events into the life for the purpose of gaining clarity on natal issues and external "mirroring" of shadow, unclaimed portions of the native's own psyche.

Black Holes in square to the Moon provoke confused, stressful emotional states, an appearance of irresolvable conflict or division. There is often a pronounced split between diametrically opposed emotions or alternatives, sometimes resulting terminal indecision or irresolution on the part of the native when definite choices must be made. There is a "damned if you do, damned if you don't" flavor to this aspect which can be highly stressful, and the instability the square evokes can make charting a specific course difficult over time.

Sextile and trine aspects are the most manageable, displaying an ease of integration of Black Hole energies which eludes the harsher aspects. Black Holes in sextile to the Moon produce opportunities, but these are not always apparent; trines are much more obvious, although their permanence may be in doubt. In both instances, active engagement with the alternatives offered in necessary to fully utilize their potential.

The inconjunct from a Black Hole to the Moon tends to produce mild tension, of a low-grade, chronic nature. There is a continual need to redirect energies, make adjustments, tweak the format, and this background hum of ever-present alteration can be felt as an underlying sense of insecurity or instability, generating an emotional need for detachment which may be at variance with the native's true nature. The changes evoked may be dramatic at times, but if so, will be experienced as fleeting; it is the seemingly innocuous, more minor shifts wrought by the Black Hole which over time combine to produce truly momentous alterations in realities.

The Moon linked with multiple Black Holes tends to compart-mentalize, divide focus and splinter, emerging as less effective in all departments. The Moon's nature is to change, wax and wane in intensity, and allied with multiple Black Hole foci syphoning energy, this tendency is vastly augmented, to the point where the native may feel so emotionally drained as to be incapable of effec-tive response.

# BLACK HOLE MERCURY

Mercury/Black Hole natives are deep thinkers, keen and penetrating, possessed of an ability to see things which others cannot. This combination also promotes a very powerful intellect capable of assimilating and processing complex data, and vast amounts of it. It is as if the Black Hole becomes the repository of all their life experience and education, waiting to be called up at a moments' notice, like some vast cosmic hall of records. This can create the potential for becoming lost in petty details, unable to see the forest for the trees. They are unusually creative thinkers, but may become mired in the universes of possibility, to the extent that they are virtually paralyzed and unable to bring any of these insights into the reality of our 3-D world. It can be difficult to ascertain in advance which options may be practical in this reality, and which are merely pipe dreams.

They see, not the ways things are, but the ways they could become, and this often creates a barrier of perspective and distance between themselves and their peers, who are not able to grasp, or are unwilling to accept, the ramifications of what the Black Hole/ Mercury native sees so clearly. This can be a useful perspective, but it also often a thankless one, as others lag behind the vision, do not fully understand it, or are threatened by its scope. Cassandra-like, many will find many doubters when they express their vision. They are able to see to the heart of the matter and can easily throw off societal conditioning and intimidation, but they often find that others are unwilling to hear what they have to say, or to take it seriously. Others may fail to heed their warnings or respect their visions of future consequences of present actions or decisions. Their greatest challenge is in finding metaphors others can understand for the insights they receive, and thus finding acceptance for their thoughts. There is the danger of becoming trapped within an inner world of thoughts and fears, unable to function adequately in the Light World of everyday reality as the native retreats into an interior dialogue, frustrated by abortive attempts to truly communicate with others and be fully understood.

Pattern-seeing is also enhanced with this placement. Foresighted, able to pick their way among the potential futures and describe the ramifications of any given action many plays ahead on the board, these individuals can become restless or discontent with the status quo and seek to manipulate it, usually with the best intentions but often not the best results. Paradoxically, decision-making can also be problematic for Black Hole Mercury individuals, who may find that they are often torn between two or more avenues, unable to pick a course of action. They can be overwhelmed by the choices presented by their connections to the potential realms in the parallel universes beyond the Black Hole's singularity, and see all too clearly the multiplicity of possible outcomes with each path, so that a paralyzation occurs and the native delays important decisions, waiting on time and events to decide for them.

They are more than usually susceptible to misinterpretation, misunderstanding, misrepresentation, and downright deceit from others, but often have a well developed sense of truth, and an ability to detect falsehood. They are also capable of projecting deceit, and may be overly secretive or keep their counsel closely, making it difficult for others to know what they truly think. They guard secrets well, both their own and others.'

Black Hole Mercury sometimes seeks to obfuscate or hide its true meaning, delighting in double entendre and word games which veil a deeper agenda, hiding their true intent in shades of meaning. They can be selective about whom they allow into their innermost world and private thoughts. There is a possibility of outright deception or subterfuge with this placement. They can be changeable, espousing first one approach to a situation and then another course of action seemingly at complete odds with the first one. This is not so much inconstancy as an ability to see the issue from a broad variety of viewpoints.

The memory may also be subject to revisionism; that is, it is possible for Black Hole Mercury natives to become so enmeshed within their version of an event that they seize upon it as an objective Truth, when in reality it is only their interpretation. At its worst, the native may not even be aware of speaking falsely, becoming convinced that this perspective is the right one, and therefore must also be true.

They can be persuasive speakers, able to charm the birds out of the trees, but there may be a danger of seeming too glib or calculating in one's approach to persuasion. There is a highly developed descriptive ability and a knack for finding the right word at the right time. They are capable of building logical, well-thought-out arguments, but often they may feel marginalized, and may find it difficult to get their message across. It can be as if their message cannot escape the confines of the Black Hole's supergravity, remaining trapped and unable to penetrate into everyday reality.

Black Hole Mercury natives grasp new facts and theories easily, and are always prepared to look at any given set of facts from a new and radically different perspective. Often their thought processes are unintelligible to others, and they may be 'ahead of their time' in their proposed solutions to problems which they encounter (in general, galactically-inspired information is commonly six to twelve months in advance of its application). The Black Hole's connection with potential realms in parallel universes provides the native with access to a unique viewpoint and greatly aids in strategic matters and the ability to forestall problems before they arise, allowing the native to view circumstances in ways that divert challenges into opportunities.

They can also be skilled at adapting complex concepts for general consumption, helping to redefine and reinterpret them so as to be more accessible to others. They often have a facility of mind which allows them to quickly integrate new information and reformulate more advanced theoretical material or arguments into simpler formats accessible to less gifted individuals. Generally quick-witted, they can wound quite effectively with their speech, which can also inspire and encourage, if they so direct it. They may blurt responses, or reply before thinking through the implications of their words, uttering truths sometimes better left unsaid. Black Hole Mercury describes both extremes of loquaciousness and taciturnity.

Sensory data can be an issue as well, with some Black Hole

Mercury individuals acquiring heightened sensation, while others will experience handicaps of some sort, in hearing or vision especially. There may also be vocal difficulties or speech impediments such as stuttering, although in written form, Black Hole Mercury is usually succinct and direct, while retaining an ability to compose flowery or poetic rhetoric. There may be extraordinary sensory capacity, with the native able to perceive and interact with a variety of higher dimensional energies, and there is a greater instance of ESP with Black Hole Mercury natives than in the general population. The tactile senses can also be very acute and developed, and the hands graceful or skilled. Manual dexterity is common, and the native may find that skill with the hands in some way opens doors or allows the manipulation of reality in ways which would not ordinarily be possible. Despite a common tendency to be deft or facile, some Black Hole Mercury natives can be unduly clumsy; Black Holes always tend to extremes, whichever way the cat jumps.

Black Hole Mercury natives may have had difficulties with early education—as with retrograde Mercury, they learn in ways dissimilar from most individuals, and may not initially test well. They understand the material, but find it difficult to conform to rules and dogma, and jump through academic hoops set up by others. There may also be increased susceptibility to learning disorders, particularly dyslexia, which by its very nature implies a variance in the way information is received. Alternately, there is the type who can perform perfectly in an academic setting, but feels out of sync with the mainstream. They may have found themselves feeling unchallenged and bored by the standard curriculum, and if no access to accelerated learning programs was available, may have fallen behind academically simply through ennui. Often these perceived or actual difficulties cause the Black Hole Mercury native to overcompensate intellectually, both in primary and higher education, channeling vast amounts of energy into academic pursuits, and many obtain advanced degrees or certifications which may never be fully utilized or put to practical application. Some Black Hole Mercury natives show an advanced facility with numbers, able to solve complex math problems in their heads.

The native thinks and processes data differently from others, and may have been considered a 'square peg in a round hole' in early education, finding it problematic to fit in and meet teachers' expectations. Although the mind is retentive and the memory sharp, in some instances photographic, they may have trouble simply regurgitating knowledge onto paper at command. Despite being gifted with an agile and creative mind, many find it hard to understand or anticipate those elements in their education which others would consider important. In time the native is generally able to overcome early difficulties and perform well in a testing environment. This requires a period of adaptation when the native learns how to reproduce what is expected, but typically this is resolved by the age of 10. After that, academic excellence may well ensue, and many Black Hole Mercury natives go on to become well-respected academicians and thinkers; many of these individuals become known for their unorthodox or genius-level thought processes, ideas, and inspirations.

Their relationships with all things Mercurial—among them children, pets, neighbors, siblings and lesser relations, trade or technical school, cars and transportation—are subject to change at a moment's notice, and may require greater and greater amounts of energy to manage. All of these are also subject to the Black Hole's quixotic behavior patterns, a tendency toward the volte face, that sudden, unexpected and dramatic reversal of events, where what comes into being is so completely different from what pertained before as to be virtually unrecognizable. All these are on the shifting sands of the Black Hole's capricious nature, which gives with one hand and takes with the other, and any can become a source of energy drain, stealing precious resources of time and energy which the native would prefer to utilize elsewhere. From time to time these Mercurial arenas may erupt in the native's life, impairing clarity of judgement and requiring the expenditure of vast amounts of energy to resolve the situation. Some of these may be areas in which the native takes energy from others, while some will cause the native's own energies to drain, but they are all potential focal points for energetic redistribution.

In particular, cars and transportation may be an issue, with vehicle breakdowns which leave the native stranded, and frequent repairs necessitating large financial outlays; or commuting difficulties which absorb much time and focus daily. Likewise, other Mercurial matters such as plumbing, electrical wiring or cables (any connective, linking energy is Mercury-ruled) or water supply issues could be problematic. Communication devices can malfunction, or need to be frequently replaced due to defect. Similarly, relations with children and young people could be draining from time to time, or responsibilities relating to them seemingly overwhelming. Pets may require a great deal of attention and upkeep and many Black Hole Mercury natives expend a great amount of energy on animals and their issues.

Black Holes also operate as liminal guardians, door wardens into altered realities, and having Mercury allied with one can afford unexpected opportunities for change and advancement. These must be acted upon quickly, however, for the Black Hole does not open doors for long, and rarely opens the same door twice. The native functions as an intermediator between these alternate realities and parallel dimensions, but it is often difficult to determine which of these are "real," and which the products of the native's own psyche. The mind can play tricks on itself, remembering things that never happened in this reality.

The particular difficulty in having one's message heard is more common with the conjunction than other aspects like the square. It can be as if the message is trapped within the confines of the Black Hole's supergravity, unable to escape or penetrate to its audience. In conjunction, others may be unable to comprehend the message, but with the square it is more likely that the native is heard, but is not accepted—conflict arises when their view of reality is expressed. Galactic information being commonly six to eighteen months ahead of its time, in many instances further development will bear out the accuracy of the native's views later, but this is cold comfort for the native in the present, and this verification of their veracity is no guarantee of their acceptance by others in the future. There is an enhanced ability to conceive and understand complex or abstract ideas or theories, but there may be a lack of capacity to communicate these in ways others can integrate or incorporate, rendering these insights less than useful.

In opposition, Black Hole Mercury natives may experience a sense that others are incomprehensible to them, or others may be instrumental in catalyzing their impressions, helping to formulate them into a more coherent format. But they can also act as a sort of interpreter for others, helping them to clarify their own thoughts and ideas into forms more generally accessible. There is a heightened understanding and perception of other's motivations, an ability to penetrate the workings of others' minds, facilitating communication.

The square is the most problematic of the aspects, combining as it does a stress or tension in expression and communication with the sense that there is a constant need to decide between two alternatives, neither of which may seem to resolve the situation at hand. While a normal square, despite its conflict, brings energy, a square to a Black Hole drains energy, until often only the conflict remains. In aspect to Mercury, this can indicate continual difficulty in communication, not so much in expression (as with the conjunction) but in misunderstanding and resultant conflict. There is a sense that the native is constantly on the defensive, a stance which itself requires the expenditure of a great deal of energy to maintain.

As 'soft' or benefic aspects, sextiles and trines are supportive, or as supportive as any Black Hole energy can be. At least they do not lend the fractious quality of the square or opposition, which would work to enhance the more negative elements of the Black Hole's inclination toward disruption and instability. These benign aspects tend more toward the creative, original or inventive end of the spectrum of Black Hole potential, providing unique perspectives and easy access of communication. With the trine in particular, the native may be gifted with an ability to "re-set" communication skills to match the audience, making for an excellent interlocutor or advocate.

The inconjunct aspect from a Black Hole to Mercury requires frequent adjustment of communication style, revision of concepts, and adaptability to incremental shifts in the status quo reality. There is a need to rethink and re-imagine communication skills, redirecting or diverting content to repackage it in a more universally acceptable form.

Mercury in contact with multiple Black Holes can lead to dissociative break-down or mental fragmentation. The mind is pulled in so many directions at once that it may be difficult to focus and marshal thoughts into coherent arguments. Distracted and disordered, the native may appear confused, bewildered, or discombobulated, unable to convey data in logical sequence or follow a line of reasoning through to its rational conclusion.

# BLACK HOLE VENUS

Venus linked with a Black Hole often manifests as one over-powering, all-devouring passion, either for an individual or for a cause. The Black Hole seeks to attract what it desires to fulfill its insatiable appetite for energy, and the Venusian arenas of love, intimacy and romance, finances, and creative expression are among the most deeply felt in the human experience. Others may see the native as flighty or too fixated on superficialities, and there is the likelihood of at least one radical reappraisal of values over the course of the life.

Long term relationships may be difficult to achieve with this placement, or when they do manifest, may prove ongoing sources of energy drain and require a great deal of attention to maintain. Many relationships are short-term, volatile and unstable, and the native tends to form attachments quickly, almost unguardedly. The life history may be fraught with unsuccessful love affairs, unre-quited love, love gone wrong, love manifest but obsessive. There may be frequent "dry periods" where the native may not be roman-tically involved, and when with a partner, it may not always be the way they envisioned such a relationship to be.

Romantic partners tend to appear out of nowhere, unexpectedly; passions burn bright, but then are dimmed just as suddenly, leav-ing the native frustrated and abandoned. Infidelity can be an issue, with either these natives or their partners simultaneously embark-ing upon illicit romances which are kept hidden from view. Black Hole Venus relationships require a great deal of attention and work; much energy can be expended in romantic matters, which are never on a sure or certain footing. The Black Hole foundation for relation-ships is quicksand mixed with tar; impossible to extricate onself from, impossible to maintain the status quo or any relative balance.

Natives with this placement tend to fall for what they think is the ideal mate, and to fall hard. There are rarely halfway measures with Black Hole Venus; it is all, or nothing at all.

Frequent misunderstandings, disagreements or impassioned conflict are common. Turmoil and unexpected upset in relationship can be the rule, until the native understands that cultivating a loving relationship with oneself must precede forming lasting bonds with another. This can also be the signature of the individual who "loves too much," and tremendous amounts of energy can be funneled into relationships or partners' needs. There is a great capacity for love, but also a tendency to cling to the object of affection, perhaps to the detriment of the relationship if jealousy or rancor ensues.

Black Hole Venus commonly attracts partners whom others see as unsuited or inappropriate; often there is a huge age, social status, or economic disparity between the individuals. Black Hole Venus relationships are rarely traditional, and may be quite bizarre to others, though they often work quite well for the participants.

Black Hole Venus indicates that the course of true love may not always run smoothly for the native. There is the potential for a deep and lasting, transformative love, but the journey may be a complicated and uncertain one. This does not negate the possibility of stable, lifelong partnerships, especially those forming later in life, but even these relationships tend to be severely codependent, with the affection often feeling more like addiction. Black Hole Venus loathes to release what she has once acquired. But once the fire of experience has burned away the dross of Venus' fanciful expectations, Black Hole Venus natives can attain the gold of true love and commitment. In the meantime, Black Hole Venus can be obsessive and compulsive, and utterly engaged in things superficial or frivolous.

There is a very real possibility of eventually finding one's "soul mate," a loving partner to whom one is perfectly suited, but the native may need to kiss quite a few frogs before finding a prince. It should be noted that the purpose of these relationships is not "love," per se, but rather, as a learning tool, so once the lessons have been mastered, the relationship has run its course and it's time to move on. There is a choice to be made here, between the reality and the ideal. The native may expend a great deal of energy in finding the perfect mate, or the time and energy may be spent on trans-forming oneself or the loved one into someone that will better fit the bill of what is desired. This is a nonproductive exercise, particularly as applied to changing others, but Black Hole Venus has a strong desire to create through love and intimacy, and often its tack is to attempt to alter existing conditions to attain perfect union.

Black Hole Venus natives may have issues with rejection and control or manipulation, on either end of that spectrum or both in turn. The desire to completely possess the love interest, or be pos-sessed by him or her, can be overpowering. Black Hole Venus indi-viduals may often be said to love not wisely, but too well. Obsession is never far away when Venus' desire to attract is combined with the Black Hole's rapacious capacities to do so. The native tends to invest heavily in romantic matters, the heart can be easily committed, and there can be a profound sense of bewilderment when despite this effort relationships wither on the vine. As they age, Black Hole Venus natives find it easier to deal with the romantic confusion and uncertainty, and often find a stable, reciprocal partnership just when they despair of having one. At this point the deep reserves of love and affection the native has harbored all life long can become the basis for a lasting relationship.

Similarly, financial matters are likely to be marked by unstable conditions throughout. The theme is uncertainty and changeability, but this can manifest as change for the better or the worse, depend-ing on what current conditions pertain. The Black Hole Venus native often has the sensation of being a revolving door financially—whatever comes in, just as quickly goes out. This is not to say that finances cannot prosper; many Black Hole Venus natives are highly acquisitive and do well in the long term financially. But there are often frequent and unexpected financial reversals and money mat-ters require constant attention, sapping much of the native's ener-gies and resources.

Finances can be difficult to stabilize, and may require constant attention. Unexpected major expenses arise at least as often as un-looked-for income, and many Black Hole Venus natives spend their lives just trying to break even. The native's finances may be suscep-tible to wild swings, with windfall profits followed by devastating loss. In general, there will usually be enough money to sustain the needs of the moment, but often unexpected expenditures will mean that as money flows in, it also flows out, leaving the native in balance but unable to make progress toward financial goals. In time, however, many Black Hole Venus natives manage to acquire large amounts of capital, though it may be restricted or held in such fashion that it is not easily accessed.

Finances in general, even when good, tend to require a great deal of attention and focus; when bad, they promote worry and stress. The native can be drawn toward purchases which others consider to be of a frivolous, self indulgent, or foolish nature. Financial projection can be tricky; costs will vary, but usually exceed estimates or expectations. Money, or the lack of it, can become an obsession with this placement. In these instances, it is not always possible to plan for every contingency, but a solid, structured financial plan, with ongoing and careful monitoring, will go a long way toward ameliorating the more deleterious effects of these contacts.

There may be serious issues with self-worth and self-valuation, and feelings of being unloved or unlovable. But there is also an inherent and well-developed sense of aesthetics and beauty, and a love of the arts, as well as a strongly creative nature which needs to be expressed.

Creative expression is likely to be heightened by Venus' conjunction with a Black Hole. These natives have a unique, perhaps startling, creative or artistic perspective, culled from the infinity of parallel potential universes beyond the singularity of the Black Hole. Artistic or creative talent is augmented by connection with these potential realms in nonphysical dimensions and realities, but the danger here may be that the native's creative output is ahead of its time, and not easily understood, integrated or accepted by the mainstream, and thus not immediately recognized for its worth. If the native can take what is envisioned and channel it into a form which others understand and find pleasing, they will do well with their projects and efforts.

These natives can expend much energy in creative pursuits, which involve them deeply, becoming completely immersed in the act of creation. This can claim their attention to the extent that they seem transported beyond the normal boundaries of time and space when engaged in creative work, to the point where they lose contact with the world about them. They have the ability to conceive and depict, not just the observant reality, but the ways things might appear, and to express this creatively in their projects and when in the act of creation. Artistic expression is favored, with some inclining to a more free form, abstract expression, while others with Black Hole Venus become very focused on mastery of classical techniques and disciplines. These natives' unique perspective allows them to see beauty in things many others would not.

The desire nature can also be very intense, with these natives wanting what they want, and brooking no dissent, riding roughshod over whatever stands between them and the attainment of their desires. Personal values and ethics are also extremely important to the native, and while tolerant of others' points of view, there is no regard for those who exhibit no value system at all. The native has very definite values, strongly expressed, but also subject to reversal or dramatic revision at some point in the life. Similarly, ethics may prove more situational than static.

With Venus tied to Black Holes, women or love interests are likely to prove important agents of transformation or development throughout the course of the life. They may exercise a greater-than-usual influence or focus, but the demands they impose upon the native may also be considerable.

Ultimately, Black Hole Venus is about prioritizing values—self-esteem and self-love are worth more than attraction or appearance, and lead to more satisfying interactions with others. But Black Hole Venus can be torn by the things of this world, and frivolous or vain pursuits can become the focus here. Focusing on one's own self-improvement and ethical action will yield greater rewards in the long term than a fashion make-over.

As with all Black Hole contacts, the conjunction is the most intense and inescapable, but also affords the native the best opportunity of interfacing or working with the energies. The native comes to see the Venus areas of life through the filter of the Black Hole, and the instability, energy drain or volatility becomes the norm, the native learning to roll with the punches and even perhaps eventually able to make positive benefit from what others would consider a chaotic or distracted existence. There is a sense that the chaos is self-engendered, and flows naturally from the native, rather than being imposed from an outside source.

The opposition tends to play out via the actions or input of others, who appear to be the catalyst for the Black Hole disruptions which plague the native. There is a pattern of projecting issues onto others, saying, "it's not me, it's them," which is understandable but not strictly accurate, and counterproductive to finding the best way through the difficulties that others seem to present. Although seemingly the font of these difficulties, careful, mindful interaction with others can also be the route to clarity of one's own Black Hole Venus issues, as they provide awareness of patterns or habitual responses of which we may not be aware. For this to be successful, a conspiratorial, partnership-oriented, "we're in this together" approach is the most useful, rather than one accusatory in nature or focused on condemning or blaming others.

Venus squared by Black Holes finds difficulty in resolving conflicts which arise, and is too often torn between unpalatable alternatives, paralyzed into action by an inability to choose among them. This is the most highly stressful of the aspects, and there is no sense of any ingrained, internal locus from which the issues arise, s with the conjunction; nor is there a clear external source on which to focus blame, as in the opposition. Squares being the most energetic aspects, and Black Holes being receivers, transmitters and transducers of energy *par excellence*, the presence of a Black Hole in square to Venus indicates continual stress on Venus systems, and difficulty finding a safe space, a calm between the storms. With no natural outlet for the energies released, the native can become deflated and exhausted by the constant need to protect vital life energies from exposure or depletion.

When the aspect from the Black Hole to Venus is a sextile or trine, and is thus benefic, the more deleterious effects will lessen, or fail to intrude to a great extent. There is still likely to be some degree of romantic and fiscal instability, but in most cases, the native will "trade up" from existing conditions to better ones, even if the ride can be a bit rocky in getting there. The opportunities presented by Black Holes in benign aspect to Venus are many and varied, but they are also short-lived, and Black Hole doors, once shut, rarely re-open, so it becomes necessary for the native to recognize when opportunity is knocking and to marshal resources to take advantage of these quickly, maximizing possibilities and potential benefits.

The inconjunct aspect again provides more incremental change, which may nevertheless prove significant in the aggregate. The level of drama in these manifestations is not so unwieldy as to be disabling, but that very quality of moderation can belie the importance of what has occurred, so that when more drastic changes ensue, the native is unprepared for the harvest reaped.

Venus tied to multiple Black Holes often finds so many outlets for its energies that it becomes impossible to properly focus on any single creative project or intimate relationship, to the detriment of all. "Too many irons in the fire" about sums it up, with the native spread too thinly over a variety of efforts, any of which could prove profitable or rewarding if singled out for special attention or follow-through. The native may be unable to sustain long-term relationships due to a lack of sustainable focus, and financial matters can be particularly distracted or without proper structure or direction.

# BLACK HOLE MARS

Black Hole Mars indicates fluctuating or variable energy levels, an uneven feeling of vacillation between the two poles of vibrant action and listless torpor, with periods of hyper physical activity alternated with periods of lassitude and withdrawal. The native may be buoyant and active one day, and lethargic or debilitated the next. There can be a great deal of energy at the native's disposal, although tapping into it may not be easy.

There may be a tendency toward accidents, with a tendency to rash, impulsive action, as the native may act precipitately, without due consideration of the consequences of these actions. There may also be a tendency toward clumsiness, with reacting so quickly as to trip over one's own feet in the response, with the native tending to leap before looking, and action is often an immediate response to stimuli. The native may be inordinately stubborn or willful, from the perspective of detractors, or resolute and determined, from the perspective of supporters. Black Hole Mars can be excitable and energetic, with an enthusiasm that is contagious, but the native may become overly stimulated and require periods of rest or retirement to recuperate. Regeneration usually follows quickly, however. The native may put a great deal of energy into Mars arenas, such as sexual pursuit, exercise regimens, sports or outdoor activities

Mars linked with Black Hole energies indicates an unusual relationship with sex. The native is compelling, magnetic and attractive, able to easily draw in partners, as desired. There may be a tendency to go to extremes, as Black Hole Mars denotes both the celibate ascetic and the debauched libertine; sometimes both will manifest in the same individual alternately, or at different phases of life. Most Black Hole Mars natives fall somewhere in between, but there is an undeniable attraction for taboo or forbidden practices, and same sex attraction is common.

Sexual matters can become obsessive, and there is a greater than usual tendency to keep sexual matters secret or hidden; deception from or toward the native is also possible. There is further the increased probability of the native maintaining a "second," secret life in sexual matters, and even one's closest intimates may be unaware of these elements. There is generally a large sexual appetite with this placement, one others may consider excessive.

Sexual impulses may also be erratic and overpowering when at peak, with again, periods of intense activity punctuated with long "dry" spells without sexual contact. During these periods, indeed, at all times, the native may be very active with autoerotic practices. Sexual magnetism is enhanced, with the native attracting others easily, albeit somewhat haphazardly. Partners may appear suddenly, without expectation, and disappear again just as quickly once the passion burns itself out.

Black Hole Mars can also be experimental and predatory in sexual matters, inclining to partners or situations whom others see as inappropriate, unworthy or offensive. There may be an attraction for secretive, unsafe or daring, even dangerous, practices or partners, and the sexual nature can be consuming. A great deal of energy may be expended in sexual pursuit and conquest, and the native may be psychologically fixated on the subject. The native is unlikely to be satisfied with a single partner, nor is serial monogamy preferred by the these individuals, who have a marked propensity to stray, always seeking new experience. There can be an element of thrill-seeking.

Black Hole Mars may generate issues with aggression as opposed to assertiveness, and the native may have difficulty either expressing anger, or controlling it. Black Holes incline one to extremes, so sublimation of even justified anger into simmering resentment is one possibility, and having a reputation for temper tantrums is another. Often the Black Hole Mars native will repress anger until the breaking point is reached, when volatile, even violent reactions ensue. This repressive Black Hole Mars can create internal conflict and sometimes disease. When the anger is released, it can be all the more shocking for being so unexpected and atypical of the native's usual response.

Anger and aggression may be major issues in the life, with some Black Hole Mars natives justly renowned for their short tempers and intense reactions. Anger may be quick to flare, and burn brightly for its time, but is just as quickly cast off and forgotten, as a summer storm dims the horizon, hurls its lightning, and then recedes to reveal a refreshed landscape and a cleared atmosphere. Easily provoked, the native does not generally hold a grudge, but reacts to stimuli, sometimes explosively, and then moves on. There may also be periods of extreme, even violent anger, which can be set off suddenly and unexpectedly, even by apparently trivial provocation. The challenge here is to become assertive without being overly aggressive; in extreme cases, anger management or assertiveness training may be advisable; cultivating methods of relaxation, such as meditation or yoga, is essential to modulate the native's temper. It is also possible that if these natives, for whatever reasons, find it difficult to express or own this tendency, they may attract others into the life to act out this pattern.

Black Hole Mars natives can be courageous or cowardly; again, the tendency of Black Holes to go to extremes can just as easily describe either alternative. Often what passes for courage with this combination is in reality an inability to assess risk, and to act abruptly, without due consideration. Sometimes this ends well, at other times the results are less fortunate.

Competitive sports are favored, with many Black Hole Mars natives becoming professional players, or devoting large amounts of time to amateur team sports. Individual, "one on one" competitions are also popular manifestations of these energies, with many Black Hole Mars natives holding records in the sport of their choice. Military careers can frequently be attractive to the native, and the combination can indicate proficiency with weaponry, although tactical expertise is not indicated by this contact. Hunting and fishing are common recreational activities for these individuals, who often betray a strong desire to shed blood in some form. There may be an attraction for, or fascination with, death, either as a concept or in its reality.

Health-wise, a vibrant constitution is generally present, although the native may be prone to accident or injury, often due to carelessness or precipitate action, and internalized stress can be a problem.

Blood pressure and blood sugar should be monitored carefully, and the native is more than usually susceptible to blood diseases, diabetes or sexually transmitted diseases.

Black Hole Mars individuals tend toward very active lifestyles. A daily physical regimen is essential for regulating and properly distributing excess energies which might otherwise manifest as misdirected anger or turned inward into depression. Many become overly focused on exercise regimes and physical activities; there is a danger that involvement in these interests may become excessive or obsessive. Black Hole Mars individuals may be prone to abuse or violence, directed outwardly to others or vented by others upon them. Quick to agitation, there may be a daily background 'hum' of discontent and fractiousness, as the native upsets easily and allows outside elements to disrupt equilibrium.

With Mars conjoined a Black Hole, the native's energies may be overly directed inward, with difficulty expressing these outwardly. There is a greater risk of self-focus to the extent of isolation, or an inability to interact with others normally which can leave the native alienated. Sexuality can become compulsive, and anger self-directed, resulting in depression and health-related concerns. There are very powerful internal reserves of energy with the conjunction, but there may be difficulty processing or distributing these for daily use.

If the danger of the Black Hole Mars conjunction is sexual compulsion, the risk in the opposition aspect is obsession, or objectification of others sexually. The need to attain the desired object may result in fixation or dependency; at minimum, an unhealthy preoccupation. Anger is similarly directed outward, to the other, and these individuals often see themselves as victims, put upon by others and at the mercy of events or persons beyond their control.

The square aspect yields the most disruptive and unstable manifestations, and the native may feel at times under siege, a prey to the slings and arrows of outrageous fortune. Where the conjunction may afford some self-control, and the opposition provides a useful "other" to confront, the square's effects are more random and not necessarily subject to any logical provenance. This dramatically increases the stress in situations and circumstance which arise from the Black Hole Mars pairing, and leaves the native in a constant state of apprehension, waiting for the next blow to fall.

Paranoia, mistrust and suspicion may result, preventing the native from completely relaxing without withdrawing into a privacy or solitude where the price of security and peace is isolation.

Sextile and trine aspects provide opportunities to augment or enhance our Mars realities. Emotions along the anger-aggression-assertiveness continuum are more easily regulated, and energy levels are not in as much flux or turmoil as with the harsher aspects. Positive benefit can accrue from the doors opened by the Black Hole, if the native is perceptive enough to recognize these opportunities when they present themselves.

The inconjunct aspect can provoke stress ailments, likely of a chronic nature. There is a continual need to adjust energy outputs, but difficulty in determining proper focus or application of these energies, once released. Manifestations lack drama and are often not measurably disruptive, but in combination over time can produce significant alteration or the status quo reality.

Mars in aspect to multiple Black Holes can experience scattered focus and extreme fluctuation of energy levels. This is a combination which does not favor constancy or monogamy, and tends to increase secretiveness and compartmentalization of areas of the life which would conflict if they interacted.

# BLACK HOLE JUPITER

In general, Jupiter linked with Black Hole energies indicates one who shifts belief systems and philosophical ground with relative ease, though there may be some degree of dogmatism about the current beliefs in each one of the various stages of this spiritual development. Black Hole Jupiter individuals tend to have a more free-flowing belief system which they adapt frequently as new data becomes available, or fresh insights influence their thinking. There is a strong likelihood that the native will endorse at least two radically different belief systems at different times throughout the course of the life, and the final determination, if there is one, will belong to no particular system, but rather will include an eclectic mix of ideas from widely differing traditions. The native's own spiritual views are likely to be strong, and perhaps unorthodox, with the probability of at least one major "conversion" experience in the life, where belief systems took a dramatic turn; others may consider their views eccentric or downright bizarre. Black Hole Jupiter individuals tend to an extremely personal, unique life philosophy, and do not easily adhere to or endorse the spiritual authority of others. Leaders rather than followers, this pairing is the archetype of the mystic and the seeker—the one who penetrates deeply into the tenets of a faith, but is also flexible enough to adapt and integrate new ideas and precepts when understanding expands to include them.

As with Black Hole Mercury, there may be difficulties with education, particularly higher education, often stemming from a difficulty or inability to work within the system, obey rules, or honor hierarchies. Jupiter/Black Hole natives may also have difficulty performing in an academic setting. They learn differently than most individuals, and are often loathe to play by the rules so important in the higher education realm. This can manifest as frustration and a lack of accomplishment in these fields, or as a great deal of energy expended in academic pursuits. There may be blocks or problems to attaining degrees or accreditation, but this placement can also describe one who has earned many degrees and spent the better part of life in institutions of higher learning. Others have a reaction similar to retrograde Jupiter, namely, a difficulty dancing to another's tune and working within the limitations or confines of the academic setting. Jumping through bureaucratic hoops is not to their liking, and their insights and theories often run counter to accepted standards, and so can be marginalized by traditional academics. They may not test well, and find it irksome to conform to others' expectations. This would not preclude the attaining of degrees or other educational goals, only a certain uncomfortableness in dealing with the types of institutions that provide them, and the individuals that one typically encounters in such a setting.

Jupiter allied with a Black Hole indicates a deep and penetrating intelligence, and the ability to grapple with complex philosophical or academic issues. The native has a natural attraction for deep philosophical constructs, but Black Hole Jupiter also craves knowledge and revels in the functions of the higher mind—logic, reason, abstract thought, etc.—and thus many Black Hole Jupiter natives are self-taught. For many of these individuals, the learning and study is an end in itself, and does not necessarily translate into worldly success due to the enhanced education. But often Black Hole Jupiter natives are actually more educated than others, as Black Holes can indicate where we put our focus and attention, or direct our energies, and thus Black Hole Jupiter can indicate the perpetual student, one who has piled on degree after degree and seems trapped within the confines of academia. Sometimes this will manifest as a career in education as well, and Black Hole Jupiter natives are among the most innovative educators, often working with intellectually disadvantaged or challenged populations. For many Black Hole Jupiter natives who pursue multiple degrees in compensation for a perceived inadequacy, often the degrees they earn are not put to practical use, and thus their effort in attaining them can be said to have been in some sense wasted.

Matters of education, travel, philosophy and religion can be more than usually transformative for these individuals, who may find that contact with foreign places or persons, or those in academic fields, can be a powerful catalyst for their growth and development, may become unusually formative or influential in the life, and often prove pivotal to it.

Generally considered "lucky," Black Hole Jupiter natives usually find themselves in the right place at the right time, to advance their goals. There is a possibility of amassing considerable wealth, as Jupiter in combination with Black Hole energies can lead to significant gain via gaming, speculation, or investment.

There may be a tendency to overextend one's self, to promise more than can be delivered, to bite off more than one can chew, or step out on a limb before being assured it can support one. Gregarious, generous and open-handed, these natives may have difficulty refusing requests, and others tend to see them as somehow larger than life.

A Black Hole in conjunction with Jupiter expresses as integrated fully into the native, an essential, formative part of the individual which is there consistently throughout. There is no separation, no sense of division, between the 'normal' Jupiter functioning and the Black Hole's effects upon it; it is simply how things are, and becomes the standard by which the native measures Jupiter issues. The heightened ability to conceptualize, theorize, and deduce which Black Hole Jupiter can bring can lead to isolation from others with this placement, as the native's own experiences can be so vastly different from others, there is little common ground on which to meet. Philosophically, in particular, there is often an adherence to concepts which others find bizarre or counter-intuitive, but which have appeared consistent and logical to the native from infancy.

In opposition, the Black Hole Jupiter native may feel threatened or thwarted by the opinions or ideas of others, which seem counter or contrary to those the individual espouses. Others can help to clarify the native's concepts or make them more accessible or palatable to others, but there can be difficulty in achieving the meeting of the minds necessary to do so effectively. Others may encourage the native to take on more than can be reasonably managed, or delve into areas for which the individual is unprepared.

In square, the Black Hole acts at cross purposes to the native's intent, leading to confusion, stress or alienation from others with whom the native wishes to interact, but to whom he may appear disordered, muddled, or uncooperative. There is a sense that whatever the native does, however he expresses abstract concepts, theories, or ideas, true communication and sharing of thoughts is impossible, with genuine understanding or intellectual give-and-take elusive. It is as if the two parties are speaking different languages, or using metaphors which the other does not understand, and bridging the gap in mental acuity can seem a thankless task, doomed to defeat. Fortune varies, with the Black Hole at times eliciting unexpected advancement, and at others seemingly snatching defeat from the jaws of victory, leaving the native stunned and staggered at the sudden reversal.

Sextiles and trines are far less inimical, and can assist the native in elevating thoughts and ideas into an art form, creating connections with others which allow them to conceptualize even the most complicated or abstruse subjects. Translation and integration of foreign languages or concepts is favored with these aspects, which also favor mediation, diplomacy and the finding of common ground between opposed parties. These are "good luck" aspects, where shifting conditions which manifest suddenly and without warning will often elevate the native to a more fortunate circumstance, or allow greater scope or success than was anticipated.

The inconjunct aspect often manifests as a tedious need to continually revise and review the beliefs held by the native, which help co-create that individual's reality. As with all inconjunct aspects, change is more incremental than typical of Black Hole interactions, but over time can become substantial and significant, altering the native's reality in important and lasting ways.

Jupiter linked with multiple Black Holes betrays an intellectual inconsistency which may appear to others as situational or based in the native's self interest of the moment. In actual fact, the native may simply be pulled in many directions intellectually, and finds difficulty crafting a single coherent philosophy. There is a tendency to attempt too much at once, to have too many irons in the fire, and subsequently to fail to follow-through or support any of these goals to a successful conclusion.

# BLACK HOLE SATURN

Saturn combined with a Black Hole promotes a high degree of turmoil or instability in work or career matters, as well as allowing the native to bring exceptional focus and energy to whatever work-related task is at hand. Black Hole Saturn natives find that work and career demands can impinge heavily on their resources and energies, but workplace stability may be difficult to achieve. There may be difficulty choosing a career, and it is likely that the native will have embarked on at least two completely unrelated careers in the life, sometimes simultaneously, more often serially, as Black Hole energies tend to facilitate major shifts and changes of direction. Also, job-hopping is common, with the native shifting employment regularly, especially early in life. This is particularly common in response to changing conditions such as business closures, layoffs and downsizing, or the native's own peripatetic movements, which require a new job search due to relocation. Many of these changes may be sudden and unexpected, and not all are likely to be at the native's behest, and may seem to be to the native's apparent detriment. In general, however, though there may be temporary set-backs, career progress will be steady, if erratic and unpredictable. There is the possibility of excelling in the chosen career, but such success is likely to be perceived by others as sudden or 'overnight,' when in reality the native is likely to have been very focused on career matters for a very long time. Black Hole Saturn natives do not always function well as subordinates; they tend to have control issues and problems with persons in authority. They act best in supervisory or managerial capacities, and most favorable is self-employment, or a situation in which they are left to their own devices and allowed greater control over the ways they organize themselves and their work output. Black Hole Saturn often describes the "workaholic" who is focused on career to the detriment of every other area of life. This combination can also describe the tireless second-in-command, the one who does all the work but never gets the credit. There may be a tendency to become a scapegoat for others' failures, and a sense of being blocked in aspirations by the powers that be. On the other hand, power accrues naturally to these individuals, who may wield considerable influence, especially behind the scenes. The career path can be a twisted one, and though prominence can result, it may not be lasting, as Black Hole Saturn delights in pulling up the rug just as one begins to feel comfortable; the native may never feel secure in what has been attained. Promotion often comes unexpectedly through the sudden absence of superiors.

In general work matters and concerns will take a greater than usual amount of the native's focus and attention. Black Hole Saturn individuals tend to be hard workers, putting enormous amounts of effort into their careers; this may not always be acknowledged by the powers that be, and it may take years, or decades, to work through until this advancement is achieved. Highly organized and serious-minded, the native is responsible and may be considered the authority, or "go-to" person at work, whatever their actual job title; often Black Hole Saturn natives perform tasks and responsibilities well above their pay scale or job description. There is a great ability to focus and a natural affinity with organization conferred by this placement. Detail oriented and performance-driven, Black Hole Saturn natives make excellent project managers, though they may have difficulty in delegating even the simplest tasks to others, as they have high standards of perfection which they may think others incapable of attaining. The Black Hole can also open unexpected doors and reveal unconsidered alternatives; it is always incumbent upon the Black Hole Saturn native to be aware that what seems like a roadblock may be a detour sign to better things.

Black Hole Saturn also affects the native's relations with the Father and authority figures in general. The Father may have been seen as either distant and unapproachable, or as devouring and manipulative, a figure of dominance and harsh criticism which the native has internalized as a driving force for perfection. There may be actual separation from the father early in life due to death, divorce, or abandonment. This early image reverberates throughout the life, creating conflict with persons in authority over the native, who may also be unduly critical of self or others; they tend to judge quickly and harshly. This may extend to one's own inner critic, which may be very harsh and uncompromising, creating a struggle for a perfectionism which is not humanly attainable. This could translate into the native's relations with others, particularly those over whom one is in a position of authority, such as children. This pattern of dissonance between generations may repeat with the native's own children, with the native reprising the role seen in the father during youth. There may also be blocks to parenthood, or enforced absence from the children's lives due to divorce, career commitments, etc.

The Black Hole Saturn native is very disciplined and capable of a high degree of self-mastery and focus, though it may take decades for these traits to fully develop. Black Hole Saturn can be very detail oriented and works inveterately to accomplish its tasks; it is structured and self-disciplined, and plans ahead. Not all these plans will be successful, some may lead to blind alleys or dead ends, others may pay off further down the road, or provide access to unexpected opportunities much later, long after they have been deemed unproductive. Practical and pragmatic, Black Hole Saturn individuals are in general extremely competent, but often lackluster.

In conjunction, although there are still disruptions and unexpected developments which intrude upon the native's plans, it is easier to detect a pattern within the apparent chaos. The native has some degree of control over career direction and the responses made to both set-backs and unanticipated opportunities. Again, the pattern of frequent job changes or loss of employment is so ingrained in the native's experience, that this seems natural, and coping mechanisms have likely long ago been developed to deal with it.

In opposition, it is others who appear to be frustrating the native's goals and aspirations. There can be a tendency to project blame onto external sources, rather than looking within to see where the individual's own performance, or lack of same, has affected the desired outcome of the efforts extended in career matters. But others can also be major catalysts in the native's career path, offering advancement or extending advice and the benefit of their experience, which, if the native accepts this assistance, will propel the individual to the next stage of the process.

As always, the square produces the most unpredictable, chaotic conditions. Often the native finds that two diametrically opposed alternatives will present themselves, and deciding what to do for the best can seem an impossible task. High stress situations arise in the work place or when making career choices, frequently with options which cannot be resolved to the satisfaction of all concerned.

Sextile or trine aspects from Black Holes to Saturn tend toward positive results, often to the amazement of others, from whose perspective the native does not seem to have done much to earn such reward. There is excellent timing conferred with this combination, and being in the right place at the right time often yields advancement which far exceeds expectations. Also common is advancement due to the unexpected removal or absence of superiors.

With the inconjunct aspect, the accent is on regular but gradual or piecemeal change, alteration which at the time seems unremarkable, but which later proves to be key to future advancement. This less dramatic adaptation of circumstance, whether positive or negative, can be tedious to endure, but is in the long run much more stable than the volatile changes brought by harsher aspects.

Saturn in combination with multiple Black Holes may experience difficulty in finding focus in career matters. So many possible avenues or alternatives may arise that the native feels paralyzed by the options, unable to commit to any single one, to the potential detriment of all. Fragmenting of work energies, multiple career paths embarked upon simultaneously, diverted focus and lack of consistent direction can all result.

# BLACK HOLE CHIRON

Chiron on a Black Hole indicates a potential to act as a guide or facilitator to others in need, acting as a catalyst for growth to others in crisis or transition, aiding them in connecting with others and helping them to resolve their own conflicts and hurts. This can lead to a mentoring, teaching role that may involve education per se, or simply fulfill the role of leading others through the labyrinth of their pain into a fuller, more meaningful existence. The native has deep internal scars from past experience, both in this life and former existences, and these can seem overwhelming and threaten to completely immerse the native in their own concerns. Interaction with others is vital to breaking out of this dynamic, and Black Hole Chiron individuals are often led to a life of service in dealing with literal, physical pain, via work with health care in some form. There is a strongly maverick streak to the native, a desire to strike out on one's own path, regardless of others' opinions, and this can seem an all-consuming need at times as the native grapples with a need, on the one hand, to conform enough to fulfill the imperative to be of service to others, and on the other, to remain true to who they uniquely are, free of restriction or hindrance.

In conjunction, the pattern of reality-altering intrusion on the life is well established, and the native has some degree of control over the effects, which are more organic and centered on the individual, seemingly arising from within. Coping mechanisms have been developed which help to offset the worst effects.

In opposition, the native looks to others as the root cause of the difficulties, projecting blame and refusing to own any responsibility for the circumstances. Active communication with others can lead to greater awareness of the native's issues and nonproductive patterns associated with the natal planetary energy.

In square, difficult choices present themselves between unpalatable alternatives, more conflict and stress is evoked, indecision and stagnation can result. The native tends to alternate between dramatically differing approaches to dealing with crises as they present themselves, but is never certain they have made the best choices.

By sextile or trine, unlooked for, positive opportunities for growth or advancement can present themselves. Beneficial circumstances accrue naturally, without obvious effort on the part of the native, but require active participation to achieve their utmost potential.

With the inconjunct, change is incremental but builds to critical mass, when major alterations can occur. There is a constant background hum of tension due to the need for continual adjustment in circumstances, procedures, or approaches to issues as they arise.

When Chiron is linked to multiple Black Holes, it becomes difficult to maintain focus or concentrate upon essentials relating to Chirotic areas. Distraction and fragmentation are likely, with the native's energies pulled in many directions at once.

# BLACK HOLE URANUS

U ranus on a Black Hole indicates a strong need to feel free of restriction, and as the master of one's own fate or destiny. This combination can convey genius-level insights, but also describes madness, which is the flip side of the coin. There is a strong urge to individuate and express one's uniqueness, which may manifest as extreme rebelliousness and a satisfaction in shocking others' sensibilities just for the fun of it, or the cultivation of a nonconformist, maverick persona. Creative thinking and a unique perspective which favors problem solving are among the potential benefits conferred by this combination, but it can also be stubbornly willful and unconcerned with the ramifications for others of one's actions. There may be problems with high tech gadgetry such as computers and communication devices, which may malfunction or require frequent replacement. Black Hole Uranus natives have a natural facility for the sciences, and may devise brilliant theories or inventions, though these may be in advance of their time, and difficult if not impossible to implement given the current circumstances.

In conjunction, the pattern of reality-altering intrusion on the life is well established, and the native has some degree of control over the effects, which are more organic and centered on the individual, seemingly arising from within. Coping mechanisms have been developed which help to offset the worst effects.

In opposition, the native looks to others as the root cause of the difficulties, projecting blame and refusing to own any responsibility for the circumstances. Active communication with others can lead to greater awareness of the native's issues and nonproductive patterns associated with the natal planetary energy.

In square, difficult choices present themselves between unpalatable alternatives, more conflict and stress is evoked, indecision and stagnation can result. The native tends to alternate between dramatically differing approaches to dealing with crises as they present themselves, but is never certain they have made the best choices.

By sextile or trine, unlooked for, positive opportunities for growth or advancement can present themselves. Beneficial circumstances accrue naturally, without obvious effort on the part of the native, but require active participation to achieve their utmost potential.

With the inconjunct, change is incremental but builds to critical mass, when major alterations can occur. There is a constant background hum of tension due to the need for continual adjustment in circumstances, procedures, or approaches to issues as they arise.

When Uranus is linked to multiple Black Holes, it becomes difficult to maintain focus or concentrate upon essentials relating to Uranian areas. Distraction and fragmentation are likely, with the native's energies pulled in many directions at once.

# BLACK HOLE NEPTUNE

Neptune conjoined a Black Hole is strongly escapist, which can manifest as alcohol or substance abuse, but can also be evoked in any number of other ways, whatever distracts the native's focus from practical reality and one's responsibilities to it. There may be issues with addiction or codependency, but Black Hole Neptune is also highly empathetic and has a strong spiritual core. There may be a tendency to gloss over problems and difficulties, and an unwillingness to face unpleasant truths. Black Hole Neptune can have issues with clarity or lack of focus, but it is highly creative and aesthetically advanced, with musical or poetic abilities common. There can also be a facility for acting or theatrics, with the native capable of assuming other guises and characters at whim.

In conjunction, the pattern of reality-altering intrusion on the life is well established, and the native has some degree of control over the effects, which are more organic and centered on the individual, seemingly arising from within. Coping mechanisms have been developed which help to offset the worst effects.

In opposition, the native looks to others as the root cause of the difficulties, projecting blame and refusing to own any responsibility for the circumstances. Active communication with others can lead to greater awareness of the native's issues and nonproductive patterns associated with the natal planetary energy.

In square, difficult choices present themselves between unpalatable alternatives, more conflict and stress is evoked, indecision and stagnation can result. The native tends to alternate between dramatically differing approaches to dealing with crises as they present themselves, but is never certain they have made the best choices.

By sextile or trine, unlooked for, positive opportunities for growth or advancement can present themselves. Beneficial circumstances accrue naturally, without obvious effort on the part of the native, but require active participation to achieve their utmost potential.

With the inconjunct, change is incremental but builds to critical mass, when major alterations can occur. There is a constant background hum of tension due to the need for continual adjustment in circumstances, procedures, or approaches to issues as they arise.

When Neptune is linked to multiple Black Holes, it becomes difficult to maintain focus or concentrate upon essentials relating to Neptunian areas. Distraction and fragmentation are likely, with the native's energies pulled in many directions at once.

# BLACK HOLE PLUTO

Pluto conjoined a Black Hole indicates one who functions as a catalyst for others in crisis or transition, as there is a natural affinity for mediating between realities which this placement confers. There may be issues with extreme jealousy or possessiveness, and a marked tendency to act behind the scenes, to manipulate or attempt to control others. The native may become obsessed with secretiveness, guarding against revealing too much to others, and this can result in an overly closed, withholding personality. There are vast reserves of energy, but they may be difficult to access, leaving the native feeling frustrated and unable to fully manifest potential. There is a strong urge to power and extreme willfulness which, if thwarted, may degenerate into obsessive/compulsive behaviors and bizarre quirks or eccentricities.

In conjunction, the pattern of reality-altering intrusion on the life is well established, and the native has some degree of control over the effects, which are more organic and centered on the individual, seemingly arising from within. Coping mechanisms have been developed which help to offset the worst effects.

In opposition, the native looks to others as the root cause of the difficulties, projecting blame and refusing to own any responsibility for the circumstances. Active communication with others can lead to greater awareness of the native's issues and nonproductive patterns associated with the natal planetary energy.

In square, difficult choices present themselves between unpalatable alternatives, more conflict and stress is evoked, indecision and stagnation can result. The native tends to alternate between dramatically differing approaches to dealing with crises as they present themselves, but is never certain they have made the best choices.

By sextile or trine, unlooked for, positive opportunities for growth or advancement can present themselves. Beneficial circumstances accrue naturally, without obvious effort on the part of the native, but require active participation to achieve their utmost potential.

With the inconjunct, change is incremental but builds to critical mass, when major alterations can occur. There is a constant background hum of tension due to the need for continual adjustment in circumstances, procedures, or approaches to issues as they arise.

When Pluto is linked to multiple Black Holes, it becomes difficult to maintain focus or concentrate upon essentials relating to Plutonic areas. Distraction and fragmentation are likely, with the native's energies pulled in many directions at once.

# BLACK HOLE BIOGRAPHIES

# MICHAEL JACKSON

*"Like a comet blazing 'cross the evening sky, gone too soon;*
*Like a rainbow fading in the twinkling of an eye, gone too soon;*
*Shiny and sparkly and splendidly bright, here one day, gone one night."*
   –"Gone Too Soon," lyrics by Michael Jackson

*"He was, I think, one of the first artists that transcended everything."*
   –Quincy Jones, music producer

*"He was a force of nature."*

   –Debbie Allen, choreographer

On June 25, 2009 the entire world reacted in shock to the news of the sudden and unexpected death of Michael Jackson, global pop icon, who suffered a cardiac arrest at his Los Angeles home, exact cause as yet undetermined. Jackson was found in his bed shortly after noon, not breathing and unresponsive; his personal physician worked for more than 30 minutes to revive the singer before 911 was called. Paramedics arrived within five minutes and continued to administer CPR for nearly 45 minutes on site, after which he was moved to UCLA Medical Center and attempts to resuscitate continued for another full hour. Jackson was finally pronounced dead at 2:26 PM PDT.

The death sent shockwaves throughout the globe, and speculation about the cause, Jackson's testamentary arrangements, and the fate of his children began almost immediately.  A public memorial held at Los Angeles' Staples Center on July 7 was attended by more than 17,000 family, friends and fans, the latter chosen at random from internet applications submitted by more than 1.2 million people. The memorial featured performances and eulogies by Mariah

Carey, Usher, Reverend Al Sharpton, Queen Latifah, and Brooke Shields, among others, and was broadcast live over five networks to an estimated worldwide audience of nearly 1 billion.

In the week following his death, Jackson, a major influence on pop culture, music and dance, continued to set records. Sales of Jackson's music outstripped those of any living artist, with nine out of the top ten spots on the Billboard Pop Catalog Chart held by his albums, and more than 2.6 million digital downloads of his songs purchased within three days of his demise, the first time any artist has sold more than a million downloads in a week. *"Number Ones,"* a compilation of Jackson's greatest hits, sold 108,000 copies, with his 1982 tour de force *"Thriller,"* which remains the best selling album of all time, adding another 101,000 copies to its 104 million copy total. Radio play of his music increased more than 1700%.

Talented and controversial, Jackson began his career at the age of eight, as lead singer and youngest member of "The Jackson 5," composed of the elder brothers in a family of nine from Gary, Indiana. Father Joseph was a strict disciplinarian with a sadistic bent, who would sit in a chair with his belt at the ready while the group rehearsed, prepared to literally lash out at any under-performing boy. In a 1993 Oprah Winfrey interview, Michael revealed that as a child he would feel sick and even start to vomit when he saw his father, and that antipathy remained into adulthood; Joseph Jackson was left nothing by the terms of Michael's will.

After two years of extensive touring in the Midwest , often performing as opening acts in burlesque halls and strip clubs, "The Jackson 5" were signed by Motown's Berry Gordy in 1968, and their impact was instantaneous. Their first four singles, "I Want You Back," "ABC," "The Love You Save," and "I'll Be There" all hit number one on Billboard's Hot 100, the first group ever to achieve that feat. The group's crossover appeal was also unparalleled among black artists, due in large part to Michael's youth, which gave "The Jackson 5" a squeaky-clean, nonthreatening image, and to Berry Gordy's brilliant marketing of their style as "bubblegum soul." Mainstream white audiences became enthralled by Michael, and within mere months the group was being mobbed at airports and hotels in "Beatlemania" fashion.

In their heyday, "The Jackson 5" spawned an entire merchandising industry, including drum kits, stickers, posters, coloring books, and were even animated in a Saturday morning cartoon on ABC, the Rankin/Bass-produced *"The Jackson 5ive,"* which ran two seasons in the early 'seventies. Michael's solo career developed alongside the group's success, but long outlived it. In 1971 his first single, "Got To Be There" became a Top Five hit, and in 1972 he followed this with the successful title song from the movie *"Ben."* In 1975 Jackson left Motown, but continued as primary songwriter for the group, now renamed "The Jacksons." In 1978 he met music producer Quincy Jones while rehearsing for his role as Scarecrow in "The Wiz," a musical version of "The Wizard of Oz." The two formed a partnership that produced Michael's next solo album, 1979's hugely popular *"Off the Wall,"* the first album ever to score four top ten singles, including number one hits "Rock With You" and "Don't Stop 'Til You Get Enough." *"Off the Wall"* ultimately sold more than 20 million copies worldwide, but it was its successor that would catapult Jackson to a position of global super-stardom from which he never fully retreated.

1982's *"Thriller"* became the best-selling album of all time, with more than 104 million copies sold to date; at its peak, it was selling at the rate of one million copies per week. It dominated the top ten on Billboard's 200 for 80 consecutive weeks, 37 of them in the number one spot. Seven of its nine tracks were released as singles, and all hit the top ten of Billboard's Hot 100. His "Billie Jean" video broke the color barrier at MTV, Jackson becoming the first black artist played there, while the *"Thriller"* title track video, directed by John Landis, is credited with transforming music video from a promotional vehicle into an art form in itself. The 14-minute epic created a sensation; after its debut, MTV was forced to run it twice hourly to meet viewer demand. Follow-up videos for "Beat It" and "Wanna Be Startin' Somethin'" cemented Jackson's reputation as an innovative leader in the burgeoning genre.

In March 1983 Jackson arguably hit his apex, as he debuted his soon-to-be-iconic "Moon Walk" dance routine at the live airing of the Motown 25th Anniversary special, viewed by some 47 million people. Jackson performed "Billie Jean" and astonished the audience with the technical wizardry of the apparently effortless gliding motion he had perfected, soon to be imitated by many. The Moon

Walk was a further development of steps he and his brothers had pioneered in the '70s, then called "the Robot," but Jackson took the style to a level never before seen, and rarely replicated since.

But within this period of unparalleled triumph and success lay the seeds of his future eccentricities and challenges. In 1979 Jackson had broken his nose rehearsing a complex dance routine, and required plastic surgery to repair the damage. The initial surgery was botched, requiring a second procedure, and Jackson remained dissatisfied with the results, beginning a long series of rhinoplasty and cosmetic surgery which would irrevocably alter his appearance. Paired with Jackson's bizarre lightening of skin tone, which he claimed was caused by vitiligo, a skin disease altering pigmentation, and the straightening of his hair, abandoning the various styles of Afro he had previously worn, these changes gave rise to frequent speculation about his motivation in transforming his image. Was Jackson rejecting his genetic inheritance and aspiring to be white? As the singer became more and more self-conscious about his appearance, he began to retreat further into his own private world when not performing, eventually resorting to bizarre tactics such as face masks, veils, head scarves and shrouds when in public.

In January 1984 Jackson's hair caught fire during the filming of a Pepsi commercial, and he was seriously injured, with third degree burns to his scalp. The painful recovery began a confrontation with another of Jackson's demons, addiction to prescription medication, initially pain killers, then anti-depressants and sedatives, which likely ended by taking his life.

In 1985 Jackson teamed with lyrics legends Paul McCartney and Lionel Ritchie on a variety of projects. He joined with Ritchie to write "We Are the World," and was one of 39 artists who performed on the recording. The single sold more than 20 million copies and raised millions of dollars for famine relief in Africa, the first major effort by the US entertainment industry to intervene in world suffering. While partnering with Paul McCartney on several songwriting efforts, including "The Girl Is Mine" and "Say Say Say," Jackson became intrigued by the business opportunities available in owning other people's songs, and excited by the prospect of buying the Beatles catalog as an investment. After ten months of rigorous negotiations, wherein his chief rivals were McCartney himself and Lennon's widow Yoko Ono, he purchased the catalog for $47.5 million, and it remains the foundation of his estate today.

In 1986, in an effort to promote a more masculine image for an upcoming film, Jackson underwent a fourth rhinoplasty and added a cleft to his chin. The film, *"Captain EO,"* was directed by Francis Ford Coppola, shot in 3D, and the most expensive short film to that date, featured for 11 years at Disneyland's Tomorrowland and eight years at Disney World's Epcot Center. Rumors that he slept in a hyperbaric oxygen chamber to retard the ageing process, and had purchased the bones of the Elephant Man, were untrue, but he did buy and befriend a pet chimp called Bubbles, and formed several unusually strong friendships with child stars of the time, including Emmanuel Lewis and Macaulay Culkin. Cosmetic surgeries continued, including a forehead lift, cheekbone reconstruction, and thinned lips. This was all fodder for the tabloid press, who promptly dubbed him "Wacko Jacko."

It took Jackson five years to follow-up *"Thriller."* 1987's *"Bad"* was not its equal, but still extremely successful commercially, producing seven hit singles, five of which reached number one on the charts, a record for any single album; its MTV video releases gave most Americans their first real look at what Jackson had become, further feeding speculation. During *"Bad"'s* World Tour Jackson broke attendance records right and left, including a Guinness Record when 507,000 people showed up for seven sold-out shows at Britain's Wembley Stadium. In 123 concerts he performed for 4.4 million people, and the tour grossed a cool $125 million, another Guinness Record. He also premiered his new, somewhat aggressive, military style outfits which would soon become trademark.

In 1988 Jackson used some of his earnings to purchase a 1700 acre, $17 million property near Santa Ynez, California, which would become the Neverland Ranch. With an estimated worth of $100 million in 2003, Neverland eventually included a Ferris wheel, carnival rides, a menagerie and a movie theater. Financial difficulties forced Jackson to abandon the property in 2006, and use it as collateral for loans; he still retained a part interest in the property at his death.

1991's *"Dangerous"* album continued the commercial slide that had begun after *"Thriller"*, with just three singles hitting the top ten lists, and only one, "Black or White," making it to the top of the Billboard Hot 100. Jackson himself, however, was still big news, and a huge popular draw. He incorporated his "Heal the World Foundation" in 1992, preparatory to the *"Dangerous"* World Tour, and all profits from the tour went to the charity. Jackson performed for 3.6 million fans in 67 concerts globally, and sold the broadcast rights for the tour to HBO for $20 million, yet another record. He performed live during the halftime show at Superbowl XXVII in January 1993, the first occasion at which the halftime show audience exceeded that for the actual game; 135 million people in the US alone tuned in to watch.

In 1993 came the first accusations of sexual molestation of minors, charges which would dog him and erode his public image for the rest of his life, irrevocably marking him as freakish and fatally flawed. In the spring of 1992 Jackson met and befriended 13-year-old Jordan Chandler and his family, though his relationship with Jordan's father Evan soon became strained. Jordan joined the coterie of children Jackson kept about him at Neverland Ranch, many of whom commonly shared his bed, though no prior accusation of improper behavior had emerged.

In August of 1993 Evan Chandler, a dentist, extracted a tooth from his son's mouth, and under the influence of a powerful sedative Jordan confessed to his father, and later repeated to his psychiatrist and police, that he and Jackson had engaged in kissing, masturbation, and oral sex, also giving a detailed description of Jackson's genitals. The LAPD began an investigation in mid-August, search warrants were issued for Neverland Ranch and the Jackson family home, and more than 30 children who were intimates of Jackson were questioned; all denied any impropriety. Jackson's sister La Toya accused him of pedophilia, claiming she had proof, but later withdrew her accusations, stating that her current husband had coerced her into making the charges in hope of financial gain. Jackson was forced to submit to a 25-minute strip search to verify Jordan's description of the singer's genitals, including extensive photography; doctors determined that there were significant similarities, but no definitive match. Jackson called a press conference to deny the charges and describe the humiliating ordeal; he began abusing anti-depressants and sedatives, and cancelled the remainder of his *"Dangerous"* tour. The case never went to trial; on advice from Jackson's lawyers, it was settled out of court on January 1, 1994, Jordan Chandler receiving a reported $22 million.

Less than five months later, on May 26, Jackson married Lisa Marie Presley. The entertainer's soft-spoken persona and total lack of adult romantic entanglements by age 35 caused many to assume he was gay, and suspect that this was a sham marriage to help resurrect Jackson's public image. Lisa Marie has stated that the two were sexually intimate during their marriage, which ended less than two years later; the couple remained friends.

In 1995 Jackson released *"HIStory,"* another record-setting album. Although it never received the critical acclaim or widespread popularity of his earlier efforts, its single "You Are Not Alone" gained the distinction of being the only song ever to debut at number one on the Billboard Hot 100 chart. Controversy followed the release of the album's fourth single, "They Don't Care About Us," which originally contained in its lyrics the phrase "Jew me, sue me; Kick me, kike me." The Anti-Defamation League charged Jackson with antisemitism, and he rewrote the offending lines before the album was released, but he had already performed them live in concert. The *"HIStory"* World Tour spanned five continents and saw Jackson performing for 4.5 million fans in 82 concerts.

During the tour in November 1996 in Australia, Jackson married Debbie Rowe, who was pregnant with their first child. Rowe had met Jackson as a dermatologists' assistant in the mid-'80s, when he was first diagnosed with vitiligo, and their professional relationship had developed into a friendship in the intervening decade. Jackson's son Michael Joseph Jackson Jr (renamed "Prince Michael Jackson" after his parents' divorce) was born in 1997, and a daughter, Paris-Michael Katherine Jackson, followed in 1998. The couple divorced in 1999, with Rowe ceding all custody rights to Jackson in exchange for an $8 million settlement and a house in Beverly Hills. In a 2008 interview, Rowe stated that she had been artificially inseminated, and she and Jackson had never cohabited as husband and wife. A third child, Prince Michael Jackson II (known within the family as "Blanket"), was born in 2002, to a surrogate mother whose identity has never been revealed; the conception was allegedly performed with artificial insemination of Jackson's sperm, but none of his three children betray any African American features, skin coloring or hair texture.

In 2001 Jackson released his final album, *"Invincible,"* which sold well internationally, but received a lukewarm reception in the States. Jackson's popularity abroad had not been affected by the sexual molestation charges; in Europe and Asia he was as big as ever, but tabloid-driven American audiences tended to treat him as more of a curiosity, focusing on his eccentricities, with his music a footnote. *"Invincible"*'s release coincided with a special star-studded concert in Madison Square Garden to commemorate Jackson's thirty years as a solo artist, where Usher, 'N Sync, Whitney Houston and others performed with Jackson on stage.

In 2003 film-maker Martin Bashir released his documentary, *"Living With Michael Jackson,"* an intimate portrait of the singer's lifestyle, which featured his relationship with 13-year-old Gavin Arvizo, a cancer patient whose treatment Jackson had paid for. Jackson and Arvizo appeared holding hands, Arvizo resting his head on Jackson's shoulder, and the two discussed sharing Jackson's bed. The footage created concern in official circles, and in June the Santa Barbara County Sherif's Department began an investigation; initially Arvizo's mother denied that there had been anything improper in her son's relationship with Jackson, but that story changed when it became apparent that the singer's prior financial support for the family would not be continued. In November police issued a search warrant for Neverland and an arrest warrant for Jackson.

Jackson had been performing in Las Vegas at the time, but surrendered himself to police on November 20, charged with "lewd and lascivious" acts with a minor, and posted a $3 million bail. On December 18 Jackson was charged on 7 counts of child molestation and two counts of administering an intoxicating agent. The judge issued a gag order preventing all parties from discussing the case with the press. The arraignment on January 16, 2004 was a media circus, with Jackson dancing atop an SUV at his arrival, to cheering crowds of supporters; the pop icon pled not guilty. A Grand Jury was empaneled in March, which indicted Jackson April 21 on additional charges of conspiracy, false imprisonment and extortion, to which Jackson again pled not guilty.

The trial began January 31, 2005, and continued into early June. At one point Jackson, who had tried to beg off a court appearance, citing severe back pain, was given an hour to show or face contempt of court charges; the singer duly arrived with moments to spare, still dressed in his pajamas. Allegations that Jackson had given Arvizo wine in a Coke can, showed him internet pornography, and masturbated him to orgasm were embarrassing for the pop star, but without corroborating evidence, on June 13, 2005 the jury found Jackson not guilty on all counts. Perhaps more damaging was a series of prior incidents involving minor boys, not previously made public, and raised by the prosecution to establish a pattern of abuse.

Despite his victory, Jackson retreated into his private life, spending increasingly frequent periods abroad, including lengthy stays in Bahrain and Dubai. In November 2006 he resurfaced in London to accept awards from Guinness World Records as "First Entertainer to Earn More than 100 Million Dollars in a Year," and "Most Successful Entertainer of All Time." Earlier, in 2000, Guinness had granted him a record for his support of 39 charities globally, more than any other entertainer or personality. That same month he received the Diamond Award at the World Music Awards, in recognition of more than 100 million albums sold.

At the time of his death, Jackson was heavily involved in preparation for a comeback tour, "This Is It!", to kick off with 50 sold-out concerts in London's O2 Arena, performing for more than one million fans. Set to begin July 13, 2009, Jackson's grueling rehearsal schedule, and the added strain that placed on his body, may have led directly to his demise on June 25. In retrospect, the name of the tour seems strangely prophetic—for Michael Jackson, this was, indeed, it.

Born 29 August 1958, in Gary, Indiana, Michael Jackson's birth chart shows dramatic deep space and asteroid activity which well describes his life story. The Sun at 6 Virgo is exactly conjoined a Black Hole, giving Jackson the power to mesmerize, captivate, and draw others into his orbit, but also creating a basic dichotomy between the inner man and the outer persona, one who feeds off the attentions and adulation of others, but is left ultimately unfulfilled, never feeling sated or satisfied. The ability of this combination to pull a rabbit from the cosmic hat, changing conditions in the twinkling of an eye and completely reversing what has gone before, is well in evidence in Jackson's phenomenally rapid rise to super-stardom. As described by Suzanne de Passe, a Motown executive who mentored Michael and his brothers when the group was first signed, dressing them for success and honing their choreography, "It absolutely went from complete anonymity to total celebrity in one beat." But she also confirms that it was Michael specifically, and not the group as a whole, that created their astounding success: "It became a disproportionate kind of worship for him and interest in him and obsession for the little one."

Black Hole Sun can create an unsettled, topsy-turvy, world-turned-upside down existence where up is down and black is white, a life full of drama and sudden change, with extreme ups and downs, highs and lows. Such was the case for Jackson, careen-ing from the heights of pop culture stardom and success to the depths of alleged utter sexual depravity, isolation and drug addic-tion. Black Hole Sun also speaks to Jackson's startling alteration in appearance over the last twenty-five years of his life, an all too literal "black is white" transformation that mirrors the Black Hole's abil-ity to remake or revision itself, by whatever means. 2008 *American Idol*" runner-up Adam Lambert's comments in an interview after Jackson's death neatly encapsulate this aspect of the pop icon's life, that seemingly limitless creativity with which some Black Hole Sun natives are gifted: "Michael was a genius at inventing himself, inventing music, inventing imagery."

The Sun also conjoins Pluto at 2 Virgo, dramatically increasing the potential for expression of Jackson's personal power, and iden-tifying him as a catalyst for others' transformations, but conveying a darker, hidden side, a temptation for the taboo or forbidden, and issues with control or manipulation. Jackson was extremely control-ling when it came to his creative output, although any manipula-tive tendencies he may have harbored in interpersonal relationships seem to have been projected onto others, as the pop star was noted for picking and retaining staff and assistants whom others thought unsuitable, and who were allegedly not acting in his best inter-ests. This combination is also the source of his fans' obsession, and Michael's own tendencies to act in obsessive or compulsive ways, not fully cognizant or aware of his urges and desires.

Perhaps most dramatic is an exact conjunction of the Sun with asteroid Polyhymnia, named for the ancient Greek muse of song, and nothing could be more appropriate for one of the greatest lyricists of the late twentieth century. Jackson wrote 14 number one hits, and another 15 that placed in the top ten list; his vocal artistry, another aspect of Polyhymnia, was uniquely identifiable and broadly appealing. Music *was* Jackson's life, and the Sun/Polyhymnia conjunction speaks eloquently to his self-identification with his art and the phenomenal talent with which he was gifted.

Not to be outdone, asteroid Terpsichore, Muse of Dance, is also strongly placed; significantly, she exactly conjoins the Black Hole at 13 Libra, and is in exact sextile to natal Uranus at 13 Leo, allowing Jackson the creative freedom to adopt new dance forms (Terpsichore), as if from an alternate reality (Black Hole) no one else had experienced, while becoming an innovative figure always on the cutting edge (Uranus). This Uranian contact also reflects his two most popular dance innovations, the Robot and the Moon Walk, both of which have the futuristic, avant garde tone of Uranus' contributions. Terpsichore is also conjunct asteroid Jackson at 11 Libra, a fitting combination for the man who was easily as famous for his dance moves as his songs.

Saturn's placement is also extremely significant, ruling Jackson's career as well as issues with his father and authority figures or legal entanglements. At 19 Sagittarius, natal Saturn exactly conjoins another Black Hole, indicating the potential for dramatic success and achievement, but also major, sudden reversal, and denoting huge amounts of energy expended in career pursuits. Both sides of the Black Hole coin can be seen in Jackson's career path, though the success predominates, and the reversals, born of issues in his personal life, never completely deflated his achievements, even if they tarnished his reputation. The extremely abusive relationship with his father is also a result of this conjunction, as Black Hole Saturn natives can experience their fathers as overly controlling, devouring, and unapproachable. Legal difficulties and his arrest and trial for child sexual abuse also stem from Black Hole Saturn, which further acted in Jackson's case to create an atmosphere of hyper-critical perfectionism in his career, and a grueling work schedule which would have defeated many who did not harbor a

Black Hole's virtually unlimited reserves of energy. Saturn is also closely tied to a pair of Quasars at 4 Scorpio and Taurus, by exact semisquare and sesquiquadrate aspects, and these are likely the source of his phenomenal career. Black Holes may open doors and provide unexpected opportunities, but they do not guarantee success. Quasars do promote achievement, recognition and reward, placing a bright spotlight upon our efforts and calling others' attention to them. These would be the contacts that allowed Jackson to thrust wide the career doors unlocked by the Black Hole, and push boldly through them, reaping countless accolades and awards and routinely setting multiple records.

But it is the minor celestials which constellate about Jackson's Saturn which are especially revealing, and even emerge in startling fashion in the titles of several of his songs. Asteroid Orpheus, named for the famed musician and singer of Greek Myth, stands close by Saturn at 20 Sagittarius, identifying his chosen (perhaps 'fated' would be a better word) career path, with Icarus and Industria within orb at 15 and 12 Sagittarius respectively. Icarus is the rash risk-taker, and Jackson was never averse to pushing the envelope and trying something new, always active on the cutting edge of music technology, popular appetite and dance innovation. He also acted rashly in his private life, in ways which affected his career.

Industria conjures images of hard work and self-application; no one was more industrious in work matters than Jackson, who frequently put in extremely long days and committed himself to rehearsal schedules that taxed his strength and pushed his body to, and beyond, its limits, always in search of a perfection that seemed to forever elude him. Jackson often commented that he was never really happy with a performance, always felt he could have done better, even with iconic moments such as the premiere of the Moon Walk at Motown 25; this hyper-perfectionism and self-criticism is typical of Black Hole Saturn natives, for whom nothing is ever good enough.

Asteroid Pandora at 16 Sagittarius is also conjunct Saturn, and there is a sense that once Jackson opened that Pandora's box of his career, he unleashed forces over which he was unable to maintain control—the career ran him, he didn't run it. Perhaps the most intriguing placements with Saturn are those of asteroids Narcissus at 24 Sagittarius and Panacea at 21 Sagittarius—Jackson was very self-focused in performance, seeming to enter his own separate reality at these times, like mythic Narcissus captivated by his own reflection. In footage of the Pepsi commercial accident released shortly after his death, Jackson is seen continuing to perform for a full six seconds after his hair catches fire, completely oblivious to the flames; this type of total immersion in his performance and self-absorption in the task at hand speaks to Narcissus' obsessive self-focus. Jackson also used his music as a healing force redolent of Panacea, Greek goddess of cures and medicinal healing, both indirectly, in the messages he attempted to convey of peace and harmony, and also more substantially, in the many charitable foundations he created or supported. The mythic themes of these asteroids are also reflected in two of his popular songs—Narcissus with "Man in the Mirror," and Panacea with "Heal the World." Saturn is also exactly sextile to Chiron at 19 Aquarius, another indicator of his desire to heal via the work he did, and the internal woundedness that work revealed.

Was Jackson gay, and a pedophile? Many chart indicators suggest he had issues with this. Venus at 16 Leo is exactly squared a Black Hole at 16 Taurus, a placement which often indicates the choice of partners or romantic encounters which others see as unsuitable or in some way unnatural or alien. Black Hole Venus further describes the excessive windfall profits from his music, as well as the constant financial strain of his later years and the frivolous buying habits for which Jackson was noted. Black Hole Venus can provide windfall profits and amass huge wealth, but often unexpected expenditures also arise, so that what comes in is immediately paid out, and the native plays financial catch-up throughout the life.

Venus also conjoins a Maser at 13 Leo, indicative of controversy in romantic matters as well as constellating volatile issues about appearance, such as Jackson's cosmetic surgeries produced. This is a placement which further grants an ability to provoke extreme excitement, even exhilaration, in others, stemming from one's creative output, which is certainly the case for Jackson.

But Venus' placement is even more complex than this. Conjoined by Uranus also at 13 Leo, this is a common combination in charts of gay men and women, who refuse to conform to societal norms in matters of love and intimacy, choosing instead to express their unique individuality. Venus is also broadly conjoined Mercury at

25 Leo, indicating a potential attraction for young persons, as well as Jackson's ability to retain a youthful appearance well into middle age. Minor celestials also intrude: incredibly, Jackson had asteroid Child at 21 Leo, conjoined Venus, and exactly conjunct asteroid Sphinx. His relationships with children and young people were certainly loving; the issue of whether or not he crossed any lines is one which, Sphinx-like, will probably remain an inscrutable mystery. Also in the mix are asteroid Aphrodite at 24 Leo, suggesting flirtation and affairs of the heart, as opposed to mere, base sexual gratification. Asteroid Amor, emblematic of platonic love, appearing at 12 Leo suggests that his affections were innocent, but asteroid Pecker is here also, at 14 Leo, lending a potentially much more sexual, earthy component to his interactions with minors.

Additionally, the Sun is squared by asteroid Sappho, often indicative of both poetic genius and homosexual attraction, at 7 Sagittarius, and asteroid Lust, betraying a more animalistic nature, at 5 Sagittarius, itself exactly conjunct a Black Hole, suggesting sexual passion and arousal were a very strong pull on Jackson's psyche, possibly directed by Sappho into homosexual outlets. Mars at 21 Taurus conjoins Nessus, a centaur associated with inappropriate expression of sexual urges, while asteroid Eros at 4 Aries, ruling romantic passion, combines with Trans-Neptunian Objects Eris, goddess of contention, discord and strife, at 9 Aries and Chaos, indicative of lack of control and turbulent disorder, at 7 Aries. Asteroid Circe is also here, at 8 Aries, suggestive of an irresistible siren call, one which the native cannot fail to listen to, but which leads him astray. These certainly describe the apparently compulsive nature of Jackson's repeat-offender-style interactions with young boys, and the controversy, calumny, and disruption which these created in the singer's personal and private life, a pattern of interactions to which he continued to return despite the negative experiences which they evoked.

Ganymed is another asteroid associated with gay themes, named for Zeus' cupbearer and lover, an underage boy whose beauty so captivated the King of the Gods that he spirited him away to Olympus to fulfill more than one need. Jackson has Ganymed at 22 Libra, inconjunct natal Mars at 21 Taurus, semisquare the natal Sun at 6 Virgo and conjunct natal Jupiter, Zeus' Roman counterpart, at 28 Libra. It may also be significant that Jackson's two primary accusers have asteroid variants of their names which are strategically placed in the pop star's chart. Asteroid Jordaens, for Jordan Chandler, lies at 28 Libra, exactly conjunct natal Jupiter and a Black Hole, and within orb of Ganymed. This certainly describes their relationship, that of the powerful, larger-than-life (Jupiter) adult who plucks a young boy (Ganymed) from his ho-hum everyday life and whisks him off to the exciting alternate reality (Black Hole) of Neverland Ranch, here a stand-in for mythic Olympus. The Black Hole's tendency to reversal also describes the effect Jordan's accusations had on Jackson's reputation (Jupiter), which never fully recovered. But Black Hole events are not always what they seem, and it is possible to put a kinder interpretation on the situation than that which has commonly been applied. Asteroid Gavini, for Gavin Arvizo, is perhaps even more strongly placed; at 0 Sagittarius it squares the Sun and joins the Lust/Sappho conjunction at 5 and 7 Sagittarius, again combining gay themes (Sappho) with rampant sexuality (Lust), but Lust's position exactly atop another Black Hole once again indicates that appearances can be deceiving, and nothing is cut-and-dried.

This is a tough call, but my personal feeling is that Jackson does not conform to the "typical" pederast profile. He seems to have been genuinely emotionally stunted at about the threshold of puberty, when super-stardom intervened in his normal development, and if so, then his interactions with boys of 12 to 14 are perhaps best viewed not as those of an adult with a child, but rather as peer to peer. As such, it is highly likely that, for a boy with the types of astrological and psychological inclinations toward homosexuality such as Jackson's chart reveals, some of these interactions with peers might lead to infatuation or even sexual contact typical of experimentation common to that stage of maturation. Jackson's adult self certainly knew he was wrong to make these contacts, but his child-like inner self, stuck in early puberty, simply couldn't prevent him from sometimes crossing the line, in particular with boys for whom he felt a strong bond, as noted by their asteroid namesakes' placements in his chart. It is also quite possible, with Black Hole activation, that nothing untoward ever occurred, and these allegations are nothing more than malicious fantasy directed at a vulnerable individual who is just odd enough to gain notice for his actions, and rich enough to make an irresistible target.

Key moments of Jackson's life and career show additional deep space and asteroid activity. The period from the fall of 1982 through the spring of 1983 was the apex of Jackson's career, and saw transit Pluto crisscrossing natal Jupiter, inflating his status and bringing him unparalleled opportunity and good fortune. At both the November 30th 1982 release of *"Thriller,"* Jackson's biggest success and the best selling album ever, and his now-iconic premiere of the Moon Walk at the Motown 25th anniversary special on March 25th 1983, this conjunction of Pluto with Jupiter was exact. *"Thriller"* established Jackson as a music innovator without equal, and its release was accompanied by a Sun/Uranus transit conjunction at 8 and 5 Sagittarius (Uranus exact on a Black Hole), squaring his natal Sun at 6 Virgo, with the Sun also within orb of conjunction to an exact pairing of transit Mercury and Venus at 14 Sagittarius, highlighting his natal Terpsichore (dance) at 13 Libra by sextile, and natal Venus/Uranus (cutting edge creative expression) at 16/13 Leo by trine. Transit Polyhymnia, muse of song, at 22 Virgo was squared the Galactic Center, denoting the universal appeal of Jackson's work, and exactly opposed transit asteroid Jackson at 22 Pisces, itself conjunct asteroid Michel (for Michael) exactly on the Black Hole at 28 Pisces, emphasizing the dramatic change in his status which *"Thriller"*'s release would evoke.

When Jackson first performed his Moon Walk, Terpsichore at 1 Sagittarius combined with Uranus at 9 Sagittarius and Jupiter atop the Black Hole at 10 Sagittarius, evoking the futuristic (Uranus) dance routine (Terpsichore) seemingly from an alternate reality (Black Hole), which greatly boosted Jackson's reputation and public image (both Jupiter); all points were again squared his natal Sun. Transit asteroid Jackson at 23 Aries conjoined the Black Hole at 24 Aries, while asteroid Michel at 4 Taurus was exactly conjunct an illumining Quasar, turning a spotlight on the entertainer and bringing him into further prominence.

By the time of the pyrotechnics accident during the filming of the Pepsi commercial on 27 January 1984, which caused severe scalp burns and may have led directly to Jackson's painkiller addiction, transit Pluto had moved away from natal Jupiter and was now at 2 Scorpio, exactly conjunct Jackson's natal Neptune, ruling drugs. Thus began a transformation (Pluto) in his relationship with prescription medication (Neptune) which would affect the remaining 25 years of his life. Following Pluto in quick succession were Mars (accidents, injuries) at 8 Scorpio, Panacea (healing medicaments) at 9 Scorpio, Polyhymnia (songs, singers) at 12 Scorpio and Saturn (career, restriction or limitation) at 15 Scorpio. A cluster of transit Neptune, Jupiter, and Venus at 0, 1 and 2 Capricorn, all in trine to Jackson's natal Sun, suggests the increased (Jupiter) drug use (Neptune) for the artist (Venus).

A decade later, the stress and anxiety of the sexual molestation accusations would put a further strain on Jackson's health, as he turned increasingly to sedatives and anti-depressants for relief from sleeplessness and worry. The $22 million settlement in the Jordan Chandler case came on 1 January 1994, and incredibly, shows asteroids Jordaens and Jackson conjoined at 28 and 29 Pisces, conjunct the 28 Pisces Black Hole. Asteroids Nemesis and Child combine at 12 and 14 Sagittarius, in trine to the natal Uranus/Venus conjunction, within orb of natal Saturn, and signal an undoing (Nemesis) based in an unorthodox (Uranus) affection (Venus), wrought by a child, affecting career (Saturn). A stellium of Achilles at 6 Capricorn, Venus at 7, Karma at 8, Mars and Mercury both at 9 and the Sun at 11 Capricorn, all in trine to Jackson's natal Sun, bespeaks a comeuppance (Karma) relating to a congenital weak spot (Achilles), namely his affection (Venus) for and possible sexual involvement (Mars) with youths (Mercury). Saturn and Pluto exactly square each other from 27 Aquarius, with Saturn atop a reality-contorting Black Hole, to 27 Scorpio, where Pluto activates an attention-getting Quasar, indicating the highly public case and its irreversible damage to Jackson's reputation and career. The truth or falsity of the accusations remains in doubt, astrologically—asteroid Askalaphus (named for the tale-bearing busybody who informed on Persephone's ingestion of pomegranate seeds in the Underworld, thus necessitating her annual return) lies at 19 Capricorn, exactly atop a Black Hole and conjoined both Neptune (lies and deception) at 20 Capricorn and Uranus (truth and revelation) at 21, building a case for either interpretation.

The "not guilty" verdict in Jackson's only trial for sexual molestation came at 2:13 PM PDT, 13 June 2005, at the Santa Barbara County Courthouse in Santa Maria, California. Asteroid Gavini, for accuser Gavin Arvizo, at 8 Cancer is exactly conjunct a Quasar, prominent at the 9 Cancer Midheaven, and also conjoined Venus (romance, affection) at 12 Cancer and Mercury (young people) at 4 Cancer, itself exactly on a Black Hole and exactly squared Jackson's natal asteroid Eros (homosexual attraction, sexual passion). Gavini also squares transit Jupiter at 9 Libra on the 8 Libra Ascendant, with these points and asteroid Karma at 10 Libra all conjoin Jackson's natal asteroid Jackson at 11 Libra; judgment (Jupiter) has been rendered, the past (Karma) laid to rest, Jackson (the eponymous asteroid) vindicated. Transit asteroid Jackson at 24 Taurus also exactly conjoins a Black Hole, and is semisquare to the Gavini/Midheaven conjunction.

When Michael Jackson was officially pronounced dead at the UCLA Medical Center in Los Angeles at 2:26 PM PDT 25 June 2009, the Sun at 4 Cancer exactly conjoined a Black Hole, as did asteroid Michel at 19 Capricorn and asteroid Jackson at 28 Aquarius, these three factors combining to transport the pop star into the alternate reality of death. From that degree, asteroid Jackson is conjoined by Neptune (prescription drugs, addiction) at 26 Aquarius and Chiron (wounding) at 25 Aquarius, with asteroid Atropos the Cutter, named for the Fate who severs the thread of life at death, in exact trine from 28 Gemini, from where she also exactly opposes a Pulsar at 28 Sagittarius, a deep space anomaly ruling newsworthy events and the media. Asteroids Polyhymnia (the singer) and Requiem (the funeral hymn for the dead) combine at 10 and 12 Aquarius, with asteroid Terpsichore (the dancer) aligned with the Quasar at 4 Taurus and in sextile to the Sun, turning the spotlight once again on the famed entertainer. Mercury, representing the songwriter, at 15 Gemini was tightly squared Saturn, ancient Lord of Death, at 16 Virgo.

On 24 August 2009, the Los Angeles County coroner's office determined that the cause of Michael Jackson's death on 25 June was homicide, a ruling which means that the death was caused by another, though not necessarily as a result of criminal action. Jackson's demise was brought on by a combination of powerful sedatives, including propofol, a drug normally used as an operating anesthetic and never administered outside of a hospital setting. Jackson's personal physician, Conrad Murray, who administered the fatal dose, is now under investigation for manslaughter.

Minor asteroids play a significant part in the astrological symbolism for the day. In particular, asteroids Conrada (#941) and

Murray (#1528) show prominently, with Conrada at 27 Pisces retrograde conjoined Uranus at 25 Pisces retrograde, emblematic of accidents, unexpected surprises and revelations. Asteroid Murray at 17 Cancer exactly conjoined asteroid Asclepius (#4581), named for a minor Greek god of healing, and are both squared Trans-Neptunian Object (TNO) Ixion (#28978) at 22 Libra in Jackson's natal chart (born 29 August 1958), named for Greek mythology's first murderer, providing a picture of the physician (Asclepius) Murray (the eponymous asteroid) committing homicide (Ixion). The Conrada/Uranus conjunction was also in effect for the 2:26 PM PDT official death time for Jackson on 25 June, with Conrada at the same degree and Uranus at 26 Pisces, then both direct, Conrada appearing here precisely on the cusp of the Sixth House of Health. At that time, asteroid Murray was at 20 Gemini, a degree now inhabited by transit asteroid Nemesis (#128), the karmic comeuppance, for the homicide ruling; this Nemesis now squares Saturn at 22 Virgo, a signal of undoing (Nemesis) via a professional (Saturn). Conrada at 6 Leo in Jackson's nativity is within orb of Uranus at 13 Leo, making a cosmic "threepeat" of the Conrada/Uranus energy also active at the death and the homicide ruling, and is tightly semisextile Jackson's natal 5 Virgo Sun while squared his 2 Scorpio Neptune, ruling drugs and pharmaceuticals. Panacea (#2878) is an asteroid named for another minor Greek healing deity, goddess of medicinal cures. Asteroid Panacea for the coroner's ruling lies at 5 Leo, squared Jackson's natal Neptune and closely conjunct asteroid Murray in his birth chart.

The Greeks' primary healing deity was Apollo, whose asteroid namesake (#1862) for the 24 August coroner's ruling was exactly conjoined Venus at 27 Cancer, with asteroids Icarus (#1566) and Tantalus (#2102) both conjunct from 29 Cancer. Tantalus was another noted murderer in Greek mythology, responsible for the sacrifice of his child, a young boy entrusted to his care (much as Murray stood *in medico loco parentis* to his patient), while the Icarus myth conjures images of rash, foolhardy deeds. This mini stellium, therefore, depicts the homicide (Tantalus) of an artist (Venus), killed by the reckless (Icarus) actions of his physician (Apollo). Venus/Apollo are also exactly conjunct asteroid Murray in Jackson's natal chart, which natally squares Jupiter at 28 Libra, bringing prominence to the name in Jackson's life story.

Transit Ixion for the ruling at 13 Sagittarius retrograde is tightly opposed by TNO Chaos (#19521) at 12 Gemini, a body associated with confused or disordered activity, actions reaping detriment or disaster. At 29 Gemini, transit Mars, associated with death via his traditional rulership of Scorpio, opposes Pluto, Scorpio's modern ruler, at 0 Capricorn retrograde, the pair forming a T-Square with asteroid Karma (#3811, the effect of our actions) at 2 Libra for Jackson's death, with Mars approaching conjunction with the 4 Cancer Sun of that event. The transit Sun at 1 Virgo for the homicide ruling lies trine to Pluto and sextile Mars, while conjoining Jackson's natal Pluto (death) at 2 Virgo and approaching his natal 5 Virgo Sun.

Transit asteroids Polyhymnia (#33), named for the Greek Muse of Song, and Requiem (#2254), the funeral hymn for the dead, conjoin at 2 and 1 Aquarius retrograde, conjunct asteroid Michel (#1348) at 3 Aquarius in Jackson's natal chart, while transit asteroid Jackson (#2193) is exactly conjunct transit Jupiter at 20 Aquarius, bringing prominence to the singer yet again.

Conrad Murray's birth has been given as 19 February 1953 (date unconfirmed); if so, his nativity sports a conjunction of asteroids Nemesis (undoing) and Michel at 2 and 7 Capricorn respectively, squared Mars (death) at 8 Aries and sextile asteroid Jackson at 6 Scorpio, with asteroid Jackson itself conjunct the King of Pop's natal Neptune (drugs) at 2 Scorpio. Asteroid Panacea, representing the medicinal cure, is also conjoined asteroid Michel in Murray's natal chart, from 11 Capricorn, and both Michel and Panacea were conjoined by transit asteroid Michel at 9 Capricorn for the coroner's ruling. His natal Ixion (homicide) at 18 Libra retrograde is squared by the exact conjunction of asteroids Murray and Asclepius at 17 Cancer for the coroner's ruling, while a natal combination of asteroids Tantalus and Icarus at 2 and 4 Aquarius, the reckless homicide, conjoin Jackson's natal asteroid Michel at 3 Aquarius.

Quite the tangled web, but typical of the sort of pertinent involvement evinced by significantly named minor bodies at critical junctures.

Whatever his faults or foibles, Michael Jackson's was an undeniable talent which influenced music history and impressed itself upon generations of music lovers the world over. Such an impact is rare indeed, and we are not likely to see his peer.

# CUNANAN, VERSACE & BLACK HOLE SUN

*"They called him the chameleon. He could be the man next door, the woman next door, the nun on the corner collecting money. He could be anyone."*
—Anonymous source, ABC News' *20/20*, 25 July 1997

On July 15, 1997, the nation was shocked to hear of the murder of fashion mogul Gianni Versace, latest victim of the previously downplayed serial killer Andrew Cunanan. Cunanan, who began his five-victim killing spree in late April at the time of a Mercury station and a transit Sun conjunction to his natal Saturn, with a stationing Uranus in exact square, was found dead in a Miami Beach houseboat, an apparent suicide, little more than a week after Versace's murder, leaving many unanswered questions as to his mental state and motivation for the killings.

Born August 31, 1969, Cunanan, according to a *Newsweek* article of July 28, 1997, "was a great and gaudy pretender. He improved upon his breeding, his education, his employment (he had none), even his name. He created, out of his imagination, a flamboyant persona.... Cunanan was a skillful fraud. He knew enough, was practiced enough, to fake his way into glittery worlds far beyond his means or station."

As such, Cunanan is a perfect example of Black Hole Native Type A; his victim, Versace, is a perfect example of Black Hole Native Type B.

Both men had Suns (as well as several other chart points) conjoined Black Holes (Cunanan's, at 8 Virgo, is sandwiched snugly between Black Holes at 7 and 9 Virgo; Versace, born December 2, 1946, has the Sun conjunct the Black Hole at 10 Sagittarius), both men have Sun trine Saturn (their Saturns square each other, Cunanan's conjoined the Maser at 8 Taurus, Versace's at 8 Leo, conjoined BH 9

Leo), both men were strongly activated by the Uranus station at 8 Aquarius in May of 1997 (squaring Cunanan's Saturn and opposing Versace's). Incredibly, both men had Mars at the same degree, conjoined the Black Hole at 18 Sagittarius.

The Black Hole Sun native is nothing if not compelling and chameleon-like. Cunanan's BH Sun enabled him to be all things to all people, to infiltrate the highest levels of the gay subculture, to change his appearance dramatically (an aid in avoiding capture for months) and to subsist in high style, predominantly on the kindness of strangers.

Versace's BH Sun enabled him to persuade a sizable portion of the fashion-minded world that his designs were worth paying top dollar for, and helped him to carve a globally recognized name and a $1 billion financial empire out of very modest origins.

The Black Hole native can be very attractive, very magnetic, drawing others into his orbit almost effortlessly. For one lucky enough to have a clear calling, a distinct goal, the focus and direction afforded by the Black Hole can prove an incredible asset. Witness the likes of Michael Jackson ("the King of Pop"), Bruce Lee ("the Dragon"), Muhammad Ali ("the Greatest") and Lucille Ball ("the Funniest Woman in the World"), all acknowledged masters and superstars in their fields, precisely because of the level of their concentration and focus, as well as such lesser-known BH Sun individuals as Timothy Leary, Martha Stewart, Rush Limbaugh, and Versace himself. The Black Hole Sun native who is not so fortunate as to have a clear direction in his life can wind up self-destructing like Andrew Cunanan, who betrays many of the characteristics typical of these individuals.

According to Eric Greenman, Cunanan's last roommate, interviewed by John Quinones on ABC's *Primetime* July 30, 1997, Cunanan was "very much a nocturnal person; he wouldn't wake up until about 3, 3:30 every afternoon." The Underworld connotations of the BH native make it difficult sometimes to function in the Light World.

Greenman asserted: "I saw more of him than anyone else did. He only let people see a certain side of him, which is the charming side, the entertainer side, the friendly, almost big brother side. I saw the down side at home, going through drugs and depression."

Greenman goes on to describe Cunanan's use of drugs such as prescription pain killers, and occasionally crack cocaine (Cunanan's 26 Scorpio Neptune squared the Black Hole at 27 Aquarius) and his addiction to S & M sexual practices, domination and leather, whips and sadistic pornographic materials (these predilections originating in the same Black Hole-conjoined Mars which provided the fatal link to Versace).

The Black Hole's insatiable lust for energy and power is evident also in Greenman's statement that Cunanan "lived for the power, the wealth and the admiration [that Versace had]....Power is what he wanted."

Cunanan's smooth tongue and ability to reinvent himself is typical of the Black Hole Sun native, who may not even be aware that the parallel universes he draws his reality from are different from that of ordinary mortals. According to long-time friend Philip Howe, interviewed for the *20/20* profile, Cunanan "had a way of telling these really ridiculous stories in a very believable way, and keeping enough consistency over the years that it was pretty seamless. He was incredibly pathological in his lying."

Cunanan, who had been dumped by a rich boyfriend the year before and whose credit cards were maxed out, had begun to feel the pressure of maintaining the facades and personas generated by his Black Hole Sun. The internal pressure, the gravitational pull, of the Black Hole is so intense that many natives without an outward focus feel overwhelmed by the energy required to maintain themselves in the Light World of everyday reality.

Cunanan left his apartment in San Diego and headed for Minneapolis, where on April 29 he murdered his first victim, Jeffrey Trail, a former boyfriend whom he killed with repeated blows from a claw hammer. He followed this up on May 3 with the shooting death of another lover in the Minneapolis area, architect David Madson, whom Cunanan once described as "the love of my life." The May 4 death of millionaire Chicago realtor Lee Miglin is harder to understand, though from the torture and abuse Miglin was put through prior to his death, it seems the formerly voyeuristic fantasies of the Black Hole Mars were kicking in and establishing a real-world foothold. On May 9 Cunanan shot a cemetery caretaker in New Jersey, apparently for his truck, which he used, with stolen North Carolina plates, to drive to Miami Beach and stake out Versace for a period of almost two months.

These early murders were apparently under the auspices of the Uranus station forming (complete on May 13) in square to his Maser-conjoined Saturn. Maser energy is extremely volatile and erratic, and Uranus, of course, is disruptive and impulsively hot-headed. The situation was doubtless aggravated by Mercury's retrograde station at 9 Taurus, atop Cunanan's Maser/Saturn, on April 15, just two weeks before the first murder, and the transit Sun's conjunction with his natal Saturn, from where it squared transit Uranus, on April 28, just one day before Jeffrey Trail was murdered.

The timing of the Versace murder is even more elegant in its geometry. Who says Grand Trines are fun? On the day of the shooting, transiting Venus at 19/20 Leo had just formed a trine to Cunanan's and Versace's Mars, both at 18 Sagittarius atop the Black Hole there while transiting Saturn completed the Grand Trine from 20 Aries.

That day the pattern became a Kite, with transiting Jupiter at 20/19 Aquarius retrograde exactly opposing Venus, an apt image of the high profile death of a fashion mogul. Transiting Mercury was conjoined Versace's natal Pluto at 13 Leo (itself conjoined a Maser and opposed a Black Hole), bringing news of his volatile death.

Cunanan's life, crimes and death are a dramatic image of the potency of Black Hole contacts and Deep Space energies in the realm of mere mortals. The energy needs of the Black Hole, always insatiable, became at last fatal. In the words of *20/20*'s reporter Juju Chang, "Cunanan was nothing if not a chameleon....In the end, he could not escape from himself. He was a middle-class kid with high-class airs. It was a facade he created, that crumbled."

# PRINCESS DIANA, THE MEDIA & BLACK HOLE MERCURY

*"She was very special because she had the power of communication....*
*She was wonderful at communicating with other human beings."*
—Baroness Margaret Jay

*"[Prince Charles] happened to marry this amazing woman who*
*turned out to be one of the greatest communicators on earth."*
—Lord Jeffrey Archer

On August 31, 1997 the world was astounded and in despair at the news of the tragic death of Diana, Princess of Wales. Even years later, not all the details of the events and circumstances surrounding this ill-fated night are known, and they probably never will be. Although we will each remember Diana in our own way, the image that predominates is of the Tragic and Triumphant Princess, tragic in her unpreparedness for the role fate thrust upon her, triumphant on her wedding day; tragic in her life with an unloving husband and the closed, cold Royal Family unit, triumphant in her love for her children, and the people's unwavering affection for her; tragic in her personality flaws that led her to bulimia and depression, triumphant in overcoming them and sharing her story with others; tragic in her separation and divorce, triumphant in building a new life from the ashes of the old; tragic finally in the circumstances of her death, but unbelievably triumphant in the apotheosis of the global mourning that followed.

Despite the quasi-divine honors showered on her in the week after her death, Diana was human, and a rather flawed human, at that. But it was just those imperfections that endeared her to the world, made her a being of flesh and blood which we could identify with, not stone and ice, as the rest of her adopted family can often appear. Rather than deny or cover up the scandals and sorrows,

Diana openly confessed them, and allowed us to share her pain, empathize with her trials, rejoice in her triumphs. The outpouring of affection and the expressions of grief and loss following her death were of truly astounding proportions—fully 10% of the population of the British Isles came out to witness her cortege on the route to the funeral, with a global satellite audience estimated at over one billion, nearly a quarter of the world's population; over one million floral offerings were left at Kensington Palace and her other residences, not to mention the millions more that showed up outside British embassies and consulates the world over. Memorial services for her in Chicago and New York attracted thousands; dozens, perhaps hundreds, of Internet sites sprang up almost overnight, and even the Queen broke precedent both by delivering her first live address in 37 years, and honoring the fallen princess by bowing the royal brow when Diana's cortege passed.

To what may we attribute this amazing ability to impact the lives of others? Astrologically, and from a Galactic viewpoint, there can be little doubt that the principal player in Diana's life was the Black Hole Mercury in her natal chart, which alternately deified and dogged her throughout her life.

Black Holes, those Deep Space stellar remnants whose gravitational forces are so great that not even light can escape them, have been the makers and breakers of many of the powerful and famous on this planet. In her birth chart (cast for July 1, 1961), Diana sports a powerful Sun/Mercury conjunction, with Mercury retrograde at 3 Cancer, just past conjunction with the Black Hole at 4 Cancer, and the Sun at 9 Cancer, just past conjunction with the Quasar at 8 Cancer. Quasars, also known as 'white holes,' may be the polar opposite of the Black Hole, ejecting back into space/time all the matter engorged by the associated Black Hole, and shining with the brilliance of a hundred million suns. For Diana, it was this brilliance which captivated the world, shining through her Sun, illuminating her deepest essence; it was her Mercury that pulled us in, her power to communicate that attracted us like moths to the brilliant flame that was her life.

In the days following the tragedy, many commented on this extraordinary gift: close friend singer Elton John stated that "She could connect with everybody, make everybody feel special. She talked through her eyes—they were the most incredibly expressive eyes you could ever imagine." NBC's Katie Couric, on the day of Diana's funeral, noted that "She instinctively seemed to know what to say, what to do, to talk to these people and project an image of compassion," while BBC commentator Lord Jeffrey Archer, former MP, had this to say: "She loved children, she loved grown-ups; she could talk to them and they could talk to her."

But that Black Hole Mercury, great communicator though it is, is a two-edged sword. More than anything, it was Diana's involvement with the Mercury-ruled Media which made her, marred her, and made her again. Her volatile love-hate relationship with the Press was undoubtedly the most significant factor of her public existence. That Sun/Mercury conjunction, straddling as it did a Black Hole/Quasar polarity, drew the Media into her net, and they elevated her to the status of Super-Royal. Undeniably the most photographed woman in the world (Neptune in the natal chart is itself conjunct a Black Hole and trines the Sun/Mercury conjunction from 8 Scorpio), Diana has graced the covers of almost every conceivable magazine; within hours of her death, bookstores in major metropolitan areas had sold out of her biographies. It is interesting that she first met the man who was to become her reluctant groom as a child (Mercury), while he was at a book (Mercury)-signing (Mercury) for a children's (Mercury) story (Mercury) he had written (Mercury).

Amazingly, the Sun and Mercury were once again conjunct in the sky on the day of her death, also conjunct a pair of Black Holes, with Mercury (again retrograde!) at 8 Virgo, just past the Black Hole at 9 Virgo, and the Sun at 7 Virgo exactly conjunct a second Black Hole. This 'hot zone' surrounding these two Black Holes is active in many of the key moments and players of Diana's life—her own natal Pluto lies there at 6 Virgo [and what better astrological imagery can we have for her death (Pluto) in a car (Mercury) in a tunnel (Black Hole), forever extinguishing the light of her life (Sun)?], while Prince Charles' Saturn lies close by at 5 Virgo. On the date of their marriage (July 29, 1981), Venus was conjunct these points at 6 Virgo; her eldest son William (born 21 June 1982) has Mercury in square to this zone from 9 Gemini, younger son Harry (born 15 September 1984) has Mercury right there at 5 Virgo, and the Sun of the final divorce decree (August 28, 1996, almost exactly a year before the fatal crash) also lies at 5 Virgo.

But the story doesn't stop there. Black Hole Mercury has dogged her public life from the start. Mercury at 24 Cancer on the date of the marriage lay within the event horizon (astronomically, the outermost boundary of the Black Hole's influence; astrologically, its orb) of the Black Hole at 28 Cancer and in exact square to the Black Hole at 24 Aries (Charles' Mercury, incidentally, lies exactly on a Black Hole at 6 Scorpio, conjunct her natal Neptune). When their separation was announced by British Prime Minister John Major on December 9, 1992, Mercury at 27 Scorpio was conjunct a Quasar and exactly square the Black Hole at 27 Aquarius. Diana's announcement that she was retiring from public life came on December 3, 1993, with Mercury at 25 Scorpio opposed the Black Hole at 24 Taurus, and reads like a Mercury keyword list, a stunning exposition by the native herself of the effect this configuration has had in her life: "You [the public (Mercury)] have also given me an education (Mercury), by teaching (Mercury) me more about my life and living than any books (Mercury) or teachers (Mercury) could have done." And she rounded out the statement with an indictment of the Press that had built her up only to knock her down again: "When I started my public life twelve years ago, I understood the Media might be interested in what I did. I realized then their attention would inevitably focus on both our private and public lives. But I was not aware of how overwhelming that attention would become, nor the extent to which it would affect both my public duties and my personal life in a manner that's been hard to bear."

The now infamous BBC interview, unsanctioned by Buckingham Palace and the Queen, which opened the last act of the marriage tragedy, came on November 20, 1995, with Diana's revelations about bulimia, depression, and her own and Charles' affairs, and saw Mercury returned to 27 Scorpio, its exact degree at the separation announcement. When Diana agreed to getting the divorce, February 28, 1996, Mercury at 19 Aquarius was exactly sextile the Black Hole at 19 Sagittarius on her Ascendant, and when the terms of the roughly $25 million settlement were finalized on July 13, 1996, Mercury had returned to 24 Cancer to conjoin its placement in the marriage chart, squaring the 24 Aries Black Hole. When the divorce became final on August 28th of that year, Mercury had just arrived on the singularity (the center) of the supermassive Black Hole center of Galaxy M-87 at 1 Libra, the largest anomaly of its type of which we are aware.

Many bore testimony to Diana's strange and addictive relationship with the Press. An ABC newsman on their special report, "Diana, The Royal Tragedy," broadcast the night after the accident, commented that "It was her moxie and shrewd manipulation of the Press which, more than anything, elevated her status in the U.S." Jane Pauley, anchoring MSNBC's flashback coverage of Diana's life on their newsmagazine "Time and Again," stated that "The Princess knew how to take advantage of the [Media] spotlight that inevitably fell on her, using it to bring attention to the causes she cared about," a sentiment echoed by Director General of the British Red Cross Michael Whitlam when he said, "She had an incredible gift to attract the Media and work with them so the message got to the people who needed to see it."

How ironic, then, to see the Media so active in the manner of her death. Despite the reports of drunkenness on the part of the limo's driver, despite the rashness implied by the couple's decision to flee at possibly very high speeds, the fact remains that if there had been no relentless pursuit of the details of her private life by the Press and paparazzi, Diana and her companion Dodi Al Fayed would have driven calmly to his Paris apartment that August night, and today Diana would be somewhere in the world, drawing attention to the plight of AIDS sufferers, the scourge of anti-personnel land mines, or one of her many other charities.

But that is not the way it happened. There were photographers and reporters, Diana did flee them, and she died. And in dying, she unleashed a global mourning that cut to the very heart of many who never knew her, never would know her, knew only what she represented, the fairy tale princess, the Cinderella plucked from obscurity into the white hot light of fame, only to find that there was no happy ending unless she made one for herself, on her own, outside the shadow of her husband and official position. A new world myth was in the making that week, or perhaps just the retelling of one as old as time, but in either case, Diana joins the ranks, perhaps at the lead position, of those latter-20th century icons who have left us too soon, and so ensured their immortality—James

Dean, Marilyn Monroe, Elvis, JFK.

Image or substance? Who can tell, in this era of Media manipulation? Perhaps NBC's "Dateline" reporter Dennis Murphy said it best when he stated, "So now we have only the images. When we think of [Diana] we will probably think of that gallery of still photos."

In closing, I want to pass on this quote from an op-ed article by culture and religion analyst Jean Houston, which came to me via several interlaced e-mails.

"Princess Diana went into that tunnel passage to death, on the Cours de la Reine (the Queen's Road) beneath the Place de l'Alma (Place of the Soul) as a woman like the moon, resplendently beautiful, changeable, sometimes shadowed by clouds, but willing to shine light in places many of us are afraid to go; she went in accompanied by three men who should have been her guardians, for she needed guardians; she went in, as other women have reflected ruefully, as a princess and a passenger, therefore still dependent; she went in flight from those who wanted to sell a piece of her; she went in at an explosive speed. That passage into the tunnel became the scene of a shocking tragedy. But the mythic story is not only about who she was going into that tunnel; it's who has emerged from that tunnel of death and rebirth to join the feminine stories in our souls. That Diana [has] taken up residence in our mythic imaginations, and if we allow [her], can shine brightly within us, providing more care and greater love to this most precious planet and all its inhabitants."

# ELIZABETH TAYLOR & BLACK HOLE VENUS

L ong acknowledged as one of the most beautiful women in the world, Elizabeth Taylor's screen presence has captivated genera-tions of men across the globe for decades. The personas she creates, from the ingenue Kay in *"Father of the Bride"* to the tempestuous Maggie in *"Cat on a Hot Tin Roof"*, the slightly seedy call girl Gloria in *"Butterfield 8"*, the stunningly regal *"Cleopatra"* or the blowsy nut-cracker Martha in *"Who's Afraid of Virginia Woolf?"* combine to form a kaleidoscopic representation of womanhood in its myriad forms. Taylor's off-screen life was at least as complicated as the charac-ters she portrayed, with eight marriages, seven divorces, and the announcement of yet another engagement in April 2010, at the age of 78. So it's no surprise to find that Liz's Venus is no stranger to Black Hole energies, which drain huge amounts of energy from romantic entanglements and confer a chameleon-like ability to adapt herself to whatever feminine role she chooses, in public or private.

Born at 2:15 AM GMT on 27 February 1932 in London, England, Taylor's 17 Aries Venus is an exact match for her natal Uranus (likely source of those stunningly exotic amethyst eyes), and this pair forms a Galactic T-Square with natal Pluto at 20 Cancer and the Black Hole at 19 Capricorn, both squared Venus. Venus linked with a Black Hole indicates definite issues in romantic relationships and partnering, a difficulty in maintaining stable unions, and a ten-dency to high drama with intimates. There are potential financial issues as well, both positive and negative.

Taylor's love life is chequered with dramatic ups and downs. Of her eight marriages, seven have ended in divorce, with her third husband, Michael Todd, killed in a plane crash and leaving her a widow at just 26 years old. Her first marriage, at age 18 in 1950, with Nicky Hilton, heir to the Hilton hotel fortune, ended barely a year later, followed closely by another unsuccessful, five year union with actor Michael Wilding, which ended in January 1957. The very next month she was back in the saddle again, with Michael Todd, and after he died just 13 months later in March 1958, she took up with singer/performer Eddie Fisher, Todd's best friend, already married to actress Debbie Reynolds.

A highly public and acrimonious divorce between Fisher and Reynolds followed, and in May 1959 Taylor and Fisher were married, but the marriage was not a happy one. While filming *"Cleopatra"* in 1960, Taylor met co-star Richard Burton, and the two began a doubly adulterous affair, as Burton also had a spouse at the time, and their awkward situation was not regularized until Taylor divorced Eddie Fisher on March 6, 1964, marrying Burton just nine days later. The romance with Burton was the most memorable and publicized of her life, and lasted the longest, ten full years, until June 1974. The marriage was notably stormy, with Burton, an inveterate womanizer and playboy with alcohol abuse issues, treating Taylor to a series of embarrassing peccadilloes and public scenes. But the Taylor/Burton connection was a strong one, and the couple remarried in October 1975, just 15 months later, only to divorce a second time, in July 1976, their reunion lasting only nine months.

By this time, Taylor had had enough of involvements with fellow actors, though, truth be told, the defect was in *her* stars, not in the ones she married. Taylor seemed to have an inability to be alone (a common Black Hole Venus manifestation, which can cling to love as desperately as the Black Hole clings to the matter it engorges), and barely four months after her second divorce from Burton, she married US Senator John Warner (R-VA), a complete departure from her former uxorial pattern.

When they married, Warner was a former Navy Secretary; in 1978, he ran for Senate in the GOP Virginia primary, finishing second to Richard Obenshain. In a strange repeat of history, another plane crash figured prominently in Taylor's life when Obenshain was killed two months later, and Warner was given the nomination instead. It was Taylor's popularity and notoriety that enabled Warner to eke out a slim victory that November, when he gained the Senate seat he would hold for thirty years. His marriage to Taylor, however, would not be so long-lived. Bored with the tame life of a politician's wife, Taylor put on weight and became increasingly unhappy. The couple divorced in 1982.

Taylor remained single for almost a decade, but in 1991 married Larry Fortensky, a former Teamster she met while taking treatment for alcohol and prescription medication abuse at the Betty Ford Clinic. They were wed at Michael Jackson's Neverland Ranch, and divorced just five years later. Since then Taylor has remained unmarried, but announced her ninth engagement, to Hollywood talent agent Jason Winters, aged 49, in April 2010; Taylor is 78.

Black Hole Venus often expresses as unions with persons whom others see as somehow inappropriate or unsuited to the individual, as witnessed in Taylor's marital history by the publically censured adulterous involvements with Eddie Fisher and Richard Burton before marriage, the bizarre, out-of-the-box choice of politician John Warner, the social status gap with construction worker Larry Fortensky, and now this latest engagement, to a man almost thirty years her junior. The continual need for relationship, the eternal search for love, is another hallmark of Venus' interaction with Black Holes, and individuals with this placement typically lurch from one relationship/encounter to the next, with very little "down time" between them. Alternately, they can become enmeshed in a pattern of "feast or famine," punctuating a series of short-lived affairs with long periods of time utterly alone, which may account for Taylor's two partnerless stints between Warner and Fortensky, a gap of nine years, and the 14 years since that latest divorce.

Finances can also be affected by Black Hole Venus, which can make or mar fortunes, and Liz Taylor, when she signed her "*Cleopatra*" contract in 1960, set a fiscal record for Hollywood, becoming the first actress to earn a million dollars for a single role. Taylor's current net worth is an estimated $650 million, much of it in the form of jewelry, her enjoyment of which is justifiably famed. This accent on adornment also squares with Black Hole Venus, as the goddess of love is also the arbiter of fashion. Many of the gems in the Taylor collection were gifts from successive husbands, with Burton's offerings among the most expensive, including a massive diamond and emerald necklace worth more than $1 million at the time, and the famed 33-carat Krupp diamond, valued then at a quarter million dollars. The fact that these were gifts and not expenses she made herself is another Black Hole quality, as these insatiable graspers revel in accumulation, but loathe output. But Taylor can give as well as receive, spending $750,000 for a clip pin at a 1987 auction of the effects of the Duchess of Windsor. She also reportedly settled nearly $2 million on Larry Fortensky at their divorce, and loaned close friend Michael Jackson some $20 million for his costs in settling the first sexual molestation case against him. Black Hole Venus also figures prominently in her line of perfumes, spearheaded by "White Diamonds," which have netted the actress an estimated $12 million.

Taylor's magic ways with money have benefitted others as well, primarily in her charity work with AIDS. In her role as national chair of AMFAR she has overseen the raising of more than $250 million for AIDS research, and the Elizabeth Taylor AIDS Foundation has distributed more than $10 million globally to AIDS organizations focused on practical assistance for those affected by the disease.

As an icon of twentieth century femininity in its many forms, Elizabeth Taylor has been the focus of the psychic projections of literally millions of men and women, either as desired object or role model, who saw her as their ideal. The Black Hole contacting her Venus has been happy to absorb these projections, feeding off the energies of her fans, and giving in exchange an image of Venusian attraction and loveliness that will long endure.

# PAT TILLMAN
## & BLACK HOLE MARS

Pat Tillman, the rising NFL star who gave up his career to serve his country in the war in Afghanistan after the 9/11 attacks, makes for a fascinating case study of Black Hole Mars in several of the key areas it rules. Born 6 November 1976, at 9:39 AM PST in Fremont, California, Tillman's athletic skill as a starting player for the Arizona Cardinals, his military prowess as an elite Army Ranger and the bizarre circumstances of his death all qualify him as Black Hole Mars exemplar par excellence.

Tillman's 19 Scorpio Mars makes several Deep Space contacts, exactly sextile the Black Hole at 19 Capricorn, exactly sesquiquadrate another at 4 Cancer, exactly semisextile a third at 19 Sagittarius, and broadly opposed a fourth at 16 Taurus. But most telling is the exact semisquare to the Black Hole at 4 Capricorn, paired with another semisquare to the Quasar at 5 Libra, with Mars on their midpoint, effectively combining the Black Hole's ability to open doors and alter realities with the Quasar's ability to promote visibility, achievement and success. The Sun conjoins Mars from 14 Scorpio, and together they square Saturn at 16 Leo, so this Mars was not just central to his being, a way of identifying himself (Sun), but pivotal in his career choices (Saturn) as well. The Sun is also exactly conjunct a Pulsar, another Deep Space anomaly which is informational in nature and often indicates heightened media attention or a newsworthy quality to the individual. Tillman's life, and more specifically his death, certainly made headlines.

Tillman's football career began in High School where he was a star player with 31 tackles to his credit, and received a sports scholarship to Arizona State University in 1994. No academic slouch either, he graduated summa cum laude with a marketing degree and a 3.84 average in 1998. His outstanding performance as a linebacker on the college team earned him the title of Pac 10 Defensive

Player of the Year his senior year, followed by an NFL Draft pick by the Arizona Cardinals. Black Hole Mars often excels at sports and athletics, and Tillman was named by *"Sports Illustrated"* to its 2000 All-Pro team after just three seasons. Huge amounts of energy are funneled into Mars areas when aspected to Black Holes, and Tillman was noted for playing hard and working hard, with that Saturn touch urging him on to perfect his game and attain mastery.

In 2001 he turned down a $9 million five year contract with St. Louis out of loyalty to the Cardinals, who paid him just over $500,000 per year. The 9/11 attacks strongly affected Tillman, who in an interview for NFL films the following day, commented: "My grandfather was at Pearl Harbor and a lot of my family has gone and fought in wars. And I really haven't done a damn thing." The following May of 2002 he did something, rejecting a proposed $3.9 million contract with the Arizona Cardinals to enlist in the Army and serve his country. He never discussed his decision publically, but expressed his intention to return to pro football once his service had been completed. In addition to Mars squared Saturn, indicating a career in a Mars-related profession, Saturn is also conjunct asteroid Achilles at 12 Leo, making soldiering specifically a good fit for Tillman, and inclining others to see him as larger-than-life, a hero. After finishing basic training that September, Tillman entered the Ranger Indoctrination Program, and was assigned to the second battalion of the 75th Ranger Regiment, then deployed to Iraq, a war he deplored.

Tillman's enlistment had been trumpeted as a shining example of sacrifice for one's country, and used effectively to boost recruitment. But once deployed, Tillman saw a very different face of the "War on Terror," which he described a "fake," deriding the invasion of Iraq, in which he participated, as "so fucking illegal." This *volte face*, the sudden, complete reversal of circumstance or opinion, is typical of Black Hole energies, which promote the activation of dramatically opposed realities in turn, an up-is-down, black-is-white quality of revisionism.

In September of 2003, Tillman was redeployed to Afghanistan, the war he had enlisted to fight. But his objections were becoming ever more vocal, and an embarrassment to the Pentagon. Through a mutual friend, Tillman had arranged for a meeting with author

Noam Chomsky, an early and prominent critic of the war, after his return from Afghanistan. He died there on 22 April 2004, in circumstances which initially had his sacrifice held up to the nation as a model of heroism, described as dying "in the line of devastating enemy fire," ambushed by overwhelming hostile forces near the village of Sperah, about 25 miles southwest of Khost at the Pakistani border. He was given a posthumous promotion and awarded both the Silver Star and Purple Heart.

But that was only the beginning of the story. In true Black Hole reality-warping fashion, his death was not the simple story of a heroic fall against insurmountable odds, which the Pentagon and the Bush administration promoted as useful PR for the war effort, as they had done with his enlistment.

Within days Army investigators were aware that the official version of Tillman's death was untrue. These facts were known before Tillman's memorial service on May 3, 2004, but the truth of his death was kept from the public and family members; several comrades from his unit present at the funeral were ordered to lie about the circumstances of his death, which are still in some degree of doubt.

Despite initial reports that Tillman was killed in an ambush by overwhelming numbers of hostile forces, forensic evidence shows that he in fact died from friendly fire. The second version of his death stated that two allied but separate units came together without warning, and in the confusion and resulting melee, Tillman was accidentally shot. But Army doctor reports indicate that Tillman was shot three times in the head at close range, a pattern that may point to a deliberate incident of fragging, or intentional killing of a comrade. No other Americans died in the altercation, although one Afghani militia was killed and two other Rangers were wounded. In the aftermath, other soldiers in the unit burned Tillman's body armor, uniform, and field notebook, in blatant disregard of protocol, and the Pentagon has never released Tillman's diary.

Tillman's family was not informed that his death was caused by friendly fire until weeks after the memorial service, and alleges Army fraud and cover-up in the incident, stating they were told "outright lies" about their son's death. Patrick Tillman Sr., in a letter responding to a *Washington Post* story on the Pentagon's official version of the death, wrote: "With respect to the Army's reference to 'mistakes in reporting the circumstances of [my son's] death': those 'mistakes' were deliberate, calculated, ordered (repeatedly) and disgraceful—conduct well beneath the standard to which every soldier in the field is held."

In August 2005 the Pentagon Inspector General opened an official investigation into the circumstances, followed by a March 2006 criminal investigation instituted by the US Department of Defense. Congressional hearings followed the release of this report in March 2007, which characterized the death as negligent but accidental. Before Congress, Tillman's younger brother Kevin, also an Army Ranger, testified that "The deception surrounding this case was an insult to the family: but more importantly, its primary purpose was to deceive a whole nation. We say these things with disappointment and sadness for our country. Once again, we have been used as props in a Pentagon public relations exercise."

The repeated misrepresentations, lies, and distortions surrounding Tillman's death are very evocative of the Black Hole, which creates false fronts or images, representations of alternate realities which have no material substance but seek a foothold in our physical reality. The sense of things hidden, that all is not as it seems, of power plays behind the scenes or an underlying reality not in evidence, and of obfuscation or obliteration of the truth in the attempt to re-create a reality that is more convenient, useful, or manipulative, are all emblematic of Black Hole involvement. In repackaging what was at the least a terribly tragic mistake, and possibly a calculated murder, into a heroic act of self-sacrifice, the Pentagon attempted to substitute an altered reality which would better serve their ends. A Pat Tillman who gave up a promising pro sports career and then died a hero's death was far more useful than one who sacrificed his career only to decry the underlying hypocrisy, deception and illegality of the conflict in which he had enlisted to serve.

In his extensive athletic ability, his elite military training, and the dramatic, fabricated story of his death, we see all the hallmarks of pervasive Black Hole interaction with Mars, such as Pat Tillman's birth chart displays.

# SECTION II:
# BLACK HOLES
# IN MUNDANE CHARTS

# BLACK HOLE PROFILES

While Black Holes active in the birth chart indicate where a pattern of energy drain or sudden reversal, creativity or alternate reality may be experienced or anticipated throughout the life, when Black Holes are contacted in the daily transit sky, they evoke the actual events and circumstances which go to form and fulfill those patterns. As such, mundane events have a great deal to teach us about the ways Black Holes interact with our everyday reality, shifting and shaping, making or marring, creating the new realities which then become our status quo consensus reality, as individuals or the global whole.

A brief overview of Black Holes active in the charts of nations and formative events indicates a high level of deep space involvement, particularly in the case of communist, totalitarian or repressive regimes, institutions exerting great power or influence, and events having global import, breaking precedent, setting records or establishing new norms. The Black Hole tendency to birth new realities and upset old circumstances to enact alternative ways of being is well in evidence in the examples given below.

## BH 24 ARIES

This Black Hole has the usual contacts to communist states; Kampuchea's (formerly Cambodia) Venus conjoins at 23 Aries; Cuba's Venus squares from 23 Capricorn. Strong man Saddam Hussein's totalitarian Iraq, which gave more than a little trouble to the world at large, had Mars conjoined at 25 Aries. The U.N.'s ineffectiveness in bottling up that powder keg may be seen in that organization's Mars/Saturn (military/limitations) conjunction at 23/24 Cancer, in square to BH 24 Aries and Iraq's Mars.

BH 24 Aries is also present in the charts for the dawn of the nuclear era, with Jupiter at 24 Cancer in square for the first controlled nuclear reaction (12.2.42), and the Sun at 23 Cancer for the first atomic explosion (7.16.45), also in square.

The chart for the first manned lunar landing (7.21.69), one of the most paradigm-shattering events of all time, shows an appropriate opposition, signifying awareness, understanding, and fruition, from the 24 Libra Moon in that chart to BH 24 Aries.

The Sun conjoins BH 24 Aries yearly on or about April 13.

# BHs 26/27 ARIES

There are actually two Black Holes theorized at this degree, at varying range off the ecliptic. Their current interactions with the mundane world include a conjunction with the 26 Aries Saturn of the New York Stock Exchange (5.17.1792), effective throughout the period of the 1929 crash and the 2008 implosion, and speaks volumes for the market's variable volatility. This is opposed by a 27 Libra Neptune, the likely source of the economic "bubbles" of fantasy-based investment regularly pinpricked and deflated by reality-focused Saturn, creating the cycles of boom and bust with which we are all too familiar. This opposition was bisected at the time of the Great Crash of '29 by transit Saturn on the Galactic Center, in trine to BHs26/27 Aries, and again in 2008 by Pluto at its station degree of 28 Sagittarius.

BH 26/27 Aries is also involved in the chart for the division of Vietnam into North and South states. Those countries sported Sun/Chiron oppositions from 27 Cancer to Capricorn, which BH 26/27 Aries neatly T-squares.

True to form with the Black Hole affinity for high-level energy, BH 26/27 Aries is seen also at the first successful detonation of a nuclear device, an underground (!) explosion in Alamagordo, New Mexico, July 16, 1945, which immediately preceded the dropping of the bomb on Hiroshima. BH 26/27 Aries sits comfortably at the Midheaven, exactly squaring the 27 Cancer Ascendant.

The Sun conjoins BH 26/27 Aries yearly on or about April 16.

# BH 16 TAURUS

Perhaps this Black Hole's most dramatic recent interventions have occurred during US general elections. On November 8, 1994 the transit Sun exactly opposed it on Election Day in the U.S., eliciting a topsy-turvy rebalancing act in Congress, which went from a solid Democratic majority to a Republican stronghold overnight. Six years later, on November 7, 2000, ths opposition was also in effect for the most bizarre presidential election in modern US history, leading to a litigated recount extending 45 days and culminating in the US Supreme Court's *Bush v Gore* decision, which handed the White House to George W. Bush. This Black Hole also figures prominently in U.S. history with a conjunction and square to the Moon/Jupiter square of the chart for the Civil War (Moon conjunct at 15 Taurus, Jupiter squared from 17 Leo) and a square to the Sun of the Confederate States of America at 15 Aquarius.

BH 16 Taurus' other current involvements in world politics include a semisquare to Rwanda's genocidal Moon/Mars conjunction at 1 Cancer, a square to Israel's Saturn at 16 Leo, a conjunction with the Ascendant of Iran's Islamic Republic at 17 Leo, and a sesquiquadrate to disaster-prone Bangladesh's Pluto at 1 Libra.

As is typical of Black Hole involvements in mundane matters, it figures prominently in the charts of communist states. Kampuchea's (formerly Cambodia) Ascendant and communist Cuba's Mars conjoin it, and Cuba's Uranus is also in square from 15 Leo, the same degree as North Korea's Pluto. Squares from 17 Leo include communist China's Pluto, Neptune for the formation of the U.S.S.R., and communist Czechoslovakia's Saturn.

Also typical of Black Holes, BH 16 Taurus is present in the chart for the nuclear holocaust at Hiroshima, semisquare the 1 Cancer Venus and sesquiquadrate the 1 Libra Chiron.

And finally, we find this Black Hole in the charts for large, energy-hungry institutions: the United Nation's Mercury opposes from 15 Scorpio, as does the CIA's Jupiter (at 17 Scorpio), while the Venus of the European Economic Community squares from 15 Aquarius.

The Sun conjoins BH 16 Taurus yearly on or about May 6.

# BH 4 CANCER

This Black Hole seems to have an affinity for India; that state's Sun squares it from 4 Aries, and its Midheaven opposes from 3 Capricorn. BH 4 Cancer bisects the Mars opposition to Jupiter/Pluto of the great Indian spiritual leader and pacifist Mahatma Gandhi with a semisquare to Jupiter/Pluto at 17/20 Taurus and a sesquiquadrate to Mars at 18 Scorpio. Another great Indian philosopher and teacher, Krishnamurti, instrumental in the Theosophical movement, has his Jupiter conjoined this point, while it also bisects a similar axis in his chart, semisquare his Sun at 20 Taurus which opposes Uranus at 17 Scorpio, to which the Black Hole is sesquiquadrate.

Israel's Venus exactly conjoins BH 4 Cancer, and as is typical of Black Hole involvement in mundane affairs, we see it represented also in the charts of the First Manned Flight at Kitty Hawk in 1903 (Neptune conjoined at 4 Cancer), the dropping of the first atomic bomb at Hiroshima (Neptune squared from 4 Libra) and in the charts of communist states (communist Czechoslovakia's Ascendant conjoined at 4 Cancer, communist Bulgaria's Neptune squared from 3 Libra, communist Ukraine's Pluto conjoined from 3 Cancer, as does the Uranus of communist China).

The Sun conjoins BH 4 Cancer yearly on or about June 26.

# BH 28 CANCER

Venus conjoined this Black Hole on August 25, 1993, which witnessed Michael Jackson's collapse from dehydration while on his "Dangerous" Tour, following the scrutiny brought to bear on his relationships (Venus) after allegations of child sexual abuse first became public.

Mercury is often associated with weather conditions, and the Mercury retrograde of July 2, 1993 conjoined BH 28 Cancer, and coincided with the worst weeks of the Mississippi Valley flooding, contemporaneous to which thousands lost their lives in floods in India and Bangladesh. But this Black Hole has its helpful side as well; the Mars retrograde of November 1992 at 27 Cancer coincided with U.N. relief efforts in Somalia, spearheaded chiefly by

U.S. troops in a Black-Hole-typical reversal of their usual life-taking function. Somalia's nativity (July 1, 1960) shows Mercury posited at 29 Cancer, and when that famine-ravaged nation found her voice (Mercury) to call for aid, this Black Hole was not immune to her cries. Of course, what started as a humanitarian venture soon degenerated into involvement in local politics and civil war, costing the lives of hundreds of U.S. and other U.N. servicemen, a not unexpected ramification considering the Black Hole's penchant for reversal. The last U.S. troops were withdrawn, with famine and civil strife looming again on the horizon, in late March 1994, just after Pluto's Quasar station in trine to this point from 28 Scorpio.

The Sun conjoins BH 28 Cancer yearly on or about July 21.

# BH 2/3 LEO

The Sun of the CIA conjoins this anomaly from 2 Leo, appropriate for an organization focused on hidden (Black Hole) matters, and responsible for the overthrow of unfriendly regimes across the globe. Energy-sucker U.N.'s Sun squares from 1 Scorpio, while the Mercury of one of its most controversial, distracting and energy-draining members, Israel, conjoins from 4 Leo. Israel has been the focus of more U.N. resolutions (Mercury), both pro and con, than any other member state. Energy-rich Saudi Arabia's Mercury opposes from 2 Aquarius, a symbol of the vast wealth beneath its sands.

Communist North Korea's Venus conjoins from 3 Leo, and it's Mars squares from 5 Scorpio. Qaddafi's Libya has its Venus also conjunct at 5 Leo, while the Mars for the first manned flight at Kitty Hawk NC opposes from 4 Aquarius. The USSR's Neptune conjoined from 2 Leo, while its Jupiter lay in square at 2 Taurus, and Khomeini's Iran has Jupiter conjoined from 3 Leo. North Vietnam's Saturn squares from 2 Scorpio and Idi Amin's Uganda had Saturn opposed from 4 Aquarius. Ethnic-cleansing Sudan has Uranus conjunct at 1 Leo, while Killing Fields-famed Kampuchea has its 0 Scorpio Uranus in square.

The Sun conjoins BH 2/3 Leo yearly on or about July 26.

# BH 9 LEO

On a mundane level, Jordan, Lebanon, Syria, and communist Bulgaria, Poland and Yugoslavia all sport Plutos conjoined BH 9 Leo, as do Vietnam's 1945 independence chart and the detonation of the first atomic bomb in Alamagordo, NM. Communist China's Mars also conjoins from 8 Leo, while Khomeini's Iran has Mars opposed at 9 Aquarius. Venus for the Wright brothers' first flight squares from 8 Scorpio, and the Saturns for both the first lunar landing and Qaddafi's Libya square from 8 Taurus, with the Pluto of the U.S. Civil War there as well. A more recent activation of this point can be seen in O.J. Simpson's Saturn placement, which exactly conjoins this point. The peak years of World War II coincided with Pluto's passage from the singularity of BH 2/3 Leo to that of BH 9 Leo.

The Sun conjoins BH 9 Leo yearly on or about August 1.

# BH 6/7 VIRGO

Terrorist-sponsor Syria's Mars/Uranus union at 5 Gemini squares this Black Hole, and the Moon of the Islamic Republic of Iran also squares from 6 Gemini. The chart for the start of the US Civil War shows Mars in square from 6 Gemini, perhaps not surprising when we note that it was thus conjunct the USA's natal Uranus at 8 Gemini, which is also squared BH 6/7 Virgo. The Saturn for the first controlled nuclear reaction also lies at 8 Gemini in square.

The former Soviet Union's Midheaven conjoins this anomaly from 5 Virgo, while oil cartel OPEC, arguably the single most powerful multi-national organization in the world, has its Pluto conjunct at 6 Virgo. Totalitarian Myanmar's Mars conjoins from 7 Virgo, and Iran's Islamic Republic has Saturn at 8 Virgo.

The Midheaven for the first manned flight squares from 5 Sagittarius, the same degree as Vietnam's Ascendant and communist China's Chiron. Communist Czechoslovakia's Sun opposed from 5 Pisces, and apartheid South Africa's Sun squared from 9 Gemini with its Chiron opposed from 6 Pisces. The USSR's bellicose Sun/Mars pairing at 8 Pisces also opposed.

The Sun conjoins BH 6/7 Virgo yearly on or about August 30.

# BH 9 VIRGO

This Black Hole's discovery was first made public in mid-January 1995, contemporaneous with the Chiron station square the Galactic Center. The testimony phase of the O.J. Simpson trial began then as well, and many of the persons involved show close contacts to BH 9 Virgo. Prosecutor Marsha Clark's Sun lies at 8 Virgo, between BH 6/7 Virgo and BH 9 Virgo, while defending counsel Robert Shapiro and Alan Dershowitz both have their Suns smack on the singularity at 9 Virgo.

This point's involvement in world affairs is typical of a Black Hole, with perhaps a more than usual accent on the nuclear. BH 9 Virgo forms a T-Square from the Sun/Saturn opposition of the chart for the first controlled nuclear reaction (12.2.42), with the Sun at 10 Sagittarius and Saturn at 8 Gemini both in square. Venus formed an exact square from 9 Gemini for the first atomic explosion at Alamagordo in July 1945, followed a month later by the dropping of the bomb on Hiroshima, when Mars filled in Venus' seat at 9 Gemini.

BH 9 Virgo's presence is apparent in the field of flight as well. The Moon at 10 Sagittarius for the first manned flight (12.3.03) squares, as does Saturn at 9 Sagittarius in the chart for the launch of Sputnik, the first orbiting manmade satellite.

And, as is common with Black Holes, it is represented in the charts of communist, or reactionary regimes, as well as large economic organizations. The MC of communist Bulgaria conjoined at 10 Virgo, as does the Sun for the coup in Libya which set up Qaddafi's regime, while the Saturn of Iran's Islamic Republic lies smack between the singularities of BH 6/7 Virgo and BH 9 Virgo, at 8 Virgo. The Sun for the bombing of the World Trade Center in 1993 by Arab terrorists also lies in direct opposition from 8 Pisces. OPEC's Ascendant squares from 9 Sagittarius.

The Sun conjoins BH 9 Virgo yearly on or about September 2.

# BH 1 LIBRA

Supermassive BH 1 Libra is the largest Black Hole we are aware of, and is likely to remain so, so it is perhaps fitting that the location of this energy sucking vacuum should be in Libra, symbol of the interpersonal relationships that can drain more energy than any other area of life.

Imaged by NASA's Hubble Space Telescope on May 25, 1994, by pinpointing its accretion disk, a brightly glowing ring of super-heated infalling matter which is the only visible part of a Black Hole, BH 1 Libra lies at the center of Galaxy M-87, and has a mass estimated to equal two billion of our Suns. The temperature of the disk, which is roughly 60 light years across, is an estimated 18,000 degrees Fahrenheit, and is rotating at a rate of 1.2 million miles per hour!

According to Philip Sedgwick in *The Astrology of Deep Space*, BH 1 Libra's event horizon, the surrounding region of time/space beyond which nothing can re-emerge, is estimated at 326 light years across. This staggering figure can perhaps begin to be contemplated by comparison with the size of our entire system and its near neighbors. Pluto is five light hours from the Sun, about 3 billion miles; Alpha Centauri, our nearest stellar neighbor, is 4.3 light years away (about 20 trillion miles), barely 1% of BH 1 Libra's' girth; we are but an olive on the relish tray of the banquet this Black Hole makes daily. Over 130 galaxies are kept in rotation by its massive gravitational thrall. Now *that* is a big hole!

BH 1 Libra's impact can be overwhelming, even at these distances. The Sun conjoined this anomaly for the launch chart of the Mars Observer in 1992; so much for that mission (the Observer disappeared without a trace 11 months later, just as it was preparing to enter orbit around Mars). President Clinton ill-advisedly chose to present his Health Care Plan to the nation while the Sun was conjunct BH 1 Libra in September 1993; not only would his proposal have created one of the largest bureaucracies in the history of the nation, but the President's popularity and executive standing were completely eroded by the attendant wrangling and partisanship which consumed both houses of Congress over the issue, and led eventually to Senate Majority Leader George Mitchell announcing the death of National Health Care in September 1994, almost a year to the day from its proposal, with the Sun again conjoined this anomaly.

BH 1 Libra's appetite for energy is insatiable; if the Universe is fated to die a heat death wherein all matter cools to the temperature of absolute zero, this point and other supermassive Black Holes like it will be the principal assassins.

The Sun conjoins BH 1 Libra yearly on or about September 23.

# BH 13 LIBRA

The United States' Saturn is conjoined this Black Hole from 14 Libra, and our chief executives (Saturn) do seem to die in office with alarming regularity, a percentage noticeably higher than in other elected democracies.

Both Vietnam and Iran have Suns conjoined BH 13 Libra. Lebanon's Mars opposes it, an apt image of the decades-old civil war which has plagued that nation, and this Mars exactly opposes Syria's Ascendant (conjoined BH 13 Libra), which has played such a negative role in Lebanon, fueling the strife there, as well as in the world, as the suspected center of many international terrorist groups.

Haiti's Ascendant exactly opposes BH 13 Libra from 13 Aries, while much-flooded, disease and famine-ridden Bangladesh's Ascendant squares from 12 Cancer. Surely an impressive roster of this point's involvement in our world community.

The Sun conjoins BH 13 Libra yearly on or about October 6.

# BH 28/29 LIBRA

This Black Hole's most notorious involvement in mundane events recently has been with the explosion which destroyed the Alfred P. Murrah Federal Building in Oklahoma City; the Sun for that chart exactly opposed it, as did the Sun for the fiery Waco, Texas debacle two years previously, where David Koresh and 75 of his Branch Davidian followers died in an assault by government agents on their compound, an incident which provided the inspiration for Timothy McVeigh's retributive bombing in Oklahoma.

Some of BH 28/29 Libra's past and present affiliations include: a square to the 27 Cancer Ascendant (itself conjoined BH 28 Cancer) of the first atomic explosion in Alamagordo, NM; an opposition to the 27 Aries Sun (itself conjoined BHs 26/27 Aries) of the communist government of Kampuchea, formerly Cambodia, of Killing Fields fame; a conjunction with the 27 Libra Jupiter of the former communist state of Yugoslavia, and a square to the 28 Cancer Mercury (also conjoined BH 28 Cancer) of the first manned lunar landing. BH 28/29 Libra infiltrates world economic organizations as well—the Neptune for the New York Stock Exchange lies within its grasp at 27 Libra, as does the 28 Libra Jupiter of the European Economic Community. The USA's Pluto squares from the Pulsar at 27 Capricorn, and also in square from 28 Capricorn is Kuwait's Saturn, highlighted by both a Solar Eclipse and a Saturn Return during the First Gulf War.

The Sun conjoins BH 28/29 Libra yearly on or about October 22.

# BH 6/7 SCORPIO

The Venus of the New York Stock Exchange opposes this anomaly from 5 Taurus, an apt image of the financial volatility that institution can evoke. The launching of the first man-made satellite, Sputnik, which began the Space Race, shows a Midheaven also opposed from 7 Taurus, and the conclusion of that race, the first manned lunar landing, has its Saturn at 8 Taurus, a Saturn degree shared by Qaddafi's Libya, which was born that same summer.

The Pluto for the first controlled nuclear reaction squares this anomaly from 7 Leo, with Kampuchea's Ascendant, communist Poland's Pluto and communist China's Mars all in square from 8 Leo with China's Venus also conjoined at 7 Scorpio. Communist North Korea's Mars conjoins from 5 Scorpio, as does communist Cuba's Neptune, at 6 Scorpio. The Venus for the first manned flight in Kitty Hawk conjoins at 8 Scorpio, with its Saturn squared from 6 Aquarius.

Khomeini's Iran has both Mercury and Mars in square, from 6 and 9 Aquarius, perhaps the source of their bellicose rhetoric which receives so much global attention, and communist Kampuchea's Midheaven falls at 7 Aquarius, with that "graveyard of empires" Afghanistan's Moon/Jupiter conjunction falling at 8 Aquarius, also in square..

The Sun conjoins BH 6/7 Scorpio yearly on or about October 30.

# BHs 3, 4, & 5 SAGITTARIUS

Taken as a group due to their proximity, as with most Black Holes, the mundane affiliations of this cosmic trio are wide-ranging and numerous, tending toward involvements with earthly regimes of a communist or reactionary nature, as well as interests of large economic organizations, and those two twentieth century landmarks in human development, Flight and Nuclear Power.

The catalog of contacts to modern states reads like a Who's Who of trouble spots: Communist Kampuchea (formerly Cambodia, of the Killing Fields fame) sports a Venus/Mars square at 4 degrees of Gemini and Pisces, forming a T-Square with these anomalies; similarly the chart for Iran's reactionary Islamic Republic shows a 6 Gemini Moon and a 3 Pisces Venus, mirroring that same T-Square. Communist Czechoslovakia's Sun squared from the Quasar at 5 Pisces, while Qaddafi's Libyan regime has a 3 Gemini Moon in opposition, a degree shared by the Sun of the state of Jordan, and communist Cuba's Pluto squares from 4 Virgo. Afghanistan, that quagmire of Soviet imperialist ambitions, and currently a thorn in the side of the United States (where it has recently surpassed Vietnam as the country's longest-running conflict), has obfuscating Neptune conjunct the trio from 4 Sagittarius, while the chart for the U.S. Civil War shows a Mars/Saturn square with Mars conjunct the Maser at 6 Gemini and Saturn filling in the T-Square from 3 Virgo.

The trio are active in the chart for the First Manned Flight, at Kitty Hawk, North Carolina (MC exactly conjoined the Black Hole at 5 Sagittarius) and the First Manned Lunar Landing (Mars at 3 Sagittarius for the touchdown of the Lunar Landing Module). Likewise, the chart for the first controlled nuclear reaction (12.2.42, Chicago, IL) shows Uranus in opposition from 2 Gemini, while the dropping of the bomb on Hiroshima has a 4 Virgo Mercury in square.

The trio's resume with world economic organizations is just as impressive: The Pluto of the European Economic Community (the old Common Market) squares from 2 Virgo, while its Mars conjoins from 6 Sag; Pluto is again the player for OPEC, the international oil cartel, with a square from 6 Virgo, conjoined BH 6/7 Virgo, and the

Ascendant of the New York Stock Exchange lies in that same region, squared from 3 Virgo.

The Sun conjoins this trinity of Black Holes yearly from about November 25 through 28.

# BHs 17/18 & 18/19 SAGITTARIUS

Another pair of anomalies related by proximity to their ecliptic reference points (though not by their actual locations in space), these points wreaked the most havoc recently during the period when Pluto conjoined them in 2003-4, which saw the inception of the Iraq War, and the resulting insurgent backlash. Double Pluto stations conjunct BH 19 Sagittarius Black Hole coincided with the war's start in March 2003, and the breakdown of stability within the country in the late summer of 2004. Its involvement in this fiasco speaks volumes for the incredible drain of resources it has caused.

Communist Bulgaria's Sun squares from 16 Virgo and its Moon opposes from 15 Gemini, a degree repeated by Uranus in the chart for the first atomic bomb explosion in Alamagordo, NM in 1945. Venus for the first manned lunar landing in 1969 also opposes from 16 Gemini, and the Midheaven for the first use of an atom bomb at Hiroshima also falls at that degree, while the Ascendant of that chart squares from 17 Virgo. The CIA's Mars opposes from 17 Gemini.

Communist Czechoslovakia's Moon squares from 16 Virgo, as does the Mars of the New York Stock Exchange (from 18 Virgo), communist Poland's Jupiter (from 20 Virgo) and communist North Korea's Sun (from 19 Virgo).

The Moon of the Confederacy conjoined these anomalies from 15 Sagittarius, as does communist China's 16 Sagittarius Ascendant, the Mars for Qaddafi's Libya, Mercury for Castro's Cuba and Neptune for Khomeini's Iran, all at 19 Sagittarius. The Jupiter of the first manned flight at Kitty Hawk squares from 15 Pisces.

The Sun conjoins this pair of Black Holes on or about December 10 and 11.

# THE GALACTIC CENTER – 26 SAGITTARIUS

Philip Sedgwick, in *The Astrology of Deep Space*, makes the point that, due to the precession of the equinoxes, no horoscope is reproducible in less than a Great Platonic Year of 26,000 earth years. But the earth, traveling in the wake of the Sun, also encircles the Galactic Center, at the rate of 500,000 miles per hour.

When Galactic Points and their relation to the celestials of our system are considered, this time frame of unique individuality is increased to 250 million earth years. No two horoscopes will be exactly alike within that (literally) astronomical time frame.

If we see the Galactic Center as the ground of our being, the source of our individuality and personhood, we can more fully appreciate the uniqueness which is our birthright, born of a cosmic evolutionary cycle of a quarter billion years. By this frame of reference, life on earth has seen the same skies only 12 times in its 3 billion year history; each day is a truly unique experience.

Until recently scientific thought has been divided on the make-up of the Galactic Center. Some considered it to be the birth place of a trillion billion just-forming Suns. Others theorized a massive Black Hole at the very heart of our galactic system, a feature which is the driving force behind our galaxy's spiral motion. It is the latter interpretation which has gained rapid credence as more and more data is acquired from advanced imaging techniques, which plot the movement of stars at our galaxy's center, and lead inescapably to the supposition of the existence of a supermassive Black Hole there. As the Great Maw of the Milky Way slowly but inexorably draws in all of the matter in the system, that "great sucking sound" you hear is the gurgle of the cosmic drainpipe.

Located at 26 Sagittarius for most of the last century (the G.C. will shift to 27 degrees early in this millennium), the G.C. forms a primal polarity with the Quasar at 26 Gemini and the Pole Star Polaris at 27 Gemini. Energy absorbed and imploded by the Black Hole core of the galaxy is disgorged by the Quasar opposite; the two function as a perfect pipeline for the cosmic round-robin.

Polaris, as the star closest in alignment to our North Pole, represents our highest aspirations, our drive and determination to be different, to become what we uniquely are. Generations of seamen have steered their course by this star, a perfect metaphor for the journey we all take through life's uncharted waters.

The G.C., on the other hand, represents both the source and the ending of the journey, the cosmic womb/tomb which birthed our system and which will one day in the far distant future reclaim it.

The G.C. emits massive amounts of infrared radiation, which Sedgwick describes as both "arousing the subconscious portion of the brain" and providing "intense stimulation for the root chakra." This activation of the subconscious promotes the retrieval of information from the past, the past of this life and other lives, which may interact with the self-preservation instincts of the root chakra, creating some uneasiness or tension.

The G.C. is closely grouped with a pair of Pulsars which provide "information parentheses" about it. The Pulsar at 24 Sagittarius, two degrees before the G.C., provides information relating to the past of an event; that at 28 Sagittarius, two degrees after, provides information relating to the future of an event. Those with connections on either side of the G.C. will more naturally tend to orient information in one of these two directions. Balance may be sought by meditation with the alternate point, using the G.C. as the fulcrum between past and future.

Lying as it does just four degrees from the Winter Solstice Point, which is surely no coincidence, the G.C. provides a convenient frame of reference for aligning with cosmic consciousness. Whenever the Sun makes one of its seasonal ingresses, it is within days/degrees of a major aspect to the Center. These two frames of reference will come into alignment in the middle years of the third century of the new millennium, when the G.C. moves to conjoin the Solstice Point of 0 Capricorn.

The Galactic Center's appearance in mundane charts suggest a global or universal import to the event or nation state contacted. Bismarck's German Empire, the root of the militaristic behemoth which eventually became Nazi Germany, had its Moon conjunct from 24 Sagittarius, and Khomeini's Islamic Republic of Iran, which continues to disturb global politics to this day, has its MC there as well, at 25 Sagittarius, with its Mercury/Mars conjunction squared from 25/27 Pisces. Qaddafi's Libya, one of the first state sponsors of the terrorism which has since grown into such a serious global threat, has its Pluto (ruling terrorism) in square at 24 Virgo. Communist China, the world's most populous nation, with its 1.3 billion people representing a fifth of the global total, has its Sun/Midheaven conjunction in square from 27 and 25 Virgo respectively. The OPEC oil cartel, possibly the leading influence on global economics, has Mars exactly opposed the GC from 26 Gemini. Those landmark pivots of twentieth century human development, the first manned flight at Kitty in 1903 and the first manned lunar landing in 1969, both of which reframed our reality definitively, are also represented, with the Sun/Uranus (flight) for Kitty Hawk at 24 and 25 Sagittarius, and the moon landing's Midheaven exactly conjunct the GC, with its Ascendant squared from 24 Pisces. The launching of Sputnik, the first man-made earth satellite, has Mercury at 17 Virgo in square.

The Sun conjoins the Galactic Center yearly on or about December 18.

# BH 4/5 CAPRICORN

This Black Hole's affiliations with current mundane charts are the same as those of BH 4 Cancer, which opposes it, and have already been chronicled in that profile. Its most dramatic involvement in recent world events is its conjunction with the Sun at 5 Capricorn for the disastrous Indian Ocean Tsunami of 26 December 2004, which also showed a Full Moon at 5 Cancer in opposition. The deep sea earthquake of 9.0 magnitude (the largest in more than forty years) which initiated the event comprised the force of an estimated 23,000 atom bombs, and created a tidal wave as much as 50 feet in height in some areas. More than 400,000 people died in countries ringing the Indian Ocean, even as far away as Somalia, almost 3,000 miles from the quake's epicenter.

The Sun conjoins BH 4/5 Capricorn yearly on or about December 27.

# BH 19 CAPRICORN

Among the energy-sucking institutions which bear allegiance to BH 19 Capricorn are: the United Nations (Ascendant at 20 Aries in square), the C.I.A. (Ascendant at 20 Libra in square) and the New York Stock Exchange (Moon at 20 Aries in square). This Black Hole seems to have an affinity with vast energy and mass destruction— the Midheaven of the chart for the First Controlled Nuclear Reaction conjoins it from 18 Capricorn, while the Moon of the first use of the atom bomb at Hiroshima opposes from 18 Cancer. Oppressive nation states seem to gravitate to it as well, as witnessed by the 19 Libra Saturn, in square, of the 1922 Soviet Union chart (following the several revolutions and Civil War of 1917-22) and the 19 Cancer Saturn of Tito's Communist Yugoslavia, in opposition, not to mention the Pluto of Iran's Khomeini-led Islamic Republic, in square from 18 Libra.

The Sun conjoins BH 18 Capricorn yearly on or about January 9.

## BHs 11/12 & 12/13 AQUARIUS

Among this pair's mundane affiliations are the Midheavens of both Iran's Islamic Republic (at 10 Taurus, in square) and Qaddafi's Libya (squared from 12 Taurus) and the Plutos of both the United Nations (opposed from 11 Leo) and the CIA (opposed from 12 Leo). Uranus from Sputnik's launch opposes from 10 Leo, wehile both Khomeini's Iran and Hitler's Third Reich have Suns in conjunction at 11 Aquarius.

The Sun conjoins this pair yearly on or about February 1 and 2.

## BH 27/28 AQUARIUS

The Moon for Sputnik's launch conjoins this anomaly from 27 Aquarius, while the Moon of the 1917 Russian Revolution, which led ultimately to the formation of the Soviet state, opposes from 29 Leo. Communist North Korea's Ascendant squares from 17 Scorpio, as does the Neptune of the first manned lunar landing (from 26 Scorpio), the Ascendant of Hitler's Germany and the Sun of the New York Stock Exchange (both from 27 Taurus), and the Mars for the Alamagordo atomic bomb test (from 25 Taurus).

The Sun conjoins BH 27/28 Aquarius yearly on or about February 17.

# BH 28 PISCES

A quick roster of this Black Hole's current contacts in the mundane world may serve to illustrate its effects. Kuwait, the emirate whose vast wealth derives from some of those Underworld sources, and which has proved such a magnet for energy during the First Gulf War, has a 27 Gemini Sun in square to the anomaly.

Interestingly, the Descendant of the European Economic Community conjoins BH 28 Pisces from 29 Pisces; their growth in partnerships (Descendant) continues apace, with three new members officially admitted in January 1995, for a total of 15, while the new democracies of Eastern Europe chafed for the opportunity to cast their lot in as well. By 2009 those countries had their chance, and the EEC now has 27 member states.

Regular devastation seemed to be the theme of famine-stalked and flood-stricken Bangladesh, perhaps not surprising when we see that nation's Pluto planted firmly in opposition at 28 Virgo. Israel, who does seem to have the luck of the Irish, Judaism notwithstanding, and whose diplomatic and alliance history is chequered with stunning reversals, has Jupiter at 27 Sagittarius in square.

Black Holes do seem to have an affinity with Communism, and BH 28 Pisces is no exception. The chart for Mao's proclamation of Communist China (the state officially took another week to form) shows the Sun in opposition from 27 Virgo, while Castro's Cuba has a 29 Sagittarius Saturn in square.

Although I cannot find the reprint of the chart he references, Nicholas Campion in his *Book of World Horoscopes* lists an Ascendant for the American Civil War (presumably based on the firing on Fort Sumter, SC) of 27 Pisces, and this dramatic tale of civil strife and brother against brother may be one of the most poignant examples of this point's energy addiction.

The Sun conjoins BH 28 Pisces yearly on or about March 19.

[All mundane reference chart data taken from Nicholas Campion's *The Book of World Horoscopes*, The Aquarian Press, 1988.]

# DETAILED EXAMPLES FROM
# MUNDANE EVENTS

# BLACK HOLE ELECTIONS

Three pivotal elections in recent US history show the power and impact of Black Holes on the outcome of our political system. The Republican take-over of Congress in 1994's midterm election runs a close parallel to a similar Democratic resurgence in 2006, but for Deep Space drama and weirdness, both are vastly eclipsed by the presidential election of 2000, the strangest ever.

Occurring 8 November 1994, 7 November 2000, and 7 November 2006, all three have the Sun in opposition to the reality-warping Black Hole at 16 Taurus, indicating a day for major upheaval, dramatic reversal of the status quo, and the imposition of major change in the body politic. It is perhaps just as well that US elections rarely occur this late in the month, tending as they do to evoke turmoil and disruption. Mercury, arbiter of voters and the votes they cast, as well as the machines that record those votes and the methods by which they are counted, is galactically active in all three cases as well, with conjunctions to the Black Hole at 29 Libra in 1994 and 2000 (upon which date it made a direct station exactly conjunct the anomaly) and in 2006 conjoined the Sun opposed the 16 Taurus Black Hole.

The 1994 and 2006 elections, which both saw stunning reversals of power between the two major parties, and in which voter disaffection and anger played a lead role, also share a circumstance of Saturn in contact with Quasars. Saturn represents the ill will and desire to punish the party in power, while Quasars heighten and augment whatever they touch. In 1994 Saturn came to its direct station just one day after the election, exactly conjunct the Quasar at 5 Pisces, bringing immense power to the pervasive voter irritability and discontent with the status quo, creating a Democratic rout in the Senate and the House of Representatives. In 2006, the

Republicans were similarly unseated in both Houses, with Saturn at 24 Leo closely opposing the 25 Aquarius Quasar, which it would aspect exactly at its station retrograde the next month.

Of the two, 1994 was the more memorable, with the GOP taking control of both Houses and a sitting House Speaker, Tom Foley (D-WA), being the first to lose this position since 1862. The Republicans wrested the House from Democrats after a 40-year-long minority, and having run the House only four years out of the previous 72. 54 House seats changed hands that day, with the Democrats waking up that morning with a 256-178 majority, and the day after in the minority by 228-199. In the Senate the numbers were almost completely reversed, with a 56-44 Dem advantage yielding to a 52-48 GOP majority, which became 53-47 when Alabama Senator Richard Shelby switched parties to the winning side a day later. Republicans made devastating gains in State Houses across the country that day as well, and the residents of Governor's mansions also reversed, flipping from a 29-20 Democratic majority to a 31-17 GOP sweep.

Twelve years later, the positions were reversed, with a Republican-weary electorate ready to give the Dems another chance. Bush fatigue was cited as tolling the death knell for 1994's Republican Revolution; when the dust cleared the day after, Democrats were back in control of both Houses, with a 233-202 advantage in the House, a thirty vote pick-up, and a slim 51-49 margin the Senate, where they gained six seats. The picture on the state level also reflected a reversal of the 1994 results—before the election, Democrats controlled just 21 more than half of the 7382 state legislature seats; afterward they numbered a 667 seat advantage. Democrats gained control of both upper and lower Houses in 23 states, up from 19 and the largest margin since 1994, while the GOP lost ascendancy in four states, dropping from 20 to 16.

These dramatic reversals are typical of Black Hole interaction, which frequently yields stunning change, fundamentally altering realities in the blink of an eye. But for sheer drama and bizarre outcomes, the 2000 election stands alone.

Held 7 November 2000, but not decided until the supreme Court gave the nod to George W. Bush on December 12, it became the longest presidential election in US history. Two major factors decided the lack of outcome on Election Day—a Solar Galactic T-Square in fixed signs involving Uranus, two Pulsars and a Black Hole (Mars also tied into this pattern by minor aspect), and the incidence of a Mercury Direct Station exactly conjoined another Black Hole. The Sun at 15 Scorpio was exactly conjoined a Pulsar and opposed the Black Hole at 16 Taurus while in square to Uranus exactly conjunct the Pulsar at 16 Aquarius. Additionally, Mars at 1 Libra was exactly conjunct the supermassive Black Hole center of Galaxy M-87, the largest anomaly of its type of which we are aware, and tied into this pattern by semisquare (45 degrees) to the Sun and sesquiquadrate (135 degrees) to both Uranus and the Taurean Black Hole. This pattern shows a shocking or unexpected development (Uranus), conflicting information and an excessive involvement by the media (the squared Pulsars), and a stubborn, heels-dug-in quality to the proceedings (Mars and the Fixed Sign T-Square).

But the true culprit, galactically speaking, was undoubtedly Mercury. Turning retrograde on October 18 from the exact degree of the Election Day Sun (!) while conjunct the Pulsar at 15 Scorpio, Mercury was about to finish its retrograde period. At 2:28 AM EST on Election Day, Mercury backed into Libra briefly, and into the waiting arms of the Black Hole at 29 Libra. Mercury rules the decision making process, the electorate, the ballots, the vote itself, and the counting and recounting process, as well as the media. With its firm stance on the quicksand foundation of an alternate-reality-inducing Black Hole, is any wonder the nation found itself leaderless, evenly divided, and unable to come to a conclusion in the election process?

Mercury turned direct from the Black Hole at 29 Libra at 9:26 PM Election Night, less than half an hour before pandemonium broke loose with the reneging of the media's call of Florida's electoral votes for Gore at 9:54 PM, and the following day edged back into Scorpio at 4:42 PM November 8, within minutes of Florida Governor Jeb Bush's assurance of a fair and impartial recount at 4:30 PM, and VP Gore's message to the nation urging patience and a full and fair accounting at 4:36 PM.

Interestingly, key events in the overnight election coverage occurred within moments of the Moon's activation of the T-Square pattern. At 2:15 AM the Moon ignited the Sun by sesquiquadrate

(135 degrees) from 1 Aries, also opposing Mars and in semisquare (45 degrees) to Uranus. At 2:18 AM CNN called Florida and the election for George W. Bush (earlier in the evening the major networks, based on exit polling, had called Florida for Gore, then retracted and put the Sunshine State back in the 'too close to call' column, where much of the nation spent most of the evening).

Shortly thereafter, Gore called Bush to concede the election, and headed for downtown Nashville to make his public concession speech. Suddenly, things changed. New numbers were coming in from Florida, putting the outcome once again in doubt. In a cliff-hanging nail-biter too real for Hollywood to invent, top aides on jammed-out cell phones tried to reach Gore, riding in the lead car of the procession, pleading with him not to step out on the stage and make that speech. At 3:41 AM Gore placed a second call to Austin, retracting his concession to Bush. At 3:42 AM the Moon, still at 1 Aries and opposing Mars while in sesquiquadrate to the Sun, made its exact semisquare to Uranus.

The battle for Florida, and the presidency, was on.

The major fronts in this war were the courts and the recount process. Joining the lexicon and lore of American elections during that time was the infamous "Butterfly Ballot" in West Palm Beach County, whose confusing design awarded some 3000 votes to also-ran Pat Buchanan and invalidated 19,000 others, which were inadvertently double-punched for two candidates. The nation became engrossed in the seemingly endless recount process, requiring a crash course in the chad, those tiny bits of paper which drop off, or are supposed to, when a voter punches his or her ballot, and which come in a dizzying variety of styles. There are hanging chads, where all but one of the four corners has been detached, swinging door chads, with two corners still intact, tri chads, with only one corner detached, and even pregnant chads, those pierced by the stylus but with all corners intact, and dimpled chads, ones where an indentation has been made but no hole punched.

It would take Mercury on a Black Hole to create this kind of confusing, frustrating, energy-sucking situation, a quantum-level gap in the fabric of electoral reality, into which, pell-mell like a herd of stampeding buffalo, we release the lawyers, with at one time no fewer than 24 separate court cases pending related to the election in Florida, with appeals to the Florida Supreme Court, the Federal Circuit Court, and the U.S. Supreme Court. The spate of legal rulings made each and every day after the election was held a roller coaster ride equivalent to, perhaps surpassing, that of Election Night itself, with first one camp and then the other appearing to gain the upper hand, only to lose it in the subsequent ruling.

With the Supreme Court's termination of the Florida recount process, despite lagging behind Gore by some half a million popular votes nationally, George W. Bush was selected and installed in the White House. It was far and away the most bizarre and controversial election in US history, the ramifications of which continue to reverberate in the national psyche and the world stage, in true Black Hole revolutionary fashion.

# McGREEVEY'S OUT
## (IN MORE WAYS THAN ONE)

*"My truth is that I am a gay American."*
—Governor James McGreevey (D-NJ), 12 August 2004

We might have expected much from a Mercury retrograde which started at 8 Virgo, exactly between a pair of Black Holes at 7 and 9 Virgo, but few were prepared for the stunning revelations by New Jersey's Governor, which followed later in the week of the Mercury station. On Thursday, August 12, Democrat Jim McGreevey called a press conference to announce that he was gay, that he'd had an extramarital affair with a man, and that he was resigning as Governor effective November 15.

Stunned doesn't begin to describe it.

The Governor has been married twice and is the father of a daughter by each wife, and was about to be sued for sexual misconduct by his former homeland security advisor and reputed lover, Israeli-born Golan Cipel. McGreevey cited issues of distracted focus, the effect on his family, and the vulnerability of the governor's office to blackmail in his decision to come out publicly to avow his sexuality and the affair, and resign.

But that wasn't the only high profile gay-themed news that day. The California Supreme Court by unanimous decision declared that San Francisco Mayor Gavin Newsom had overstepped his bounds in directing the county clerk to register same sex marriages last February, and those marriages were annulled.

Even a novice political astrologer will see a pattern here, and the Deep Space Detective was not long in launching an investigation. Sleuthing for clues to the celestial puzzle involving human sexuality, we will of course look for activity involving Venus and Mars; and for sexuality deviating from the norm, we'll want to see if Uranus, Neptune or Pluto is active in aspect to them.

As further qualifiers of sexuality, or at any rate, sexual attitude, we also have a variety of asteroids to consider. For the purposes of these news stories, and particularly McGreevey's, I chose to ascertain the whereabouts of asteroids Sappho (an early Greek lesbian poet), Ganymede (Zeus' cupbearer and bun boy), Antinous (Roman Emperor Hadrian's deified male lover, whose cult once far eclipsed that of Jesus Christ), Lust (for obvious reasons) and Pecker (which speaks for itself).

First, as to the day in general—the Sun at 19 Leo was exactly trine Pluto, already conjoined a Black Hole at its upcoming station degree of 19 Sagittarius. We can expect some secrets to be revealed with this linkage, muck-raking (Pluto) which is perhaps self-exposed (Sun). Taken in tandem with Mercury still at its station degree of 8 Virgo and sandwiched between two Black Holes, we can expect the revelations to be bizarre and unexpected, and as Mercury is retrograde, these will likely involve reversals of opinion or status quo. The conjunction with Mercury to both Mars at 0 Virgo and Ganymede at 3 Virgo shows the disclosures to be of a sexual (Mars) nature, particularly emphasizing homosexual energies and a possible abuse of power via a socially imbalanced affair (both Ganymede). Ganymede is further exactly conjoined a Pulsar, guaranteeing a high public profile and "newsworthiness" to the announcements.

Venus, arbiter of romance and intimacy, is exactly conjunct the Black Hole at 4 Cancer, indicating a dramatic reversal or disclosure in matters of the heart. Venus is also closely conjoined by Antinous at 3 Cancer, reiterating the gay theme on the intimacy side of the human sexual polarity, as Ganymede with Mars reinforces the purely sexual aspects.

Uranus at 5 Pisces is exactly conjunct a Quasar, promoting pervasive manifestation and a high profile or public visibility, and opposed the Virgo stellium while closely trined Venus/Antinous. Uranus linked with Venus and/or Mars often signifies deviance or variation from the norm in intimate/sexual matters, the social outcast or iconoclast, maverick and eccentric. Asteroid Lust at 9 Pisces retrograde is conjunct Uranus and opposes Mercury closely, prompting the press conference (Mercury) about the unorthodox (Uranus) extramarital affair (Lust).

Jupiter and Saturn both tie to the Sun/Pluto axis; Jupiter at 20 Virgo being semisextile the Sun and square Pluto, Saturn at 21 Cancer being semisextile the Sun, sextile Jupiter, and inconjunct Pluto. Jupiter tends to inflate the situation, and also implies a prominent role for a judiciary in the day's events, which we see in the California Supreme Court's decision. Saturn involves a chief executive, resignation, and legal status, and again indicates lawyers or legal professionals, particularly ones placed in high authority.

Although largely unaspected to the rest of the day's celestial patterns, Neptune, Sappho and Pecker were all galactically active that day as well. Neptune at 13 Aquarius is exactly a Black Hole and indicative in its galactically-sensitive position of a huge disappointment or massive deception, a revelation of a parallel reality till then unsuspected. Sappho at 27 Taurus is exactly conjoined a controversy-provoking Maser, and Pecker at 10 Gemini is exactly opposed the Black Hole at 10 Sagittarius Pecker is also squared Mercury, Uranus and Lust.

So we are clearly dealing with variant human sexuality, controversy, deception and disappointment, legal standing and judicial rulings; when we look closer at the charts of the major players in the day's events, Jim McGreevey and the State of California, the picture becomes even clearer.

McGreevey (born 6 August 1957) sports a rather unfortunate mid-Virgo stellium of Lust at 20, Ganymede at 21, and Sappho at 23 Virgo. Attached to Venus at 13 Virgo on one end, and Jupiter at 29 Virgo on the other, it clearly shows a strong same-sex attraction, one which would be difficult to repress and ultimately impossible to conceal, given Jupiter's tendency to boast and brag, inflate situations, and overplay one's hand. His own Mercury at 9 Virgo, exactly conjunct a Black Hole, squared and shored up by natal Saturn at 7 Sagittarius, helped him immeasurably to construct and retain the facade he hid behind the first 47 years of his life, but ultimately betrayed him when transit Mercury returned to its natal place for its powerful retrograde station.

Transit Jupiter had recently crossed that Mercury, and was currently exactly conjunct McGreevey's natal Lust, while the Pluto retrograde period which ended later that month had highlighted each of these asteroids in turn, beginning with the station exactly square Sappho the previous March. This one-two punch of revelatory celestials was simply too much pressure to be ignored, particularly as corruption may be involved (his lover and accuser Cipel was admittedly completely unqualified for the position he held in the McGreevey administration, and was subsequently forced to resign), the exposure of which is dear to Pluto's heart and high on his agenda.

His Sun at 13 Leo, exactly conjunct a Maser, indicates one who has the potential to be controversial and disruptive in the extreme. It was currently exactly opposed by Black Hole-conjoined Neptune, indicating coming to terms with one's true self, revealing deception and coming forth honestly to speak one's truth. Neptune also is exactly inconjunct natal Venus, an apt image of the disillusion and disappointment his wife and family must be feeling at this time, as well as the deception surrounding the extramarital affair. Transit Neptune further conjoins McGreevey's natal Chiron at 14 Aquarius; hopefully in the long run, this wounding will bring healing for himself and those closest to him.

McGreevey's natal Mars at 28 Leo closely conjoins his Pluto at 29, and together they fill in the missing leg of a T-Square of galactic energies at 28 degrees of Fixed Signs, as well as being trine the Galactic Center, implying a universality or unusual prominence to the native's sexual expression. Pluto/Mars further indicates sexual variance, and the high probability of secretive amours. These are squared by McGreevey's Pecker at 29 Taurus, itself conjunct the Maser at 28 and the concurrent position of transit Sappho at 27 Taurus.

Transit Mars and Ganymede in early Virgo are closing in on natal Mercury, and Mars at 0 Virgo is exactly sextile his natal Neptune at 0 Scorpio, another reiteration of the sexual deception theme, including the self-deception and attempted abnegation of his true nature which McGreevey states he has struggled with since childhood. Transit Saturn at 21 Cancer is sextile the Virgo asteroid stellium and conjunct natal Antinous at 19 Cancer, which reinforces the Ganymede energies of romantic liaisons with social inferiors, and elevating them to positions of power or prominence without regard to their suitability for these positions.

When we look at California (admitted to the Union on 9 September 1850) we see a clear picture as well.

The transit Soli-Pluto trine becomes an exact Grand Trine with the inclusion of California's Saturn at 19 Aries, also representing its supreme judicial body. The transit Uranus/Lust opposition to Mercury/Mars/Ganymede ignites California's natal Neptune/Quasar at 5 Pisces (Uranus in exact conjunction), detailing the disappointment doubtless inherent in the decision for the 4,037 couples involved. California natally sports a strong Sappho/Ganymede conjunction at 27 Scorpio and 1 Sagittarius, straddling the manifestation-evoking Quasar at 28 Scorpio and making the state a natural Mecca for gays and lesbians, who will have a high profile there due to the Quasar conjunction, which is analogous to setting a beacon on a hill. On the day of the ruling, transit Sappho at 27 Taurus conjunct a controversy-sparking Maser was exactly opposed its natal position.

The state's natal Mars/Mercury conjunction at 10 and 12 Libra, within the event horizon of the Black Hole at 13 Libra, was forming a second Grand Trine with transit Neptune on the Black Hole at 13 Aquarius and transit Pecker at 10 Gemini. Pecker further forms a Galactic Grand Cross by its squares to California's natal Neptune and transit Lust at 5 and 9 Pisces, transit Mercury and California's natal Sun at 8 and 16 Virgo, and its opposition to the Black Hole at 10 Sagittarius.

Transit Pluto has been crisscrossing California's natal Chiron at 22 Sagittarius, and was particularly active last February at the time of the marriages, opening a national wound on this subject that has prompted the current administration to promote a constitutional amendment banning same sex unions.

So there we have it—two dramatic reversals and revelations, both with a gay twist, both emerging from the bizarre parallel realities evoked by Mercury's station on a tag team of Black Hole energies and heavily influenced by homosexuality-nuanced celestials. But it's just another day on the cosmos beat for the Deep Space Detective.

# HURRICANE KATRINA

*"It's totally wiped out....It's devastating. It's got to be doubly devastating on the ground."*
　　　–George W. Bush, viewing New Orleans from Air Force One, 31 August 2005

*"I don't think anybody anticipated the breach of the levees."*
　　　–George W. Bush, 1 September 2005

*"Brownie, you're doing a heck of a job."*
　　　–George W. Bush, to FEMA director Michael Brown, 2 September 2005

*"We've got a lot of rebuilding to do...The good news is—and it's hard for some to see it now—that out of this chaos is going to come a fantastic Gulf Coast, like it was before. Out of the rubbles of Trent Lott's house—he's lost his entire house—there's going to be a fantastic house. And I'm looking forward to sitting on the porch."*
　　　–George W. Bush, touring devastation in Mobile, AL, 2 September 2005

*"What didn't go right?"*
　　　–George W. Bush, to House Minority Leader Nancy Pelosi, requesting Brown's dismissal for incompetence, 7 September 2005

*"I also want to encourage anybody who was affected by Hurricane Corina to make sure their children are in school."*
　　　–First Lady Laura Bush, twice referring to Katrina as "Corina" while speaking to evacuees, South Haven, MS, 8 September 2005

*"What I'm hearing which is sort of scary is that they all want to stay in Texas. Everybody is so overwhelmed by the hospitality. And so many of the people in the arena here, you know, were underprivileged anyway so this (chuckle)—this is working very well for them."*
        –Former First Lady Barbara Bush, on the flood evacuees in
                              the Houston Astrodome, 5 September 2005

*"Now, tell me the truth, boys, is this kind of fun?"*
        –House Majority Leader Tom DeLay (R-TX), to three young
                    New Orleans evacuees at the Houston Astrodome, 9
                                                       September 2005

*"We finally cleaned up public housing in New Orleans. We couldn't do it, but God did."*
        –Representative Richard Baker (R-LA), to lobbyists, as
                quoted in the Wall Street Journal, 9 September 2005

Hurricane Katrina will go down as the most costly natural disaster in US history to date, with total loss of life rivaling 9/11, a rebuilding cost certainly in excess of $200 billion, and virtually an entire American city submerged. The complete failure of government at all levels which it revealed and the enormous expenditures it will require, class it as a Black Hole event par excellence, swallowing resources, evoking strange, parallel reality images, and exposing the true realities behind surface appearances. Upwards of a million people had their lives uprooted in virtually the twinkling of an eye, changed forever in ways that made them completely unrecognizable from what went before, with loss of home, job, community, all possessions and continuity; this is Black Hole energy with a vengeance.

The world was treated to the spectacle of its sole superpower, the most developed nation on earth, unable to feed, house and provide security, medical assistance or basic sanitary conditions for a large population of its citizens, even when granted several days' advance notice to do so. The soft underbelly of the Bush administration was not just exposed, but sliced open, dissected and read for augury: the signs were not favorable. Their unpreparedness, ineptitude, and unconcern were highlighted in bold relief to an electorate which was already quickly degenerating into two polarized camps, of realists and true believers.

The chart for Katrina's landfall in Louisiana, set for 6:10 AM CDT Monday, 29 August 2005, at New Orleans, is extremely revealing, both on the suprapersonal level of Deep Space points, and the intimate level of named asteroids which reflect the dynamics of the event.

First, the Sun at 6 Virgo is conjunct the Black Hole at 7 Virgo, a conjunction which became exact later that night as the foundered levees broke, deluging the city in as much as twenty feet of water. In true Black Hole reversal-of-reality style, the images of New Orleans under water and entire Gulf Coast communities leveled, bloated bodies floating in flooded streets or eaten by rats, masses of citizens trapped in their own squalor, dying of thirst or lack of medicine or medical attention, and citizens left behind who were looting and firing on rescue workers, contrasted sharply with the perception of New Orleans as the fun-loving Big Easy, of America as a land of wealth and order.

Opposed the Sun was transit Uranus, at 8 Pisces just fresh from his conjunction with the Quasar at 6 Pisces, lending the air of sudden devastation on a massive scale (Quasars highlight and bring into the forefront of consciousness whatever they contact). Traveling with Uranus and just approaching conjunction with the Quasar was asteroid Hazard at 3 Pisces, an apt celestial reference for the "toxic stew" which became the New Orleans streets, a heady mix of sewage, toxic waste, garbage, debris and rotting animal and human carcases.

There was much other galactic activity as well: the Maser at 27 Taurus was exactly conjunct the Midheaven, while the Black Hole at 28 Aquarius hugged the Descendant at 29. Maser energy is extremely erratic and debilitating, often violent and uncontrolled; the activation of an additional Black Hole reinforces the world-turned-upside-down quality of the Sun's conjunction with BH 7 Virgo. The Nadir was closely conjunct a manifestation-evoking Quasar at 28 Scorpio; security was the most pressing issue after relief and rescue in the aftermath of the tragedy, and the unpreparedness of all responsible agencies was brought under the harsh light of scrutiny for all to see. New Orleans has been changed and transformed to its very foundations.

Mars at 16 Taurus, denoting the loss of life and the violence which broke out in the days immediately following the storm, was exactly conjunct the Black Hole at 16 Taurus, indicating the numerically large loss of life. Neptune at 15 Aquarius is squared Mars and conjunct an information-evoking Pulsar, which often denotes a major news story; Neptune's connection with water and the sea is of course obvious, but he also rules the TV media and floods in general, as well as the oil whose smooth distribution was disrupted by the devastation.

Close by Mars/death's side was asteroid Flood; at 13 Taurus she formed an exact galactic T-Square with the volatile Maser at 13 Leo and the Black Hole at 13 Aquarius, indicating the violence and destruction of the storm, and the devastating consequences it evoked. New Orleans had a thriving gay community, and asteroid Antinous, named for the Roman Emperor Hadrian's male lover, deified after his drowning in the Nile, and whose cult at one time threatened to eclipse that of Jesus the Christ, stands conjunct with transit Mercury, ruling the dikes and pumping infrastructure, as well as the overwhelmed sewage and water systems, and the downed communications, at 19 Leo.

The Moon, representing the population as well as their needs for sustenance, sanitation and medical assistance, and herself a metaphor for the sea, was exactly conjunct the Quasar at 8 Cancer, evoking the surfeit of water and the devastation it wreaked, and both imperiling the populace and bringing a strong spotlight of public awareness of their plight.

Additional asteroids have quite a tale to tell as well. There are two which are name variants for Katrina—Katherina, which at 22 Sagittarius was closely conjunct holocaust-evoking, transformative Pluto at 21, and Ekaterina, which at 15 Leo was closely squared Mars and opposed sea god Neptune, conjunct Mercury/Antinous, and also conjunct the energetically-erratic Maser at 13 Leo. Oddly, asteroid Dike (named for a Greek goddess but a homonym for the English word for sea wall) at 25 Gemini was conjunct the Quasar at 26 Gemini and opposed both Pluto and the Galactic Center at 26 Sagittarius. Quasars evoke larger than life manifestation, circumstances which, for good or ill, are well-nigh impossible to ignore, and GC contacts often indicate a high level of general interest or universality to an event. New Orleans' importance as the nation's fourth largest port and a nexus for oil transportation and refinement meant aftershock ripples felt throughout the US economy, forcing gas prices well in excess of $3 per gallon, a situation impacting a huge number of Americans who otherwise had no direct ties to Louisiana.

Squaring the Sun was asteroid Atlantis, named for the fabled sunken civilization, at 6 Sagittarius; and opposed the Moon was asteroid Poseidon at 11 Capricorn, named for the Greek god of the sea and floods. Also with Atlantis was asteroid Ulysses at 8 Sagittarius, that most famous of ancient mariners, who spent ten years on storm-tossed seas trying to return home; his Greek original, asteroid Odysseus, was paired with Pluto at 18 Sagittarius, and in trine to Mercury/Antinous. Icarus, the rash and daring youth who flew too close to the Sun on waxen wings, only to plunge to his death into the sea, was also conjunct Pluto at 16 Sagittarius.

Even stranger are some of the more mundane connections. This incident arguably formed the nadir of the Bush presidency, and we find asteroid Busch conjunct the manifestation-evoking Quasar on the landfall's Nadir at 28 Scorpio. Quasars show us in our truest essence, and asteroid Busch at the Nadir showed "President" Bush not as the decisive leader and problem solver the GOP spin machine painted him, but in his true colors, as a vacillating, indecisive, ineffectual front man who was in way over his head in his then current occupation.

Adding to this revelation is asteroid George, which, also conjunct a Quasar at 4 Taurus, is, incredibly, exactly opposed asteroid Storm, conjunct another Quasar at 4 Scorpio. The Storm surely revealed George for what he was, to millions of Americans. Standing beside Storm is asteroid Fireman at 6 Scorpio, exactly sextile the Sun and conjunct the Black Hole at 7 Scorpio. There's a funny story about George and firemen which we'll be discussing later...

But first, one more named asteroid—Blanco—seems appropriate. Representative of Louisiana governor Kathleen Blanco, she lies at 6 degrees of leadership-oriented Aries, square the Moon/Quasar at 8 Cancer, in trine to chief executive Saturn at 5 Leo and inconjunct Katrina's Sun at 6 Virgo.

We should speak briefly about the chart of New Orleans herself, and Katrina's interaction with her.

Incorporated 17 February 1805, New Orleans sports an exact Sun/Neptune square, indicating the constant struggle between the city's very existence (Sun) and the hazards of water (Neptune) as well as the importance of oil in her economy. Falling at 28 Aquarius and Scorpio respectively, the city's natal Sun/Neptune square lies exactly on the Descendant and Nadir of Katrina's landfall. New Orleans' Pluto, the power both of destruction and regeneration, at 8 Pisces forms an exact match for the landfall's disruptive Uranus. Her stellium of Saturn, Moon and Uranus at 15 through 20 of Libra forms a close conjunction with both Katrina's stellium of Venus, South Node, and Jupiter at 14, 15 & 18 Libra, and George W. Bush's stellium of Chiron, Moon, and Jupiter at 15, 16 & 18 Libra, as well as the USA Saturn, representing the presidency itself, at 14 Libra. (Incredibly, this means Dubya was having a Jupiter Return when Katrina struck! Not the kind of "luck" I'd brag about, but, karmically, probably quite apt.)

The nation's Moon at 26 Aquarius conjoins New Orleans' Sun and Katrina's Descendant; the nation felt this loss emotionally, and struggled to understand the dramatic change in its relationship with the Crescent City. A national outpouring of relief assistance and charity highlighted the intimate involvement of the American people with this tragedy. Further, Dubya's Mars at 9 Virgo, exactly conjunct another Black Hole, is also conjunct Katrina's Sun at 6 Virgo; his actions, or lack of them, were pivotal in determining the federal response and the severity or ease of relief efforts in the aftermath.

All in all, the Bushies didn't do so well in this crisis, a circumstance which contributed further to Dubya's poll slide, with approval ratings plunging in the aftermath of the storm to the mid to upper thirty percent in most polls. Two images recorded at the time of Katrina's impact on New Orleans may well depict the Bush attitude to the suffering she wreaked. In a bizarre combination of Roman Emperor Nero and French Queen Marie Antoinette, two of the most notoriously isolated and self-centered individuals of all time, Dubya spent parts of the 29th and 30th of August making music and eating cake.

On August 29, the day Katrina slammed into the Louisiana coast and overwhelmed New Orleans' defenses, Bush appeared at a 69th birthday celebration for Arizona Senator John McCain, where they let him eat—cake. Marie Antoinette would have been proud.

On the 30th, the morning after the levees had broken and deluged the city, trapping thousands of Americans, Bush flew out of his Texas ranch; not to see to New Orleans' rescue, but to give a speech at Coronado Naval Base in California, commemorating the 60th anniversary of VJ Day. Afterward, he spent some time strumming a guitar given him by country singer Mark Wills; Nero fiddled while Rome burned, Dubya picked and grinned while New Orleans drowned.

Caught at the tail end of his five week vacation in Crawford, Texas, Dubya sat on his hands and did nothing in advance of the storm, waiting until two days afterward for a fly-over of the Gulf on Air Force One, from 2500 feet up. Black Hole Mars natives can be that way—quick to anger, long on resentment, they may find action, particularly in crisis situations, to be beyond them; it is as if the Black Hole has absorbed their capacity to react without prompting, carefully guarding the vast reserves of energy it has hoarded. Aides finally had to create a DVD of Katrina's "greatest hits" and force the commander in chief to sit down in front of the TV and watch it on the Friday after, four days later, before the notoriously isolated and incurious George could wrap his mind around the scope of the disaster.

Vice President Dick Cheney was AWOL as well, and didn't resurface in Washington or so much as make a statement until the Saturday after; he had been shopping for a $2.9 million mansion, a weekend retreat on the Chesapeake Bay, and couldn't be bothered. Defense Secretary Donald Rumsfeld, some of whose troops would be committed to the rescue and relief efforts, continued his vacation in California with a San Diego Padres ball game the night the levees broke. Secretary of State Condoleeza Rice, whose department would be instrumental in coordinating offers of aid from foreign governments, remained in New York, taking in a show of the Monty Python musical "Spamalot," and buying pairs of thousand-dollar shoes at Ferragamo's, where she was verbally accosted by a fellow shopper, appalled at Ms. Rice's indifference to the circumstances unfolding in the Gulf. Condi had security physically remove the woman from her presence.

Of course, the administration's complicity in the tragedy extends well beyond their inaction in the early days of the crisis. The tragedy in the Gulf of Mexico had much to do with the tragedy in that other gulf, the Persian Gulf—resources which might have made all the difference had been redirected to Bush's Oil War in Iraq. Money which had been allocated for a repair and reinforcement of the levee walls that protect New Orleans was cut from the budget, diverted specifically for the war effort, and changes in wetlands protection policies under Bush left the city more exposed to the effects of storm surge than it would otherwise have been. Additionally, a third of Louisiana's National Guard, and half their equipment, were serving overseas at the time Katrina struck, and thus unavailable for the missions for which they were primarily trained, helping out in just such crises. Finally, Bush's patented brand of compassionate capitalist cronyism had placed as FEMA director one Michael Brown, a man with absolutely no experience in disaster relief, formerly a lawyer for the International Arabian Horse Association, whose primary qualifications were that he was a Bush insider and the college roommate of the former FEMA director, Joe Allbaugh.

The humanitarian disaster apparently did not faze the administration, but once the enormity of the PR disaster became apparent, however, the White House spin machine went into overdrive. GOP supporters touted the failures in this crisis of the New Orleans mayor and the Louisiana governor, both conveniently Democratic, and did not forget to focus our attention on the culpability of bedridden nursing home residents who failed to evacuate themselves before the waters rose above their noses.

Dubya's initial unconcern was soon replaced by an almost hectoring ubiquity on the Gulf Coast, with five walking disaster tours and a live address to the nation from New Orleans in little more than a week. But the "live" and spontaneous quality of these visits left something to be desired.

Enter the firemen. On the Gulf Coast, local first responders were getting burnt out after days of rescue and relief efforts, but thousands of New Orleans residents remained stranded and isolated. On the weekend after the disaster, Mayor Ray Nagin of New

Orleans pleaded for replacements on national television, so his own people could get some much-needed rest. Over a thousand firefighters from across the nation were assembled by FEMA in Atlanta, and given ... eight hours of community relations training, including a class on sexual harassment. The FEMA plan? Using these highly trained rescue workers as PR officers, distributing FEMA flyers to evacuees and victims. But a small portion of them, 50 in fact, had a higher calling. Told to grab their gear and go, these brave souls were yanked from the conference and flown at top speed to Louisiana, where they were instructed to stand beside Dubya at his photo op.

Helicopters were flown in and placed strategically in the background. Evacuated children were cleaned up—not TOO much, a certain sense of pathos was desired—and placed within head-tousling distance; emergency aid stations were set up, food and water piled high for imminent distribution (these would be quietly dismantled once Dubya moved on, the region left to its debris and its corpses).

Enter the President of the United States, surrounded by axe-toting rescue workers; cue refugee children; pump the blades of those whirly-birds; big smiles, now, as we feed the victims.

Click-click those cameras, brave media. Your Emperor, Master of the Free World, has arrived.

# THE DEATH OF
# ANNA NICOLE SMITH

The Media firestorm unleashed by the death of a second-rate
celebrity on 8 February 2007 was perhaps predictable, but somewhat surprising nonetheless. Anna Nicole Smith had always been
a lightning rod for controversy and publicity—how many *Playboy*
centerfold models have cases which appear before the US Supreme
Court?

Born Vicki Lynn Hogan in Houston, Texas on 28 November 1967,
Smith's life can perhaps best be described by the title of an unpub-
lished biography written by her sister: *"Train Wreck."* Her father
abandoned the family just after her birth, and her parents were
divorced when she was less than two. It was her mother's second
marriage, and she went on to marry four more times; Smith's father
remarried twice.

Smith dropped out of High School in her sophomore year, working as a waitress at a local restaurant where she met her first husband, cook Billy Wayne Smith. They married in 1985; she was 17, he
was 16; their son Daniel was born in 1986 and the couple separated
a year later, though their divorce did not become final until 1993.
Jobs at Wal-Mart and Red Lobster failed to support Smith and her
child, and in 1991 she turned to exotic dancing and began vocal
training. That autumn she answered a Houston newspaper ad for
*Playboy* models and met oil billionaire J. Howard Marshall II; her
life took a dramatic turn.

Chosen personally by Hugh Hefner as the cover girl for the
March 1992 issue of *Playboy*, under the name of Vicki Smith, she
became an instant sensation, noted for her voluptuous (though sur-
gically enhanced) figure and stunning resemblance to 60's icons
Marilyn Monroe and Jayne Mansfield. By 1993, when she was chosen as *Playboy*'s Playmate of the Year, Vicki had metamorphosed into
Anna Nicole, and later that year Guess Jeans hired her to replace

supermodel Claudia Schiffer in their ad campaigns.

After meeting in the strip club where she worked, Smith and J. Howard Marshall, whose net worth exceeded one and a half billion dollars, began a relationship which culminated in their marriage in June 1994; Smith was 26, Marshall was 89. Despite the great disparity in their age and income, and the fact that they never lived together, Smith always averred that she married for love. Thirteen months later the groom was dead, and Smith was embroiled in an inheritance battle with her stepson, himself 28 years her senior, which continued to the day of her death. Though both original litigants are now dead, Smith's claim is being prosecuted on behalf of her infant daughter Dannielynn, and Marshall's son J. Pierce Marshall's claim is upheld by his widow.

The see-saw legal wrangling saw rulings both in favor and against Smith's claim, which was based, not on Marshall's will, but on an oral contract Smith claimed her late husband had made with her. At times she joined forces with another of Marshall's disinherited sons to wrest part of the inheritance from Pierce. A Texas probate jury denied Smith's claims, but a 1996 bankruptcy filing in California following an employee's successful sexual harassment suit brought that state's judiciary into the fray. In September 2000 a California bankruptcy judge awarded her almost half a billion dollars from Marshall's estate, but the Texas probate judge supported the earlier jury finding and struck it down in July 2001; the conflicting rulings forced the case into federal court. In March 2002 a federal judge vacated the California bankruptcy court's decision, reducing Smith's award to $88 million. This ruling was itself reversed on appeal at the 9th US Circuit Court in December 2004, a three member panel stating that the federal courts had no right to overturn the Texas probate court's original decision.

At this point the Bush administration intervened. Anxious to extend federal jurisdiction over state probate courts, Bush directed the US Solicitor General to bring the matter before the US Supreme Court, which on May 1, 2006 ruled unanimously that Smith did have the right to challenge the state probate ruling in federal court. This did not award a share of the inheritance to Smith directly, merely allowing her to pursue her claim on the federal level, which she has done. Her stepson and opponent J. Pierce Marshall died June 20,

2006, but the family has continued to pursue the legal battle.

After her initial successes with *Playboy* and the Guess Jeans modeling contract, Smith's career consisted mainly of publicity from her legal troubles and eccentric persona. She was featured in a few poorly reviewed films, but was predominantly fodder for late night comics and tabloid magazines, ultimately securing nothing but cameo roles as herself. In the late 'nineties her weight became an issue, and the once-sveldt celebrity, who had never quite overcome her white trash roots, became an object of derision.

Oddly, Smith chose to showcase this low point in her fortunes with a reality show on E! cable network, *The Anna Nicole Show*, which chronicled her troubles with money, substance abuse, dating and weight control. Toward the end of her show's two-season run, she was picked up as spokesperson by weight loss company TrimSpa, which reportedly helped her lose 80 pounds. Back at her *Playboy* fighting weight, Smith began to do awards show appearances and celebrity guest spots, but was unable to gain traction in her career.

2006 was a banner year for Smith. In May came the Supreme Court decision which breathed new life into her legal struggles, in June her longtime rival Pierce Marshall predeceased her, and September saw the birth of her daughter and the death of her twenty-year-old son, within days of each other. Smith had retreated to the Bahamas to avoid a court-ordered DNA test to determine her daughter's paternity, and her son's death, from a fatal combination of prescription drugs, occurred in her hospital room just three days after her daughter's birth. Smith was devastated, reportedly jumping into Daniel's grave at his funeral.

Although Smith declared that her longtime attorney, Howard K. Stern, with whom she underwent an informal (and not legally binding) commitment ceremony in September 2006, was Dannielynn's father, and he was so listed on the Bahamian birth certificate, this was disputed by her former boyfriend, entertainment photojournalist Larry Birkhead. Birkhead went so far as to file a paternity suit, and after Smith's death requested an emergency DNA sample from her corpse, which was denied. Also in the aftermath of her death, several other men came forward to advance a claim to fathering the infant who might now be worth half a billion dollars, including Zsa Zsa Gabor's husband, Frederic Prince von Anhalt, who alleged a ten-year affair with Smith; Alexander Denk, her former bodyguard; Mark Hatten, who lived with Smith for two years; and Ben Thompson, the realtor who sold her the Bahamian mansion to which she had retreated (and whose claim was discarded when it was discovered he had undergone a vasectomy). Not to be outdone, Smith's sister stated that Anna Nicole had told her the child was conceived with frozen sperm from her late husband, Marshall.

For several days prior to her death on 8 February, 2007, Smith had been experiencing flu-like symptoms, and reportedly had a temperature of 105 the night before she died. Paramedics were called to her room at the Seminole Hard Rock Hotel and Casino in Hollywood, Florida, to find her unresponsive; CPR and intubation were attempted, to no avail. Smith was pronounced dead on arrival at Memorial Regional Hospital. Ironically, Smith, who often likened herself to Marilyn Monroe, died in Hollywood (Florida) and was initially reported to have also died of a drug overdose, though no illegal drugs were found in her hotel room. Although the cause of death was not immediately determined, some form of pneumonia was suspected.*

Almost immediately, more legal wrangling ensued. In addition to the ongoing paternity challenge and battle over the Marshall inheritance, the validity of her commitment ceremony with Stern, the ownership of her Bahamian mansion, the legality of her will, the custody of her child, and the disposition of her remains have all been disputed.

Her burial finally occurred March 2 in Nassau, Bahamas, with the coffin, draped in pink sequin-studded velvet with tassels and feathers and borne in a white stretch limo, laid to rest beside her son's grave at the Lakeview Memorial Gardens. The private ceremony at the Mount Horeb Baptist Church was attended by 300 invited mourners and hundreds more lined the procession's route. The church was filled with roses in Smith's favorite color of pink; a special gown was commissioned by Stern for her funeral, pink with rhinestones and lace, with a heart embroidered on the bodice. Smith's mother filed a petition for the return of both her daughter's and grandson's remains to Texas, and for custody of her infant granddaughter.

Anna Nicole Smith is a virtual case study in Black Hole energies, with all the dramatic ups and downs, sudden changes of fortune, and larger-than-life qualities typical of strong galactic contacts. Born 28 November 1967, Smith's Sun is enmeshed within the Black Hole at 5 Sagittarius, and one need barely scratch the surface of her life to see its effects.

Smith essentially created herself from nothing, a common Black Hole Sun circumstance. The name change is also typical of such individuals, who have the chameleon-like ability to adapt and present themselves in whatever manner best supports their goals. Smith's breast augmentations, though hardly a rarity, speak to this desire to be something she was not by birth, as does the obsessive modeling of her persona on that of her idol, Marilyn Monroe, significantly another celebrity made up of whole cloth, right down to her name (Monroe was also a Black Hole Sun).

Smith used the attractive qualities of her Black Hole Sun to great effect, becoming the erotic fantasy material for literally millions of men with her *Playboy* layouts. Although she never created a great, or even memorable, film or television role, she maintained a high celebrity profile for well over a decade, based on a nonexistent body of work. Her face and figure were her stock in trade, and she traded well, snaring one of the richest men of her native Texas.

Similarly, her spokesperson talents, portrayed for Guess Jeans and TrimSpa, showcased her ability to attract and ensnare others with her film presence and persona. Even at the level of remove created by celluloid and print, she had the power to manipulate and persuade, both typical Black Hole Sun attributes. Smith eventually became a cult figure through her reality series, which showed an appalling side of the celebrity, seemingly permanently drugged out and incapable of managing her life. Again, the Black Hole's power to compel attention, and its obsessive need for it, ruled her existence but gave her the inner fortitude to keep on fighting for her goal, even when true success must have seemed hopeless.

Of course her legal battles are textbook examples of Black Hole energies, illustrating their advanced level of instability and unpredictability, which bounced her from success to failure and back again in her fight for the Marshall inheritance. This type of roller coaster, see-saw activity, this sense of now-you-have-it, now-you-don't, is a common manifestation for the Black Hole native, often to the point where this hectic, fast-paced turnover becomes the norm.

Her legal troubles are further described by the incidence of her 4 Virgo Jupiter, governing court rulings, also conjoined a Black Hole and in tight square to her Sun. Additionally, natal Saturn, ruling lawyers and the legal process itself, at 5 Aries retrograde is in a tight Grand Cross with Black Holes at 4 Cancer and Capricorn and the Quasar at 5 Libra. The Black Hole elements of this configuration speak of frequent reversal and an uncertain outcome, but the exact opposition to the Quasar indicates ultimate success, which unfortunately had not been realized at the time of her death, but the struggle for which will continue in her absence.

All three of Smith's "money planets" make dramatic Deep space contacts—Venus at 20 Libra is square to the Black Hole at 19 Capricorn, Jupiter conjoins a Black Hole at 6 Virgo, and Pluto at 22 Virgo is squared the Galactic Center and the Quasar at 26 Gemini. The effects on her financial status of Venus and Jupiter are variable with Black Hole uncertainty, but hold the potential for both windfall profit (as in the half billion inheritance from a 13-month marriage) and major loss (as in her bankruptcy filing). It is Pluto's position which sets the seal on the deal, allying the Quasar's achievement-oriented energies with the high visibility and global reach of the Galactic Center contact; finally, when all is said and done, Smith's estate should get those millions she fought more than a decade for, and we will surely hear of it. As of March 2009, lawyers for her estate have once again taken the case to the US Supreme Court, in hopes of lifting an appellate court stay on the payment of an earlier judgment in her favor.

Black Hole Jupiter allied with the Black Hole Sun is also the source of the dramatic weight fluctuations which dogged her, and her ability, when focused, to recover lost ground and resurrect an image that many who saw her in the late 'nineties thought was gone for good. Black Hole Sun natives frequently undergo extreme weight loss or gain throughout the life, and Jupiter's appetites added fuel to the fire, also conferring that larger-than-life presence which others found so compelling.

Her notorious drug use and the glamorous visual persona she so assiduously cultivated can be seen in a tense T-Square from natal Neptune at 24 Scorpio in exact opposition to the Black Hole at 24

Taurus and squared the Quasar at 25 Aquarius. The Black Hole tempted substance abuse, which drained much of her energies, and the Quasar gave her image star power, however little substance was evident to back it up. Neptune also conjoins Mercury at 19 Scorpio, and Smith was noted for her breathy, zoned-out communication style, part Marilyn Monroe throwback, part chemically-induced.

Black Hole Venus often manifests as love or marriage with persons seen by others as somehow unsuited to the native, and sometimes in ways considered shocking or wholly inappropriate. Such was certainly the case with Smith's marriage to Marshall, 63 years her senior. The "Love Goddess" image she built for herself, modeled on Marilyn Monroe and Jayne Mansfield, is another manifestation of this Venus and its power to attract; aspected by a Black Hole in Capricorn, the focus of Smith's femininity was her business life—in essence, love *was* her business.

Mars at 27 Capricorn conjoins a Pulsar and forms a Grand Cross with three Black Holes at 27 Aries and 28 Cancer and Libra. This certainly expresses Smith's sexual energy perfectly—no less than three Black Holes could account for the extraordinary impact Smith's sexual charisma had on virtually all who saw or met her in her heyday. At times almost achingly beautiful, at others a downright drab, Smith's sexual appetite seemed apparent, and much of her celebrity was built upon sex. One could argue that sex *was* her career, again with the Capricorn influence of the Mars placement. It also describes the bizarre pairing with Marshall, not to mention the plethora of reputed fathers of Dannielynn who have made themselves known since her death. Mars with a Pulsar guarantees that whatever her peccadilloes, we'll be hearing about them. Pulsars are informational in nature, and often indicate heightened Media involvement or interest. With her Mars on a Pulsar, Smith's affairs were always considered newsworthy, and she had a natural ability to dominate the Media with her sexuality.

That this Venus and Mars are in square aspect indicates that for Smith, love and sex were very different things, and often didn't mesh. This conforms with some of her intimates' opinion that no matter how many lovers she took, the only person she ever truly loved was her son Daniel.

Death is also co-ruled by Mars, and it is thus no surprise that

Smith's death should be at once so public and so mysterious, attracting so much attention and interest. The Black Holes in aspect each feed off the event, compelling others to invest their energies and become a part, however voyeuristically, of the demise of a national sex symbol.

A quick glance at Smith's chart in comparison with that of the US shows why the public has fed so heartily at this funeral banquet (besides the fact of the Media force-feeding them), and reveals a startling connection. Smith has two natal planets in exact conjunction with US chart points—her Pluto at 22 Virgo on the USA Neptune, and her Mars at 27 Capricorn on the USA Pluto and a Pulsar. In astrologic shorthand this spells out a national fascination (USA Neptune) with her death (Smith's Pluto) and the lifelong Media (Pulsar) obsession (USA Pluto) with her sexual persona (Smith's Mars).

On the day of her death, the Sun joined Neptune in the sky at 19 Aquarius, in exact square to her Scorpio Mercury and applying to oppose transit Saturn at 21 Leo retrograde. Here Saturn plays the part of Death, messenger Mercury bringing news of her passing via the Neptune-ruled medium of television. Sun/Neptune also indicates the fatal drug combination which took her life.* Transit Pluto on the Pulsar at 28 Sagittarius is yet another indicator of a major Media story concerning death, and exactly squares her natal Uranus at 28 Virgo, representing the suddenness and unexpected quality of the demise. That Uranus trines her Mars and is opposed the Black Hole at 28 Pisces which would host a solar eclipse in six weeks' time (just before the coroner's ruling on the official cause of death).

Anna Nicole Smith, who once graced the cover of a New York magazine issue titled "White Trash Nation" (pictured in a short skirt and cowboy boots, eating chips), was a bizarre American mix of glamor and gutter, a veritable microcosm of her times, long on image and short on substance. Salon magazine's Cintra Wilson may have best captured Anna Nicole's Black Hole qualities and the implosion that was her life in her posthumous comparison of Smith with her idol, Marilyn Monroe: "When she was able to suppress her demons enough to pull herself together and look her best, she was fabulously gorgeous. ... [but] she was not so much a candle in the

wind as a bonfire in a hailstorm. The real similarity between Anna
Nicole and Marilyn was their shimmering tension—an unsettlingly
powerful physical beauty, collapsing in real time. She was entropy
porn at its finest."

* On Monday, 26 March 2007, more than six weeks after her
death, Broward County Florida Medical Examiner Joshua Perper
announced that the cause of Smith's death was an accidental
overdose of prescription medications, citing the sleep aid chloral
hydrate as the major contributing factor, but including several anti-
depressant and anti-anxiety drugs as well as methadone for pain
relief. The transit Sun at 5 Aries was exactly conjoined her Saturn,
opposed a Quasar and trine her 5 Sagittarius Sun, finally shedding
light on her demise; Mercury at 7 Pisces opposed natal Jupiter and
a Black Hole and squared her Sun; Mars conjunct Neptune at 21
Aquarius (a drug-related death) and Saturn at 18 Leo both squared
the natal Mercury/Neptune conjunction.

# CLIENT #9 (ELIOT SPITZER)

On March 10, 2008 the political world was stunned to learn that Eliot Spitzer, Governor of New York and a past exemplar of law enforcement as the state's Attorney General, a man with a reputation for toughness, tenacity and probity in prosecution, was named in a federal investigation into the activities of an international prostitution ring. Spitzer's resignation shortly followed on the 12th. Unlike many *laissez-faire* Democrats, Spitzer was a staunch proponent of law and order, tough on crime and corruption, with a sterling record as a hard-nosed, no-nonsense prosecutor, known as "Mr. Clean." *Time* magazine termed him "Crusader of the Year" in 2002; his fall has been dramatic and complete.

Born in The Bronx to parents of Austria Jewish extraction, educated at Princeton and Harvard Law, Spitzer made waves early on with his vigorous pursuit of organized crime figures in New York, primarily the Gambino family. A long list of successful prosecutions for the District Attorney's office led to his political rise with the 1998 election, where he gained the post of Attorney General for the state of New York. In that capacity he continued his crusade for justice, taking on the securities industry, insurance companies, police corruption, the entertainment industry and computer manufacturers. He became a powerful presence in Lower Manhattan, locally known as "the sheriff of Wall Street" for his indictments in the banking community.

In late 2004 Spitzer announced his intention to run for the New York Governor's office, almost two full years before the November 2006 election. He spent most of 2005 raising his public profile by campaigning for mayoral candidates across the length and breadth of New York, making regional contacts and garnering favorable publicity. That summer three term Governor George Pataki declared he would not run again, greatly increasing Spitzer's chances of success, with an open seat and a Republican Party in disarray.

His landslide victory in November 2006 was the largest in New York gubernatorial history; Spitzer won 69% of the vote, carrying all but three counties. His January 1, 2007 inauguration was the first in more than a century to be held outdoors.

The term has not been a successful one; budget disputes and a $4 billion shortfall marred the first year, and political infighting between Spitzer and Republican minority leaders in the State Assembly increased gridlock. A proposal to legalize gay marriage was introduced by Spitzer in April 2007, passed the Assembly, but failed in the State Senate. The governor was also accused of improper use of state police in tracking the movements of political opponents. In September his executive order authorizing state offices to issue driving licenses to illegal immigrant residents of New York sparked a controversy that found its way into the Democratic Presidential campaign. Public outcry and opposition in the legislature caused Spitzer to withdraw the order's implementation that November. Just a year after his 69% victory, Spitzer's approval rating had dropped to 33%.

On Monday, March 10, 2008, *The New York Times* reported that Spitzer was part of an ongoing federal probe into a high-end prostitution ring, Emperors Club VIP; in the indictment he was identified as "Client 9." Spitzer had spent the evening of February 13 with a 22-year old call girl at the Mayflower Hotel in Washington DC, registering under his own name and address. The young woman, based in New Jersey, had crossed state lines to keep the assignation, thus making it a federal crime. Spitzer reportedly paid $4300 for the two hour session, part in compensation for those services, and part as a credit toward future calls.

This was not the first instance of Spitzer's involvement with the Emperors Club, having paid the service more than $15,000 for eight appointments in the previous year, and cumulatively perhaps as much as $80,000. His activities had first come to light when his bank reported suspicious wire transfers, in accordance with the Bank Secrecy Act, which requires that the IRS be informed of transfers in excess of $10,000. To evade this provision, Spitzer broke the fee into smaller amounts, but his request to have his name kept off the wire transfers alerted the bank to the unusual nature of the transactions. At first, bribery was suspected, but when the FBI became involved in the case, Spitzer's link to the international prostitution ring was uncovered.

Spitzer held a very brief press conference late the day the *Times* story broke, with wife Silda at his side, stating simply, "Today I want to briefly address a private matter. I have acted in a way that violates my obligations to my family and violates my, or any, sense of right and wrong. I apologize first and most importantly to my family. I apologize to the public, whom I promised better. I do not believe that politics in the long run is about individuals. It is about ideas, the public good, and doing what is best for the state of New York. But I have disappointed and failed to live up to the standard I expected of myself. I must now dedicate some time to regain the trust of my family." Speculation ensued that Spitzer was delaying resignation as leverage in crafting a deal with prosecutors. The Republican minority in the State Assembly threatened impeachment proceedings if prompt action was not taken. On Wednesday the 12th, Spitzer formally resigned his office, effective Monday the 17th.

As has been the case with former public sex scandals, galactics and asteroids fill in the gaps in our astrologic knowledge. Born 10 June 1959, Spitzer's Sun at 19 Gemini closely opposes the Black Hole at 18 Sagittarius and is exactly conjunct asteroid Eos. Black Hole Suns can be extremely secretive, living double lives and publicly espousing virtues and beliefs which in private they reject. Such is clearly the case with Spitzer, known for his zealous pursuit and prosecution of criminal activity while New York Attorney General, and commonly referred to as "the sherif of Wall Street." Black Hole Sun is also subject to the type of dramatic reversal of fortune which Spitzer's fall betrays, and in many cases, this is due to the sort of Greek tragedy-type character flaw which led to his downfall.

Eos was the ancient Greek goddess of the dawn, an apparently inapt combination, until we look more closely at her myth. Drawn into an affair with Ares, Aphrodite's primary paramour, when the goddess of love discovered this infidelity, she cursed Eos with a constant craving for erotic passion, thus effectively rendering her a nymphomaniac. Spitzer has reportedly spent upwards of $80,000 on escort services, thus qualifying him for the male version of Eos' affliction. To add insult to injury, asteroid Aphrodite lies at 19 Virgo, in exact square to Spitzer's Sun and her old rival Eos, and transforming the Black Hole opposition into a T-Square.

Mars and Venus at 4 and 5 Leo both conjoin a Black Hole at 2 Leo and square another at 6 Scorpio, but they also square a polarity of Quasars at 4 Taurus and Scorpio. Black Hole Venus inclines individuals to form liaisons with persons whom others deem inappropriate, and Black Hole Mars can exert a sexual obsessiveness that is impossible to ignore, difficult to sate. Compulsive and secretive, Black Hole Mars also tends to unconventional sexual practices, and craves multiplicity, and the native can expend vast amounts of energy and resources in sexual pursuit. The Venus/Mars combination also suggests a pairing of sex and money, central to this case (the duo is also inconjunct natal Saturn at 4 Capricorn, again linking romance or sex with business).

The Quasars promote visibility and exposure, shining a spotlight on whatever they touch; it is not possible to conceal for long what they illuminate. It is also interesting to note that Spitzer's activities were "brought to light" due to suspect banking practices, another nod to Venus' financial implications. The 4 Taurus Quasar is further conjoined by asteroid Arachne at 2 Taurus, named for that weaver whom Athena transformed into a spider, thus she is in square to Venus/Mars, and oh, what a tangled web we weave! The 4 Scorpio Quasar is also the seat of natal Neptune, lending its patented brand of confusion and an inability to see the situation clearly, also inclining the native to romantic and sexual fantasy. Indeed, one wonders what Spitzer could possibly have been thinking, or how he expected to evade detection, particularly as in making his arrangements he utilized the very methods of email and text messaging which he is on record as counseling others against. This is strongly Neptunian, an inability to see in oneself what one sees so clearly in others, and a lack of awareness as to the probable consequences of one's actions.

The Venus/Mars conjunction is also broadly conjoined natal Uranus at 13 Leo, itself exactly atop a controversy-provoking Maser. Uranus with these personal planets inclines the native to form unorthodox or unusual unions, and adds a decided element of kink to intimacy, evoking actions which others would consider bizarre or eccentric. There is again a restlessness in sexual matters, an unwillingness to be fettered or restrained, and a tendency toward impulsive action or recklessness. The Maser's presence here acts to magnify the salacious quality of the episode, evoking shock, controversy and disruption.

Uranus itself is exactly opposed by asteroid Damocles, conjunct the Black Hole at 13 Aquarius. Indeed, Spitzer's unconventional sexual activities have been a sword suspended over his head, the precise nature of the thread being cut further defined by Damocles' close pairing with asteroid Lust at 18 Aquarius, which is tightly trine Spitzer's Sun. Lust rebounds in an exact opposition to Vesta at 18 Leo, adding an element of ritualistic need, and the likelihood of a precise patterning of practices. It also defines Spitzer's passion for prostitutes, which is in fact what the original Vestal Virgins were, not chaste maidens but rather sacred whores.

Jupiter at 24 Scorpio retrograde is part of a Galactic Grand Cross, conjunct asteroid Sisyphus at 23 Scorpio retrograde, exactly opposed a Black Hole at 24 Taurus and squared to both the Quasar at 25 Aquarius and asteroid Eros at 23 Leo. Here we have that fatal combination of erotic passion (Eros) with politics (Jupiter), with the Black Hole motivating complete surrender and immersion in one's desires, while the Quasar provides the ultimate revelation of these to the public. Sisyphus, named for that Hadean worthy doomed to forever roll the same rock up a slope, only to have it roll back down again, lends a quality of compulsion and signals the repetitive nature of Spitzer's infractions. Jupiter also acts to inflate and expand Eros' passions, and its square to Lust should not be discounted. Seemingly this was a behavior over which Spitzer had no control, which eventually attained a life of its own, bringing about his ruin.

Additional galactic contacts include an exact square from natal Mercury at 28 Gemini to the Black Hole at 28 Pisces, indicating deceptive communication and flawed reasoning; and natal Saturn exactly conjunct the Black Hole at 4 Capricorn. This expresses both the accruing of extensive executive power as governor of New York, and the dramatic and sudden reversal which drove him out of office, destroying his career.

Pluto at 1 Virgo conjoins asteroid Karma at 3 Virgo, an apt image of the devastation wrought by our actions. To inveigh against lawlessness in the manner of "Eliot Ness" Spitzer, and then to proceed lawlessly, is to court a karmic comeuppance of major proportions, and a fall of plutonic thoroughness.

Minor Planet Eris at 10 Aries is exactly conjunct a Quasar, conjoined by asteroids Fanny and Pandora at 11 and 12 Aries, and opposed asteroids Juno and Pecker, both at 10 Libra. Eris is the troublemaker, tetchy and quarrelsome, evoking conflict, which was doubtless something felt very strongly by Spitzer's spouse, as represented by the opposition to Juno. The combination of Fanny and Pecker may well be an apt one, indicating what particular services Juno was unwilling to provide, and the myth of Pandora's box is evocative of the hail of troubles which have redounded upon Spitzer's head when the Quasar turned its spotlight onto these points.

The transits for the day the *Times* story broke are incredibly telling. Uranus and the Sun joined at 18 and 20 Pisces, in a tight, tag-teaming square to Spitzer's 19 Gemini Sun, disclosing the shocking revelations. Mars at 2 Cancer opposed Pluto at 1 Capricorn, itself conjoined Spitzer's 4 Capricorn Saturn, indicating the total devastation (Pluto) wrought to his career (Saturn) by sex (Mars). Mercury at 24 Aquarius, with Neptune standing by at 22 Aquarius and Venus at 26, was highlighted by a Quasar at 25, all bringing up the natal square from passionate Eros at 23 Leo to libertine Jupiter at 24 Scorpio. Saturn at 3 Virgo was exactly conjoined asteroid Karma and within orb of natal Pluto at 1 Virgo.

The asteroid placements are even more apt, with the entire cast of natal characters making important contacts in the sky that day. Transit Aphrodite at 13 Aquarius was exactly conjunct natal Damocles, while Chiron, the wounded healer, exactly conjoined natal Lust at 18 Aquarius, emphasis added by transit Icarus, the rash risk-taker, at 19 Aquarius. Arachne at 10 Libra was exactly on natal Pecker and Juno, while Karma at 9 Gemini was in a tight trine. Eros at 13 Aries exactly opposed a Black Hole and had just crossed natal Eris, Fanny and Pandora. Transit Fanny at 1 Leo was conjunct natal Venus and Mars, and transit Sisyphus at 4 Scorpio highlighted the natal Neptune/Quasar there, bringing out the T-Square to Arachne and Venus/Mars. Both Lust at 5 Sagittarius and Pecker at 16 Taurus were exactly conjoined Black Holes, Lust in trine to natal Venus/Mars, and Pecker forming a T-Square with natal Damocles, Lust and Uranus.

A truly stunning Black Hole reversal of almost biblical proportions, ending the public career of a man once tapped as potentially the first Jewish president of America, the Sheriff of Wall Street, Mr. Clean, Client #9.

# THE WALL STREET BAILOUT BILL

When Pluto made its final turn in Sagittarius on September 8, 2008, preparatory to its official passage into Capricorn, where it is scheduled to transform and purge governmental, corporate and banking structures, few imagined how quickly its effects would be felt in financial markets. But if you're an American with an IRA or a 401k account, it shortly became crystal clear just how ephemeral our digitized wealth can be.

Pluto's station degree of 28 Sagittarius fell exactly conjoined a newsy, information-evoking Pulsar, and within orb of the Galactic Center at 26 Sagittarius—suddenly the global credit crunch became big news, as within the week the bottom had begun dropping out of the Dow and other financial markets worldwide, urged by a rapid series of investment firm failures and government bailouts—mortgage giants Fannie Mae and Freddie Mac, AIG, Merrill Lynch, Lehman Brothers. From 28 Sagittarius Pluto highlights the largest grid of Deep Space anomalies of which we are aware—fully eight points are activated on this grid, including a square to the Black Hole at 28 Pisces, sextiles to additional Black Holes at 28 Libra and 28 Aquarius and inconjuncts to a fourth at 28 Cancer and a volatile Maser at 28 Taurus. Aided by personal finance-ruling Venus in square to a Black Hole, on September 15 the Dow plummeted 500 points, and another 450 on the 17th. Huge rallies alternated with massive drops for weeks, until the government decided that in order to avert a complete meltdown, a major $700 billion bailout of Wall Street was needed.

The Bush Administration's first proposal was a mere two and a half pages, but managed to combine such sweeping powers for Treasury Secretary Henry Paulson that its defeat was perhaps inevitable. Among its bizarre conditions, the bill guaranteed complete freedom of action and a total lack of oversight or accountability for

Paulson, who was empowered to do just as he liked with the $700 billion without having to answer to anyone then or at any point in the future. Coming from the Bush Administration, who used the tragedy of 9/11 to railroad through Congress the incredibly draconian provisions of the USA PATRIOT Act, this was a not surprising approach to the problem.

Despite its deficiencies, when the bill failed on Monday the 29th of September, it evoked a 777 point drop on the Dow, the biggest single day loss in the market's history, representing $1.1 trillion in market value. In addition to Pluto still on the Pulsar and squared the Black Hole at 28 Pisces, financial planets Venus and Jupiter for the 29th both showed Black Hole activation—Venus at at 6 Scorpio conjoined one Black Hole at 7 Scorpio and Jupiter at 13 Capricorn exactly squared another at 13 Libra. Congress' response was to "revise" the bill, which exploded from two and a half pages to 451, and somehow managed to add $110 billion in pork barrel projects to legislation designed to ease a financial crisis. The resulting Emergency Economic Stabilization Act of 2008 granted the government authority to purchase and insure troubled assets from banking and investment firms, in an attempt to thaw the credit freeze and promote the free flow of credit and capital. Democrats managed to insert oversight provisions and curbs on how the money is spent by the institutions which receive it (including caps on CEO compensation), and the bill was passed in the House of Representatives on Friday, 3 October 2008 by a vote of 263-171.

Fair financial winds did not result. Continuing its rollercoaster ride for investors, the Dow and global markets continued to seesaw between extremes, with record gains alternating with record losses. October 9 was a case in point—that day the Dow fell below 9000 for the first time since 2003; ironically, it was the one year anniversary of the Dow's all-time high of 14,165 on 9 October 2007, a drop of 39% in market value over that time. The Sun for October 9, 2007 was exactly conjunct the success-oriented Quasar at 15 Libra, indicating the peak performance; on October 9, 2008, the Sun was a degree further along in the zodiac, and from 16 Libra it formed an exact inconjunct to the Black Hole at 16 Taurus, evoking the major adjustment. Another record was set October 13, its 936 point gain the largest ever in the market's history. The $1.2 trillion gain ended an eight day losing streak totaling 2400 points, a drop of 22% or $2.4 trillion in market value. More Quasar activity was evinced for the huge gain, with Venus at 23 Scorpio squared the Quasar at 25 Aquarius and exactly sesquiquadrate another at 8 Cancer as well as more broadly sesquiquadrate the 10 Aries Quasar; Jupiter at 14 Capricorn lent support with its square to the 15 Libra Quasar.

Global markets remained volatile, and continued to lose over all, until March 2009, after the passing of another mammoth recovery bill. Nothing the government did in the meantime, by itself or in tandem with other nations, appeared to have any effect on improving investor confidence, and with news of negative growth in Britain and rising unemployment in the US, fears of a global recession, even depression, loomed.

Would the Bailout Bill work in the long run? A galactic analysis of its passing suggested that we were not out of the woods yet, a diagnosis borne out by nearly double digit unemployment in the US despite a generous rebound of the Dow.

Cast for 1:35 PM EDT Friday, 3 October 2008 in Washington DC, probably the most striking feature of the chart is the exact conjunction of the Ascendant with the USA's natal Pluto at 27 Capricorn. Transformative the bill certainly is, as it makes the US government, and by extension the people, a major investor in the banking system. Charges of socialism from the bill's opponents may be somewhat extreme, but it is a fact that Republican deregulation allowed capitalism to run rampant and unchecked, to the benefit of the few, creating the circumstances we now find ourselves in, which require that we spread the losses to the many. This certainly appears to be capitalism on the way up, and socialism on the way down. But the USA Pluto on the Ascendant signals this as a powerfully transformative crossroads moment for the nation, which will never be quite the same again.

The chart is more than apt as a descriptor of the crisis—Saturn, Mercury and the Sun all fall in the Eighth House of investments and shared resources, Saturn here signaling the restrictions, limitations and loss, while Mercury defines its effects on commerce and the Sun indicates the centrality of the problem, which ultimately pervades every area of our lives. Saturn in the Eighth depicts the Bear market with a vengeance, and its financial opposite, Bullish

Jupiter, is invisible and hiding out in the Twelfth House, forming an exact square to the Black Hole at 13 Libra in the Eighth which falls on the Sun/Mercury midpoint. The message is clear—optimism is a thing of the past, relegated now to some parallel universe to which we have no access.

Uranus at 19 Pisces retrograde is, not surprisingly, the sole tenant of the Second House of personal finance, ably imaging the profound shock to the bank and retirement accounts of average Americans. Its exact trine to the 19 Scorpio Midheaven suggests that more shake-ups are in the works. Venus at 11 Scorpio in the Ninth House is square to the Black Hole at 12 Aquarius and Chiron at 16 Aquarius, and rules the 19 Taurus Nadir. We are certainly at or approaching the nadir of our collective financial fortunes, and security of all types—from paper investments to psychological comfort—is a major issue now. We are facing a major reversal (Black Hole) in our philosophy (Ninth House) about money, and what "value" (Venus) truly is. The square to Chiron certainly reflects the intent of the bill, to heal financial stresses, but Chiron can be a less than tender ministrant, and its lessons may simply be that we need to stop living above our means, and find value in less consumerist, commodities-oriented things. From 11 Scorpio Venus is also exactly semisquare the Galactic Center at 26 Sagittarius, denoting this as a global issue not just restricted to the US.

Mars at 29 Libra is exactly conjoined a Black Hole and in square to the Ascendant/Descendant axis—the appearance (Ascendant) of taking assertive action (Mars) is essential to reviving confidence in our fiscal interactions with others (Descendant). Pluto at 28 Sagittarius in the Eleventh House reflects the devastation the crisis has wrought in the dreams, goals and aspirations (Eleventh House) of many Americans. Neptune at 21 Aquarius in the First House, conjunct Chiron, implies that we need to re-image ourselves, and face some unpleasant truths—we are much more vulnerable (Neptune) than we realized, and we in the US are all inextricably bound together as one (Neptune) with the global community in this crisis, not the maverick loner (Chiron) we liked to think ourselves. The Moon at 1 Sagittarius in the Tenth House shows the emotional nature of the situation, that this is, more than anything, a crisis in confidence. The continually changing nature of the Moon is a further indicator that this problem is still evolving, and may undergo many permutations and changes in fortune (and fortunes) before we reach the crisis' end.

Finally, asteroid Midas, named for that Cretan monarch famed for turning everything he touched to gold, appears at 4 Libra, again in the Eighth House of investments, conjoined the Sun and the highlighting Quasar at 5 Libra, squared Black Holes at 4 Cancer and 5 Capricorn. Wall Street may have thought it had the Midas touch, but Black Hole reality came crashing down along with the Dow, perhaps causing us to engage in a Midas-like revaluation of what it is that we possess which has true worth, value beyond the bottom line of the balance sheet.

# OBAMA, FISCAL POLICY & BLACK HOLE VENUS

As the government's bills mount higher, with no end in sight, it might be instructive to take a look at what our new Chief Executive brings to the fiscal table, galactically speaking. Every president brings challenges to the office, his personal nativity playing out on an international scale while he heads the administration that represents us. George W. Bush's Black Hole Mars brought us foreign wars and torture, not only creating huge expenditures, waste and loss of life, but also remaking and perverting our international image, all Black Hole manifestations. Bill Clinton's combined Mars and Venus, in tandem with both Black Hole and Quasar energies, brought us highly visible (Quasar) sex scandals that absorbed the focus (Black Hole) of the nation for years.

And as the massive increase in governmental spending indicates, Obama's case is no different. Among other things, Venus indicates financial matters in the chart, and Obama's natal Venus at 1 Cancer is not only within the event horizon (orb of influence) of the Black Hole at 4 Cancer, it's also exactly squared the supermassive Black Hole center of Galaxy M-87 at 1 Libra, the largest anomaly of its type of which we are aware, with a mass in excess of 3 billion suns, holding more than 100 subsidiary galaxies in its gravitational thrall. Obama has an innate ability to both attract vast amounts of money, and to accrue huge expenditures. When this personal trait is taken to the national level, it has truly disturbing implications. Add to this the fact that at 1 Cancer, Obama's Venus conjoins both the USA's Venus at 3 Cancer and its Jupiter at 5 Cancer (both straddling that 4 Cancer Black Hole), stimulating our collective tendency to overextend ourselves financially and spend too much, and we have a potentially dire situation.

Black Holes function as points of both energy drain and energy attraction, often each in turn. They create an unstable, unpredictable atmosphere, making firm foundations difficult to achieve, and commonly require huge amounts of energy, focus and resources to manage. The singularity, or center, of the Black Hole connects with parallel universes, nonphysical realms where things exist in potential, and act as cosmic conduits to birth these into our reality, thus they are often active when record-breaking events occur, as establishing a new status quo or benchmark to be equaled or surpassed.

The positive, acquisitive side of Obama's Black Hole Venus was well in evidence in 2008's never-ending election season. Long-shot Obama came out of the gate with an astounding $25 million raised for his presidential campaign in the first quarter of 2007, when he formally announced his candidacy. This total was just $1 million behind apparent frontrunner Hillary Clinton for the same period, and should have been a wake-up call for her campaign, who instead hit the snooze button until nine months later when Obama took Iowa.

The Illinois senator went on to raise an unprecedented $410 million in the primary season, then $335 million more for the general election, an astounding, record-smashing total of $745 million, garnered mostly from small donors, contributions of $100 and under. Compare this staggering amount to the 2004 election, where George W. Bush and John Kerry *combined* raised only $650 million! As is often the case with Black Hole Venus, income and expenses almost balance—after the rigorous expenditure of the 21-month campaign and a $170 million TV ad blitz in its last two months, Obama successfully retired from the field with a mere $30 million surplus, less than 5% of the total raised.

The flip side of this equation is less attractive. Within seven weeks of his inauguration, Obama had approved almost $1.2 trillion in emergency and stop-gap spending, and proposed a 2010 fiscal budget of $3.5 trillion, a new record. Not only does Obama himself own a Black Hole Venus, so does the administration, born by constitutional fiat at noon on January 20, 2009. Venus in this chart at 17 Pisces is squared the Black Hole at 18 Sagittarius, reiterating the fiscal issues of the president. Further, Venus also conjoins Uranus at 19 Pisces, indicating galactic-sized "sticker shock" and controversial, possibly erratic, but definitely forward-thinking economic policies. The administration's Venus also opposes Saturn at 21 Virgo retrograde, suggestive of tough financial times ahead, and a need to get serious about money (Obama's proposed fix of the Pentagon's procurement protocols is a much-needed step in this direction). Not to be outdone, Pluto, which has affinities with both vast wealth and the shared resources of the Eighth House, which it co-rules, lies at 1 Capricorn in the chart for the administration, exactly opposed Obama's natal Venus, and bringing out a Galactic T-Square with an exact square to the 1 Libra Black Hole.

In Obama's natal chart, the Black Hole at 1 Libra which Venus squares falls in the Eighth House of unearned income and shared resources, appropriate for both the campaign contributions, which cannot be said to have been "earned" in any normal sense, and the government spending, which by definition concerns resources shared in common by all of us. On Friday the 13th of February, the Senate passed the 1,073 page "American Recovery and Reinvestment Act," which attempts to disburse some $787 billion in federal funds to buy our way out of the economic downturn which has gripped the nation. The bill passed both Houses on highly partisan lines, with a vote of 246-183 in the House of Representatives, garnering no GOP support whatsoever. A sprinkling of 3 Republican senators contributed to the narrow margin of 60-38 in the Senate, the filibuster-proof sixty votes only acquired after extending the floor vote a precedent-breaking 5 hours and 17 minutes, allowing Senator Sherrod Brown (D-OH) to fly back from attending his mother's funeral to cast the deciding ballot.

This occurred at 10:47 PM EST, providing a chart with Black Holes at three of four angles (excluding the IC), and a loaded Fourth House, denoting an emphasis on foundational matters. Venus at 8 Aries is exactly squared the Quasar at 8 Cancer, an anomaly noted for providing a high profile and enhanced visibility, and often resulting in an inflated or magnified result. Venus is also trine Black Holes at 9 Leo and 10 Sagittarius, forming a Galactic Grand Trine which reinforces the huge financial outlays. Jupiter, another indicator of Big Money, is sextile Venus and exactly opposes the 9 Leo Black Hole from 9 Aquarius, forming a Kite from the basic pattern, focused on expansion, increase and excess.

When the proposed $3.5 trillion federal budget for fiscal 2010 was released on February 26, 2009, the Sun and Venus opposed Black Holes, with Jupiter exactly conjoined a third. This figure builds on the previous high water mark of the Bush administration, which for 2009 proposed a budget totaling $3.1 trillion. But that budget was never passed in its entirety, and funding for most of the government's departments was only secured through the first half of the fiscal year, until March 31 of that year.

Enter the Omnibus Appropriations Act, a supplemental spending bill passed by the Senate on March 10, 2009, which provides an additional $410 billion to carry government through the balance of the fiscal year, until September 30. Please note that this sum does not include any funding for the Department of Defense, by far the most costly division, nor for Homeland Security, which comes in second in overall expenditures. Nor does it include the costs of the Iraq War, which are always computed "off budget" with accounting gimmicks, and merely added directly to the national debt. When the Senate passed this bill at 7:09 PM EDT, Venus at 15 Aries was still at its retrograde station degree, exactly opposing the Quasar at 15 Libra. With Jupiter at 14 Aquarius, itself conjoined a Black Hole at 13, Venus formed a Yod with an exact Moon/Saturn conjunction at 18 Virgo, indicating the financial (Venus/Jupiter) pinch (Saturn) for the American people (Moon).

This expenditure may be necessary; it may even perform the intended outcome, and provide economic relief for the country. But it adds considerably to the already staggering $11 trillion national debt, much of it owned by actual or potential global competitors like China. And someday, somehow, it will have to be repaid.

Obama's Black Hole Venus manifests in a variety of other ways as well. Venus also rules values, desires, romantic and intimate relationships, and women in general. Women have always played a major role in Obama's life; his father abandoned the family when Obama was just two, leaving his mother as the responsible parent. She in turn did her own Black Hole fade eight years later, leaving Barack in the care of his grandparents from age 10. His American grandmother became a leading light in Obama's life, supporting and guiding him until her death just days before the 2008 election. Michelle, too, fits the profile of a strong, independent woman such as Black Hole Venus can manifest, and the domestic environment is

dominated by females; with the addition of their daughters Malia
and Sasha, Obama is seriously outnumbered at home. Black Hole
Venus can produce widely disparate manifestations in relationships—often long-term union is difficult to achieve, and the native
careens from one partner to the next in unpredictable and erratic
fashion. But the combination can also result in union with a soul
mate, someone to whom the native is inextricably bound. While it's
very difficult to assess any relationship from the outside, Michelle
and Barack Obama's seems to be closer to the latter variety than the
former.

But it is in the realm of values where Venus' Black Hole affiliations were most strongly seen in the issues raised in the campaign
itself, issues which at one point threatened to derail his candidacy.
Obama's difference, his virtual alien-ness, became an issue—just
who was he, and what was he about? Past associations with domestic terrorist Bill Ayers and current associations with pastor Jeremiah
Wright were dissected and analyzed in an attempt to determine
where Obama's true loyalties lay.

Of the two, Obama's relationship with Reverend Wright was
the more controversial, as the candidate had spent twenty years
in Wright's congregation, and when clips surfaced on YouTube of
Obama's pastor declaiming, "God Damn America!" and accusing
the government of spreading AIDS in the black community, serious
doubts began to be expressed about both Obama's spiritual mind set
and his political opinions. The furor erupted over the period from
early March to late April 2008, just as transit Pluto came to form its
retrograde station at 1 Capricorn, in exact opposition to Obama's
natal Venus and squaring the 1 Libra Black Hole, calling into question his values, and probing beneath the apparent surface reality to
reveal the hidden truths beneath. Obama's response was deft, the
candidate crafting a well-received speech on race relations the likes
of which hadn't been seen in this country for forty years, and eventually denouncing his pastor's views and withdrawing the family's
membership in Wright's church. But Black Hole Venus had opened
that window into the alternate reality of Obama's otherness, adding
a sense of being currently out of the religious mainstream to prior
concerns regarding his half-Muslim parentage and early education
in Malaysian public schools, where Islam was taught.

Further incidents marred this period—bowling (badly) in Altoona, Pennsylvania didn't negate Obama's caustic comments about the "bitterness" of rural American voters "clinging" to guns and religion, at a fundraiser in San Francisco that same month. Once again, Obama's values became the issue. Was he the latte-swilling, arugula-munching, professorial liberal elitist with the Ivy League education, or the lower middle class, up-by-his-bootstraps, hard-working community organizer from the single parent family that had been on food stamps? Preconceived notions and prejudices largely determined which side of the Obama fence you came down on, but the disconnect between these disparate views of the values that formed him resonated throughout the spring and into the early summer, creating a voter backlash that saw Hillary Clinton sweeping several important blue collar Democratic strongholds at the end of the primary season, despite a numerical superiority which all but guaranteed Obama's ultimate victory. People were spooked by the revelations, wary of a false display of solidarity with the working class belied by the glimpse into Obama's potentially radical, elitist values.

Ironically, in the final analysis, it was Black Hole Venus that assured his campaign's success, after providing the most serious stumbling block Obama had to negotiate. Buoyed by the incredible fundraising windfall it supplied, his message of change reinforced by the looming financial crisis it obligingly furnished that autumn, which distracted voters from more personal, values-based Venusian concerns, Obama's Black Hole Venus was largely responsible for sweeping him into the White House. Once there, it wasted no time in racking up huge expenditures and debt, perhaps just the tip of the fiscal iceberg the administration seems to be steering the ship of state toward.

How will it all turn out? With such mammoth expenditures looming as the overhaul in the nation's healthcare system and the likely fiscal blowback from $CO_2$ emissions "cap & trade" legislation, Obama's Venus will have much to chew on. Black Hole Venus provides a kaleidoscopic, ever-shifting panorama of potential outcomes and future realities, and predicting which manifestation pops up when Dame Fortune spins her wheel is a fool's errand. But wherever this nation is headed, Obama's Venus will have a lot to say about it.

Finally, a word or two about Venus as arbiter of peace. On Friday, October 9, 2009, the world at large was somewhat taken aback when the Nobel Committee announced that it had chosen Barack Obama as the recipient of the 2009 Nobel Peace Prize. Nominations for the honor closed on February 1, just twelve days after his inauguration, and while few doubt Obama's good intentions, there doesn't seem to have been enough substance so far to have merited the honor. Obama himself acknowledged as much in his statement several hours later: "Let me be clear: I do not view it as a recognition of my own accomplishments, but rather as an affirmation of American leadership on behalf of aspirations held by people in all nations. To be honest, I do not feel that I deserve to be in the company of so many of the transformative figures who've been honored by this prize."

We can consider Obama's Venus exactly squared the supermassive Black Hole at 1 Libra as the culprit here, greedily acquisitive for awards and honors, earned or otherwise. Venus in the sky that day was at 22 Virgo, exactly semisquare the Black Hole at 7 Scorpio and exactly conjunct Obama's natal Mars, ironic but strangely appropriate when one considers that the President was at that time deep in discussions about whether and to what extent to ramp up the war in Afghanistan. The degree is also reflected in the USA's natal Neptune, accounting for the wave of disbelief and confusion that swept across the country as the news became known. Transit Venus was also conjoined transit Saturn at 27 Virgo, apt for the choice of a chief executive (Saturn) for the Peace Prize (Venus), with this pair roughly squared the Galactic Center at 26 Sagittarius, indicative of an event having global implications.

# PLUTO BLACK HOLE STATIONS

Station degrees, points at which celestials of our system appear to slow, come to a standstill and change direction, become highly charged with the energies of that celestial, and resonate for much longer than the normal period of time allotted when the planet is moving at its standard rate. When this occurs conjoined a Black Hole, the opportunity for major change and massive transformation is dramatically increased, as an infinity of parallel universes beyond its singularity seeks expression in our reality. The contacting planet acts a sort of reflector or transducer, taking these non-physical realities and stepping them down into our 3D existence, manifesting their potential into the world around us. When Pluto is the planet making a Black Hole contact, expect titanic forces to be unleashed, altering the status quo reality in spectacular and irreversible ways.

Pluto, which rules change and transformation, also governs such things as sex, reproduction and genetics; the forbidden and taboo; huge expenditures or waste; the wealth of the underground; nuclear power and weaponry; totalitarian regimes; terrorism, genocide and war; scandals, secrets, and their disclosure; evolution and species extinction; ecological disaster and renewal; and decay and death.

The most turbulent Pluto/Black Hole station in recent memory was that of March 22, 2003, exactly atop the Black Hole at 19 Sagittarius, which fell just three days after the US-led invasion of Iraq, a conflict which is still ongoing, and has cost the country in excess of $706 billion in direct costs, with associated expenditures in support and follow-up care for veterans estimated to exceed $2 trillion. Add to that cost the almost 4300 dead US servicemen and more than 30,000 wounded, to say nothing of the Iraqi dead, possibly more than 100,000, and we see a Plutonian boondoggle of truly enormous Black Hole proportions, incorporating its governing themes of war, death, and massive expenditures. To add insult to injury, it was at the time of Pluto's backhand station direct conjunct this same anomaly, eighteen months later on August 30, 2004, that the final US report on Iraq's supposed WMDs, the *casus belli* of the invasion, revealed that no evidence for them could be found, and all that blood and treasure had been spent for nothing. [Report released 16 September 2004, two weeks after the station; earlier, on August 24, the Schlesinger Report disclosed that the abuses at Abu Ghraib prison were the result of "fundamental failures throughout all levels of command," not the work of a few aberrant soldiers; these abuses, involving torture and sexual humiliation, directly governed in Pluto's bailiwick].

When Pluto subsequently made a retrograde station at 26 Sagittarius conjunct the supermassive Black Hole at the Galactic Center, on 29 March 2006, world events clustering about this station included the 22 February bombing of Samarra's Golden Mosque, Shia Islam's holiest shrine, which resulted in major escalations of sectarian violence in Iraq (focusing on Pluto's rulership of terrorist acts); George W. Bush's March 9th signing of a renewal of the USA PATRIOT Act, including an accompanying signing statement stating that he did not consider himself bound by its requirement to inform Congress how the law was being applied (with its implications toward Plutonian themes of totalitarianism, secrecy and invasion of privacy); and the 11 April announcement by Iranian President Mahmoud Ahmadinejad that his country had successfully enriched uranium, a key step on the road to becoming a nuclear power (also ruled by Pluto). Earlier stations bear out Pluto's tendency to evoke extreme manifestations, particularly involving areas it governs, when in conjunction with Black Holes.

A retrograde station on the Black Hole at 10 Sagittarius on March 13, 1999 coincided with the release of important NASA data verifying global warming, potentially responsible for another pending mass extinction such as Pluto rules, when they confirmed an annual three foot loss in the Greenland ice shelf. Just eleven days later the NATO-led Operation Allied Force began bombing raids on Milosevic's Yugoslavia in an effort to end his support for genocidal atrocities and ethnic cleansing in Kosovo (showing Pluto as ruler of genocide, war and racially-based violence). When Pluto subsequently turned direct at the same anomaly on August 20, 2000, it was just three days before the National Institutes of Health approved federal funding for embryonic stem cell research, which has the potential to cure countless diseases, Pluto governing biologic processes on the cellular level.

In a similar incident, when Pluto stationed retrograde conjoined the Black Hole at 5 Sagittarius on March 8, 1997, it was accompanied by a federal ban on human cloning, signed by Bill Clinton on March 4th, and the first cross-adoption of their children by a lesbian couple in New York on March 7th, an early harbinger of the gay marriage rights controversy which has since enveloped the nation, and significant in light of Pluto's rulership of sexual matters and taboo. Weeks later, on 27 March, Marshall Applewhite's Heaven's Gate cult committed mass suicide at Rancho Santa Fe, California, a nod to both the self-destruction aspects of Pluto and its first Black Hole station conjunction in religious-philosophy-ruling Sagittarius.

Eighteen months later on 15 August 1998, when Pluto again stationed on this point, Clinton was back in the news, on a more personal level, with his August 17th confession to the nation of his affair with Monica Lewinsky. Terrorism, another Plutonian arena, was also highlighted, with the August 7th bombing of the American embassies in Kenya and Tanzania, and the USA's retaliatory response on al Qaeda training bases in Sudan and Afghanistan on August 20th. These incidents were among the first warning shots of al Qaeda's war on America, and a root cause of the Bush administration's Global War on Terrorism, with ramifications to this day.

The previous cycle of Pluto/Black Hole stations dates back to the late '80s, with the retrograde station of 8 February 1986 on the Black Hole at 7 Scorpio eliciting the fall of two dictators (also Pluto-ruled), Haiti's "president for life" Jean-Claude Duvalier, who fled the country on February 7th; and the Philippines' Ferdinand Marcos, who rigged the February 7th election to defeat Corazon Aquino, only to be ousted in a military coup on February 26th. In a surreal pairing of Pluto (death) and Sagittarius (exploration), America watched in horror as the space shuttle Challenger exploded on live TV just minutes after take-off on 28 January, killing the crew of seven.

When Pluto turned direct at 7 Scorpio on 17 July 1987, it was in the midst of the Iran-Contra investigation, the biggest scandal (Pluto) of the Reagan administration, featuring Colonel Oliver North, who testified that his actions had been approved by higher authorities; National Security Advisor John Poindexter, who authorized the use of Iran arms sales profits to aid Contra rebels in Nicaragua; and Defense Secretary Caspar Weinberger, who admitted to officially-sanctioned deception and intrigue (cloak-and-dagger operations being also Plutonian).

Sometimes Pluto's actions at station do not appear to be earth-shattering, their importance only noted much later. Such is the case with the 24 June 1978 direct station of Pluto on the Black Hole at 13 Libra, preceded shortly by the June 18th incorporation of the Whitewater business venture, an Arkansas sweetheart real estate deal gone wrong which would lead to investigations eventually resulting in the impeachment of Bill Clinton in the US House of Representatives, twenty years later.

On 11 June 1973, Pluto stationed direct conjunct the supermassive Black Hole center of Galaxy M-87 at 1 Libra. Just two weeks later White House Counsel John Dean testified to Richard Nixon's complicity in the Watergate cover-up, in congressional proceedings which ultimately brought down that presidency. The prior direct station of Pluto on a Black Hole, occurring 21 May 1963 at 9 Virgo, witnessed the height of racial tensions in the American south, with federal troops enforcing the integration of the University of Alabama on June 11, and the assassination of civil rights leader Medgar Evers in Jackson, Mississippi the following day. Another far-reaching consequence of that station was the May 28th initial offering of common stock in the Dow Jones Stock Exchange to the public, which has led us to this point of average Americans heavily invested in the ups and downs of Wall Street. Investments are also an Eighth House/Plutonian matter.

Pluto's first Black Hole station post-World War II fell on 8 December 1959, just after the December 1st transmission of the first color photo of Earth from space, a symbolic event noted for its concurrence with a growing understanding of our planet as one whole, an interdependent eco-system, at once fragile and enduring, and the realization that we have it within our power to preserve or destroy it.

To focus on the effects of a station closer to the present day, Pluto's station retrograde on 6 April 2010 at 5 Capricorn, exactly conjunct the singularity of the Black Hole there, proved to be plutonically inventive and destructive at once. I mean, who but Pluto could have conceived of a volcano disrupting global travel for weeks and costing billions for commercial airlines?

Pluto inhabited its 5 Capricorn station degree from February 26th through May 18th with the actual station falling midway during this period, on April 6th), but dramatic seismic activity actually began in early January, as Pluto rolled over 4 Capricorn, where this same Black Hole appeared until 1992. Pluto rules underground processes, including earthquakes and volcanism, and the 7.0 magnitude quake in Port-au-Prince, Haiti on 12 January 2010 set the stage for a series of major reality-shakers across the globe. The Haiti quake was the most dramatic in terms of loss of life, with upwards of a quarter million deaths and a complete devastation of the local economy, with reconstruction costs perhaps as high as $14 billion. But very strong quakes in less densely populated areas quickly followed—a 7.0 quake in the Ryukyu Islands, just as Pluto moved to the Black Hole's current degree on February 26, was a precursor to the 8.8 magnitude quake in Chile the following day, which took more than a thousand lives. The cost of this seismic event to the global insurance industry could top $7 billion, with a reconstruction cost upwards of $30 billion. GPS readings indicate that this quake was so powerful, it shifted the entire city of Concepcion, closest to its epicenter, 10 feet to the west, and moved the earth's axis 8 centimeters. Quite a calling card for Pluto to give its Black Hole host! These major quakes were succeeded by a 6.4 quake in Taiwan March 4, a 6.5 quake in Sumatra March 5, a 7.2 quake in Baja California April 4, and a 6.9 quake in China April 13.

On March 20 the Eyjafjallajokull volcano in Iceland erupted, hurling lava several hundred meters into the air, but with little accompanying ash from the relatively small, glacier-topped mountain. On April 14, however, the ongoing eruption entered a new phase, spewing huge volumes of glass-rich ash more than 5 miles into the atmosphere, directly into the jet stream, from where the plume quickly spread to encompass most of Europe. The ash posed an extreme risk to air travel, severely diminishing visibility and

interfering with both instrumentation and aircraft engine performance, and led to the largest shut-down of air traffic since World
War II. Most of northern Europe was grounded from April 15th
through the 23rd, stranding more than 5 million passengers worldwide, as connecting and international flights which could not be
rerouted through unaffected air space were also cancelled, greatly
increasing the scope of the disruption. Airlines collectively lost $2
billion during that eight day period alone, and continuing sporadic
disruptions into May have added to that total.

Healthcare per se is not within Pluto's bailiwick, but health insurance, as an Eighth House matter, is. When Barack Obama signed
the Healthcare Reform Bill into law on 23 March, 2010, it marked
another watershed moment for Pluto's station period. Dealing
predominantly with extending coverage to millions of uninsured
Americans and reforming insurance company policies, the legislation is expected to cost upwards of a trillion dollars over the next
ten years, a figure which is also covered by Pluto's rulership of exor-
bitant expenditures in excess of $1 billion.

Pluto not only rules the underground, but the wealth that is contained there, and the efforts to extract it. On 5 April, the day before
the actual station, an explosion of methane gas 1000 feet beneath the
surface caused the worst mining accident in the US in forty years,
when a disastrous cave-in at Massey Energy's Upper Branch Coal
Mine in Montcoal, WV, took the lives of 29 miners. In 2009 Massey
Energy had received $382,000 in fines for serious unrepentant viola-
tions in safety and ventilation systems, despite which it remained
open and fully operational. On April 28 a second, less publicized
accident occurred at the Dotiki coal mine in Providence, KY, when
a shaft roof collapsed, killing two workers.

Oil drilling and environmental disasters are also subject to
Pluto, and the blowout, explosion and resulting leakage of oil from
the Deepwater Horizon oil drilling rig 50 miles off the Louisiana
coast far eclipses the 1989 Exxon Valdez oil spill as the worst oil
disaster in US history. Deepwater Horizon had been in the news
just months earlier, drilling the world's deepest oil and gas well,
more than 6 miles deep, in September 2009. The April 20th explosion
killed eleven workers and sank the offshore drilling rig, creating
an oil gusher which continued to release as much as 20,000 barrels

(840,000 gallons) of crude oil into the Gulf of Mexico daily. Attempts in early May to cap the exposed pipe some 5000 foot below sea level with a large containment dome, followed by a smaller "Top Hat" covering, were unsuccessful. Similarly, controlled burns of the oil slick and attempts to use booms to prevent its making landfall met with only limited success.

On May 16th, BP installed a siphon pipe into the leak, which drew off perhaps as much as 1000 barrels per day, barely a drop in the oil bucket; this was the best progress made in dealing with the situation before Pluto exited its station degree on the 18th. The slick had then grown to a size larger than the states of Rhode Island and Delaware combined, encompassing as much as 12 million gallons, with much more oil remaining below the surface in vast underwater plumes. The use of Corexit, a chemical dispersant designed to assist the breakdown of the oil while still at sea, was ordered discontinued on May 20th by the EPA after it was revealed that the product is a severe toxin, eradicating perhaps as much as 25% of marine life in the treated areas. BP had already sprayed nearly 700,000 gallons of Corexit , and continued to spread the deadly chemical after its banning.

In early June, another attempt to cap the leak proved partially successful, but incomplete. The only viable option remaining to end the leakage as of this writing [June 2010] is to drill a relief well to siphon off the oil, a process taking anywhere from 3-5 months, by which time the volume of leaked oil is expected to exceed 100 million gallons. Winds and currents could carry the spill as far as North Carolina, and have already brought it to the Florida Keys. The impact on local fishing and tourism industries has been devastating, as will be the repercussions to the environment should the spill come ashore in the interconnected wetland marshes of the Gulf coast. In an effort to ensure that BP pays the full cost of the clean-up, legislation is pending in the US Congress to increase oil industry liability amounts to $10 billion, which were capped at $75 million after the Exxon Valdez disaster.

All in all, quite a devastating grab-bag of destructive effects, brought to you courtesy of Pluto's retrograde stations conjoined those reality-warping Black Holes.

# SECTION III:
# BLACK HOLES IN DEPTH

# THE ESSENCE OF THE MATTER

Matter and Essence. Once thought to be wholly incompatible, we now understand them as an inextricably bound whole.

Entire philosophies in the West, and therefore entire civilizations, have been founded upon this presumed incompatibility between the visible and invisible components of ourselves and our world. Science became the champion of this split founded in religion, and science now leads us home to a true understanding of our interconnectedness with all that is.

For centuries science strove to reduce matter to its component parts, and thought little, if any, about essence, or spirit. The focus shifted somewhat with the discovery and exploration of electricity in the late 1700s, and then electro-magnetism in the mid 1800's, but contemporaneous advances in microscope technologies retained the primary reductionist thrust of the science community, until a visionary genius named Albert Einstein fractured that worldview forever.

It is hard to imagine today's world without Einstein. Although the most visible and tangible result of his immediate work was the atom bomb, a rather unfortunate legacy for a man of genius, without the groundwork of his turn-of-the-century theories, nothing that physics has taught us since could have been developed.

Einstein's concepts of Relativity shattered the worldview that ascertained that everything scientifically measurable was also objective, by showing, among other things, that time would be measured differently by two observers in differing relative proximity to a single event. This staggering realization was the wake-up call for the philosophy of wholeness.

Einstein's theories opened the floodgates of intellectual speculation into the true nature of matter, with physicists from Max Plank to Fritjof Capra building upon this framework to radically alter our worldview and the understanding of physical reality.

The Heisenberg Uncertainty Principle, dating from the mid-1920's, is the first major plank leading us toward the knowledge of our indivisible unity with spirit. As science delved further and deeper into the atom, it became clear that things were not as they seemed. Matter had been conceived of as being composed of progressively larger building blocks, protons, neutrons and electrons building an atom, atoms building a molecule, molecules building a cell, cells coalescing to form organs which become systemically joined to form ourselves. But as science's scrutiny became more focused, it found that this was true only to a point. The particles that formed the atom were themselves created of smaller particles, which seemingly appeared and disappeared from the void at will. Even at the level of the electron, extreme uncertainty reigned.

For decades the debate raged: were electrons particles, or were they waves? Finally, Werner Heisenberg gave us the answer: yes.

Electrons are wavelike particles, which cannot be precisely measured in both their states at once. If we try to pin down the position of an electron at a given time, rating its particle-like properties, we lose all evidence of its speed, or momentum. Likewise, the converse is true when we try to measure the wavelike properties, giving rise to the concept of the "probability cloud," which stresses the importance of the observer in the act of observation and measurement.

Electrons are understood now to exist as a "cloud" or "halo" of probabilities encircling the nucleus, which remains in an unstable state until it is observed, when the cloud collapses into a single point.

The Uncertainty Principle is a primary law governing Black Hole interaction in a chart, where all the possible manifestations of a given point or aspect exist at once in a probability cloud of parallel realities, the "observed" probability being the one which has manifested in the life so far as the circumstances connected with this aspect. The Uncertainty Principle shows us that the observer, in this case the owner of the nativity, has a direct effect on the probability that manifests, and that this manifestation will change whenever the observer's attention, and thus energy, is brought to bear upon this point.

A second vital plank on the platform of our understanding of the interconnectedness of essence and matter is Bell's Theorem. Dealing again on the level of the electron, physicist John Bell determined that two particles which began their journey together as one, retain a link between them no matter how far apart they travel in space. Interactions affecting one electron are reflected in the other as well, and virtually simultaneously, giving rise to the principle of nonlocality, which states that particles need not share the same local region of space to be intimately connected.

This demonstration of interconnection at a distance is vital to our understanding of how Deep Space points can affect our lives from across the vast voids of intergalactic space, and leads us to the third and fourth planks of our holistic philosophy, namely, Bohm's Theory of the Holographic Order of the Universe, and Sheldrake's Theory of the Morphogenetic, or Morphic, Field.

Physicist David Bohm's holographic universe is a concept which should be detailed at this point. It is based in part on an alternate view of Bell's theorem, presented above. Bohm asserts that there is another way of viewing this apparent nonlocality, which is that these are, indeed, two separate particles when viewed from three-dimensional space, but when viewed from the higher perspective of six dimensions, the two particles are seen to actually be one.

Alan Combs and Mark Holland in *Synchronicity: Science, Myth and the Trickster* illustrate his position thus: consider the case of a fish in a tank, with two separate video monitors, at right angles to each other, each trained on the fish. An observer watching both monitors would seem to be seeing two different fish due to the two perspectives, but each time one of them moved, the other would, also. Once the "trick" was revealed, however, and the higher dimension disclosed (the six dimensions formed by overlapping two disparate views of a single third dimensional space), it would become apparent there was only one fish.

And so with Bohm's theory. In the holographic universe, each part is composed of all the others. Like the Hindu image of the Net of Indra, where each jewel in the net mirrors each of the others, Bohm's holographic universe shows each part enfolded within the rest. This view stresses the wavelike properties of the universe, and considers physical matter to be a more stable, "standing wave" version of the radiant energy that permeates everything, even intergalactic voids. The implications of this theory for general astrology, and especially Galactic Astrology, with its emphasis on Deep Space points, is obvious: if we each contain the cosmos enfolded within us, then as it moves, so do we, and the energies we ascribe to the planets and celestials interact inside us as surely as they do in the Heavens.

Biochemist Rupert Sheldrake presents yet another image of holism in nature, the principle of formative causation, the central theme of which asserts that the development of organisms is guided by a holistic force known as the "morphic field." This can best be described as a sort of pattern, a habit, even, which Sheldrake maintains acts as a governing agent for everything from molecular organization to patterns of brain activity that impel certain thoughts or behaviors. The basic concept here states that once a particular form occurs, it is more likely to do so again, and that over time these varying classes of forms have developed nonlocal formative elements (the morphic fields) to maintain the continuity of the form. These fields, which are not limited by location, restrict the individual's development along certain avenues, yet remain open to new information provided by the individual, which then impacts the collective once it becomes incorporated into the field.

This concept of Sheldrake's is not new; in fact, it can be traced as far back as Plato's assertion that there were Ideal Forms in existence on a higher plane of reality that served as models for the forms in our less elevated, more imperfect reality. It is in light of this connection that we can see the interaction of the Deep Space galactic points as the model Ideal Forms, which resonate on the next lower octave as the Archetypes represented by the celestials of our system, and ultimately resolve themselves into the psyches and somas of individuals on this planet. Truly, "As above, so below."

These four primary planks on our philosophical platform of holism are held in place by pegs and nails provided by dozens of others, in our own century and in the centuries prior, since the time of the ancient Greeks. In accepting this worldview, we must acknowledge the potential pearls of wisdom and self understanding to be gained by incorporating galactic points into our lives, for to know them is to know ourselves, and to understand the workings of their interactions is to understand the workings of our own psyches.

# ASTROPHYSICAL ANATOMY OF A BLACK HOLE

*"The known is finite, the unknown infinite; intellectually we stand on an islet in the midst of an illimitable ocean of inexplicability. Our business in every generation is to reclaim a little more land."*
                                                              –Thomas Huxley

Black Holes are only one possible end point of the life cycle of stellar bodies, but perhaps the most dramatic. Physicists theorize that this anomaly can result only from a star which had at least 1.5 solar masses to begin with (a solar mass, as the name suggests, is equivalent to the mass of our own sun, and is regularly used as a basis of comparison of stellar bodies, just as astronomical units, or AU's, the distance from Earth to the Sun, has become a constant in measuring distance within our solar system).

The life story of a star is a study in contrast: on the one hand, there is an urge to expansion which causes the star to radiate energy, and on the other, an equally strong urge to contraction which is what fuels the atomic collisions and fusion reactions of the nuclear furnace within, thus creating more energy to be radiated. Stellar interaction is a very volatile, but extremely delicate, balancing act. As a star ages, grows out of its comfortable middle years which astronomers term "the main sequence," very often there is a slight edge on the expansive energies which causes the star to expand to Red Giant proportions, the largest stars known. (If our Sun one day reaches this stage, some-odd billion years hence, it will grow to a size to encompass the Earth, which will continue to revolve around the center of mass as a semi-molten lump of charred rock.) Eventually, this expansion becomes fatal; the nuclear fuel at the center of the star begins to be exhausted, and the energy radiated is no longer sufficient to support the mass. The star begins to collapse in upon its own weight, and one of three things may happen: the star may explode as a supernova, spewing vast amounts of complex matter into the universe which will seed life in other systems; it may condense into a neutron star, also called a Pulsar, which is composed solely of the denser, neutron nuclei of the original atoms; or it collapses further still, to form the Black Hole, a pinpoint region of space having infinite gravity and infinite mass, and from which even light cannot escape.

This latter quality of the Black Hole is what makes it so difficult to verify experimentally: how do you image something which you cannot see? The May 1994 imaging by NASA of the supermassive Black Hole in the center of Galaxy M-87, was done by imaging its "accretion disk," a broad layer of infalling gas and matter which is superheated and glows brightly. The Black Hole itself, however, is invisible, but its presence can be intuited by observing its effects on the region of time/space which surrounds it, particularly that which is subject to the Black Hole's gravitational field, a region termed the "event horizon."

The event horizon is specifically related to two stellar factors: the parent star's Schwarzchild radius, and its escape velocity. After Einstein's new theories of gravitation and the warping of space by matter were publicized, German physicist Karl Schwarzchild began to work on the equations which would show at what point in a star's interior the laws of Newtonian gravity and Einsteinian relativity diverged; within this imaginary boundary at a star's core the spacetime curvature becomes extraordinarily large. Schwarzchild radii themselves are relatively small: the Sun's is roughly one mile, while that of the Earth is barely an inch.

The escape velocity, by contrast, is the minimum speed at which a nearby particle would need to travel to break away from a celestial body's gravitational influence (for the Earth, this is 6.8 miles per second, the speed NASA's rocket's must attain if they are to escape Earth's gravity and ascend into space).

Essentially, a Black Hole is formed when the star has shrunk to a size which falls within the limits of its Schwarzchild radius, which creates an escape velocity exceeding the speed of light. The light rays are bent back in upon themselves, and the object becomes invisible. This border region, equivalent to the old star's Schwarzchild radius, becomes the event horizon of the Black Hole. The curvature within this boundary is so great that it prevents all matter which falls within its grasp from moving in paths other than an inward spiral to the center of the Black Hole, also termed the "singularity."

The singularity is a region of unimaginable heat, pressure, and contraction. Matter here loses all semblance of its original form, becoming merely a quantum soup of superheated particles, a froth of cosmic potentiality. Astrophysicists still disagree as to the fate of matter which the Black Hole has engorged; presently Stephen Hawking, a pioneer in the field, supports the theory that eventually, after aeons of time, the energy is "leaked" by the Black Hole, which thus loses mass and gravitational attraction, finally ending up as a sort of celestial deflated balloon. But many scientists still contemplate the possibility that there is a means of egress from the Black Hole, the so-called "wormhole," a sort of timespace bridge between realities which may connect the Black Hole via higher dimensions with its polar opposite, the "white hole" (sometimes known as a Quasar), in a completely different region of timespace, or perhaps even a different universe entirely, where the engorged matter is regurgitated into 3-D physicality.

This is the life cycle and structure of the astrophysical anomaly we are attempting to decipher on its astrological level, and these astrophysical qualities have their reflection in what the Black Hole represents astrologically, and how it operates. Principally, they are these: the absorption of matter/energy is reflected in the Black Hole quality of draining energy from the areas of our lives represented by the celestial bodies it contacts; the massive gravitational pull is reflected in the inescapable quality of Black Hole interaction and the personal magnetism displayed by those strongly contacted to one; the bending of light to become invisible is reflected in the qualities of perception alteration and a strong desire to work behind the scenes, or in some sense hidden, common to Black Hole individuals. Finally, on a theoretical level, the potential Black Holes offer for access to parallel universes or alternate dimensions is reflected in the options and opportunities for altering our status quo reality and enacting any of an infinite number of parallel realities which they present.

# METAPHYSICAL ANATOMY OF A BLACK HOLE

*"Those wise ones who see that the consciousness within themselves
is the same consciousness within all conscious beings, attain eternal
peace."*

–Katha Upanishad

B lack Holes are the energy absorbers of your chart and your life.
The elderly neighbor who always needs to be driven to doctor's appointments; the faucet that keeps dripping and requires the
repairman every six months; the persistent rumor that the company you work for may be financially unstable: each of these mundane matters distracts your focus, takes precious physical, mental
or emotional energy from you. The types of energy drains can be
determined from the placements and positioning of Black Holes in
the birth chart.

The first hypothetical instance listed above, that of the elderly
neighbor's illness, might stem from a Sixth House Mercury which
trines Saturn and is in square to a Third House Black Hole. Being
responsible (Saturn) for short-term transport (Mercury) and being a
support (trine) in the health care (Sixth House) crisis (square) of an
elderly (Saturn again) neighbor (Third House) is depriving you of
valued time and energy (the Black Hole). Although this may seem
at first glance to be a matter too mundane for the cosmos' attention,
when we examine the galactic constructs in our charts we can see
emerging the very framework of how we manifest into the physical,
the patterns of interconnectedness which bring into our experience
of the physical plane mirrors of the inner landscape of the psyche.

Take another incredibly mundane example, from some poor
schlub's life. OK, let's use me. I confess I am the leaky faucet offender
of the list above, and a look at the galactics in my chart show why.

First, on a general level, we can see domestic issues being a drain quite clearly with the double whammy of a 19 Virgo Moon (the home, domestic environment) squared the Black Hole at 18/19 Sagittarius (18 degrees in the nativity, this anomaly has currently transited to 19) as well as trine the Black Hole at 19 Capricorn, and the incidence of a third Black Hole, at 11/12 Aquarius, exactly conjoined the IC (Fourth House cusp, naturally ruling the home).

But why plumbing, in particular? Well plumbing is a very Mercurial, connecting energy, and water and waste are Neptune and Pluto. Let's see how those connections factor in.

First and foremost, Mercury is at 19 Cancer, Stationary Direct, sextile the Moon, inconjunct BH 19 Sagittarius and exactly opposed BH 19 Capricorn. The former, by the way, lies in my Second House of finances. 'Nuff said? Well, in case you're still wondering, yes, the plumbing problems have caused adjustments (the inconjunct) to my bank account.

Both the Moon and Mercury aspect Neptune at 6 Scorpio, the Moon by semisquare (45 degrees) +2 and Mercury by tredecile (108 degrees) -1. The tredecile, by the way, is a "purification" aspect. Nice touch.

That Neptune is astride the midpoint of a galactic pair consisting of a Quasar at 5 Scorpio and a Black Hole at 7 Scorpio, which is roughly semisquare to BH 19 Sag.

Neptune is also sextile Pluto at 4 Virgo, which is conjoined a Pulsar at 3 and the Black Hole at 6/7 Virgo, and is exactly semisquare Mercury.

And there isn't a tight faucet on the premises. New fittings, completely new hardware, sealants, nothing lasts for more than a few months. Now, you might be hard-pressed to predict in advance that this plumbing thing would manifest from the astrological linkages above, but in hindsight, it all makes sense. Once you know what you're manifesting from a particular archetypal pattern, you can reflect on other ways that energy might resolve itself, and take steps to consciously create that.

Another personal example. I spent half the month of February 1993 getting really stressed out by my sudden tendency to spill water on or near electrical outlets, until I sat a moment and reflected that this was just a manifestation of the contemporaneous Uranus (electricity)/Neptune (water) conjunction astride the Black Hole at

19 Capricorn, which had just opposed my hands-ruling Mercury. I did a short meditation to send that energy towards the creation of a nice, safe, clean hydro-electric plant somewhere, and my hand stopped slipping.

Obviously not every pattern will be dealt with as easily (and typing was certain hell under this transit—in true Neptunian fashion allmywordsrantogether and I had a plethora of unezxpected Uranian typos—so I still had more to learn from that transit, obviously), but you can't hope to deal with something until you have identified what it is. The ancient metaphysical doctrine that to know a thing's name gave you power over it is certainly true to at least this extent, that without identification of the problem we cannot hope for a rational or lasting solution.

It may seem we have gotten a bit off the beam of our topic, but to understand the structure of a Black Hole in the birth chart, we need to see how they operate.

Astrophysically, Black Holes are composed of three theoretical parts: first, the "event horizon," which is the boundary of space within which all matter is inexorably absorbed by the Black Hole's gravitational field, and which corresponds astrologically to the five degree orb of influence on either side of the Black Hole; second, the "singularity," which is the actual center of the Black Hole itself and from which, hypothetically, a quantum of energy could escape and re-emerge into this universe (this corresponds astrologically to the actual degree at which the anomaly appears); and lastly, the most theoretical part, the "wormhole," a spacetime loop or bridge which disgorges the absorbed matter via a connected Quasar (sometimes also known as a "white hole"), either into another, parallel universe, or into a far distant corner of this one. Physicists currently debate as to whether wormholes are "stable" or "unstable," which, for theoretical purposes, would determine such things as whether they could be negotiated by space craft in the future (perhaps the modern scientific equivalent of the medieval theological conundrum, "how many angels can dance on the head of a pin?").

Astrologically, wormholes correspond to the exact aspects the Black Hole makes, both to other galactics and to the planetary positions of the nativity, these being the peripheral points from which the energy absorbed by the Black Hole might be expelled into the psyche. Aspects to natal points could be considered "stable" worm-holes, since they are ever-present; aspects activated by transiting or progressed planets might be considered "unstable," since their effects are transitory.

Basic principles of physics tell us that energy is never destroyed; it is simply converted from one form to another. The life energies absorbed by the active Black Holes in your chart can be deflected via aspect to another individual either in a general sense, or more specifically via synastric contacts.

One couple with whom I am acquainted have an exact Sun/Venus conjunction in early Leo. This conjunction is within the event horizon of the Black Hole at 2/3 Leo, and falls in the Second House of the Sun person, Ninth House of the Venus individual. The Second House Sun has always encouraged his partner to pursue a career in art, eventually paying for the education. Quite a role reversal for this individual, who, with a Second House Sun conjoined a Black Hole, is used to sudden and dramatic inflows of money attracted by the Black Hole, which in this case found its syphon in his partner's Venusian art degree.

British physicist Stephen Hawking, a pioneer in Black Hole research, has quoted Dante's "Inferno" in reference to the Deep Space anomaly: "Abandon all hope, ye who enter here." In a meta-physical sense, it might be better to amend that to "abandon all expectation," for the native with natal or progressed placements here.

By progression, especially, there is a sense of the world turned upside down (the native is used to dealing with this energy from birth and has usually learned to in some sense cope with it). There can be a sort of psychic implosion and explosion as the progressed planet makes its way into and out of the singularity.

On the trip in, the individual may become more and more intro-verted, caught in the inner turmoil of the thoughts and feelings as they implode inward, then, once the pit of the singularity has been reached, there is a gradual explosion as the individual makes his way up and out of the anomaly, a return to the Light World he or she is familiar with. This occurs almost instantaneously from the chronologic perspective of the Black Hole, but from our merely human standpoint, the journey can involve over ten years by progression for a personal planet, even longer for an outer planet or if a retrograde is involved.

Hawking unwittingly contributes a warning to the native who is unconscious of his or her Black Hole contacts, and an intriguing speculation concerning a Black Hole's orb of effectiveness as it ages. In *A Brief History of Time*, Hawking contends that "the area of the event horizon must always increase with time. [This is] reminiscent of entropy, which measures the degree of disorder of a system, which tends to increase with time if left to itself. [This] increase of disorder...is what distinguishes the past from the future, [thus] giving a direction to time."

With regard to the effect this postulation has upon orbs of effectiveness, it is unclear at this time whether Black Holes would begin with an event horizon of perhaps only a degree, building to a maximum of five degrees, or whether in fact the five degree orb might need to be increased as the native matures and becomes more conscious. But clearly, a Black Hole left to its own devices and allowed to function without any attempt to control or direct its power, is a dangerous thing, tending toward increasing disorder and random manifestation as it becomes more and more entrenched in the psyche.

How to deal with a Black Hole? There is another metaphysical dictum that may prove useful here: the more we reach out to the divine, the more the divine reaches out to us. Or, if you prefer the laws of Newtonian physics, to every action there is an equal and opposite reaction.

Working with a Black Hole, in the sense of meditating on that point and its effects in your life, or sending it a token of energy via affirmations of release (such as releasing unwanted fears, negative emotions, or "bad" habits) may prove an effective way to cultivate a relationship with this most challenging of the cosmic quartet. Once on speaking terms, don't forget that a Black Hole's connection to a parallel universe has the potential of making it almost a cosmic Aladdin's lamp: rub it the right way and the genie you release could grant you your three wishes.

But, as always, be careful what you wish for—you just might get it.

# METAPHORIC ANATOMY
# OF A BLACK HOLE

*"Everything that exists is in a manner the seed of that which will be."*

–Marcus Aurelius

What does a Black Hole represent, metaphorically?

The basic essence of a Black Hole is change, especially sudden, dramatic reversals of the status quo reality. Black Holes function astrologically as indicators of a fundamental shift in progress; what has gone before is no more, and bears little, if any, resemblance to what must now come. In the human condition these indicators often reflect "negative" situations, such as the difference before and after an accident or serious illness, or the change in status from married to divorced or widowed. However, Black Hole changes can also be things commonly viewed as "positive," such as the shift from modest means to wealth by winning a lottery, or a status change from single to married, or becoming suddenly a parent with the birth of a child.

Black Holes are metaphoric of major life passages, wherein one steps across the threshold of one reality into another, as in the passage from childhood to maturity, from adulthood to old age. Both birth and death are decidedly Black Hole moments in our life cycle, but so are cultural turning points such as starting kindergarten, leaving home for college, entering the work force, getting a first apartment, losing one's virginity, the onset of menopause, or the loss of a parent. Essentially, any major life passage can be seen as a Black Hole metaphor, passing from one state of being or awareness to another.

Black Holes are also indicators of the accretion of knowledge and the changes in one's consciousness and perspective which this induces. When we as a species stopped believing the Sun revolved around the Earth, we completed a Black Hole transformation in consciousness; when we as children stopped believing in Santa Claus and the Tooth Fairy, we did the same, passing from a world of relative simplicity and fantasy into one more harshly real.

The Black Hole, further, acts as a metaphor for where we feel trapped, dis-empowered, carried along by events outside our conscious ken or beyond our immediate control. In this same metaphoric zone we find them functioning as emblems of the loss of energy, or the wear and tear of life on our biologic systems, an entropic image of the disintegration of the life force through time.

Finally, Black Holes stand unrivaled as a metaphor for the alienation we experience in modern society. Cut off from our fellows, misunderstood, feeling like we are unable to communicate with others, we often seem trapped beyond the Black Hole's event horizon, still visible, perhaps, to our fellow man, but unable to receive assistance, aid or comfort as we spiral irrevocably towards the pit of the singularity.

Black Holes, then, are metaphoric primarily of these commonly encountered human phenomenon: volte face, that is, sudden, dramatic and usually unexpected reversals; the completion of major life passages of a cyclic and unavoidable nature; changes in consciousness resulting from increased knowledge or experience; the loss of control or energy; and the experience of alienation. As such, Black Holes function as powerful metaphors for vital and compelling aspects of the human condition.

# MYTHIC ANATOMY OF A BLACK HOLE

*"No problem can be solved from the same consciousness that created it."*

–Albert Einstein

Perhaps the simplest metaphor for the core of Black Hole mythology is the tale of Orpheus and Eurydice.

Orpheus is that worthy minstrel renowned for his use of the lyre; not only could he move rocks and trees with it, he even melted the heart of the stern god Hades/Pluto. As such he is already a good image for Black Hole functioning, which is to alter existing realities and conditions.

When we add in the tale of Eurydice, we can begin to see a primary metaphor for dealing with the resulting transformation.

Eurydice was Orpheus' wife, but Orpheus was out a lot, a wandering minstrel's life being what it is, and one day while walking alone Eurydice was molested by Apollo's half-mortal son Aristaeus, who attempted to rape her. As she flees his embraces, the hapless Eurydice treads on a serpent and expires of its poisonous bite.

Well, needless to say, Orpheus is desolate; he resolved to go to Hades and win her back. Normally entrance into the Dark Lord's realm isn't all that easy for the living, but Orpheus so charmed Charon, the ferryman over the River Styx, that he gave him free passage without a word of challenge. On the further shore his music lulled fierce three-headed Cerberus, the Guard Dog of Hades, and thus he passed without hindrance into Pluto's realm. Pluto, moved by his song and perhaps considering his own wayward behavior in the rape of Kore/Persephone, in a very rare act of grace allowed Orpheus his boon: he could return with Eurydice to the surface, but on one condition—during his passage out of the Underworld Orpheus must never once look back to reassure himself that his bride followed.

Well, you guessed it. Have you ever known an artist with restraint? Just as he is nearing the attainment of his goal, Orpheus turns at the entrance to the Light World and sees Eurydice, who had been behind him as promised, fade away into the blackness of the pit.

The image of descent and return is especially important when choosing a myth to depict Black Hole functioning. The twin-funnel-shaped, crossed X diagram which astrophysicists use to represent a Black Hole is particularly striking in this regard, for, with just a bit of imagination, it is easily converted into a stairway to the Underworld.

In the case of contact by progression with a Black Hole, there is a very real sense of the layers being stripped away, perhaps not easily, more like a whirlwind bound for the Black Hole's singularity has forcibly wrenched something from your control, carrying it howling into the pit. As such we have a perfect metaphor for this sense of loss in the image from ancient Mesopotamian myth of Inanna and Ereshkigal.

Ereshkigal was the Mesopotamian Queen of the Underworld, wife of Nergal, God of the Dead, and sister to Inanna, Queen of Heaven. No description of Ereshkigal would be complete without reference to her sister Inanna. The pair are reverse and obverse of the same coin; in fact, they were probably originally two aspects of the same goddess, and they well depict the starkly opposite nature of Black Hole manifestations, tending to extremes of circumstance and sudden, dramatic reversals.

Ereshkigal and Inanna, though sisters (i.e., in a metaphoric sense, the two halves of consciousness which arise from the same source, Ereshkigal the dark and brooding subconscious, and Inanna the bright light of reason and intelligence), are not exactly close. But when Ereshkigal's husband dies, Inanna feels it is only fitting she make the perilous journey to the Underworld to comfort her sister.

She knows the way to the Place Beneath is fraught with dangers, so, while leaving her husband Tammuz in charge of her estate (Tammuz can be seen as the egoic projection of the persona which creates a "place marker" for consciousness within the individual), she takes the further precaution of informing her father of her plans, and commands her majordomo to appeal to him in the event she does not return and her husband seems less than anxious to rescue her.

Inanna, being fully conscious, is a great judge of character.

Upon Inanna's seeking entrance to the Underworld, Ereshkigal is informed of her sister's request to pay her respects. In the bitterness at her loss, Ereshkigal charges that her sister shall be treated "according to the ancient laws" of her domain, and a painful stripping of identity ensues for Inanna, who at each of seven portals along the descent must endure the removal of one after the other of her *accoutrements* of power and position.

At each sacrifice the Queen of Heaven importunes her guide: "What, pray, is this?"

Each time the answer comes: "Be silent, Inanna, the ordinances of the nether world are perfect. O Inanna, do not question the rites of the nether world."

Only through surrender and acceptance of the processes of transformation can the subconscious be appeased, but for Inanna, though she submits with head bowed, there is no reprieve. When she finally gains The Presence, naked, beaten and bowed low, Ereshkigal casts the eye of death upon her, and Inanna is left on a meat hook to rot.

Meanwhile Tammuz is having quite the time back in Inanna's palace, lording it over the place and thoroughly enjoying his freedom. He remains deaf to the majordomo's pleas, until at last the worthy fellow appeals to the two Queens' father.

Enki considers for a bit, and then, taking the dirt from beneath his fingernails, he fashions two beings, the perfect empaths, and sends them to plea for the return of Inanna's life.

Ereshkigal is in labor when they arrive, and the two so ingratiate themselves to her with their patient sympathy and understanding in her hour of travail that she grants them a boon, whereupon they ask for Inanna's restitution and return.

Ereshkigal is happy to oblige, but there is one problem. Apparently, the books have to be kept very closely in the nether world, and the soul count is not allowed to drop by so much as a single soul once accrued.

You guessed it. Returned to life and the Light World, Inanna promptly despatches the faithless Tammuz and sends him to Ereshkigal in her place.

The image of the conscious mind being ultimately at the mercy of the subconscious is an apt one for the human condition. When Inanna appears at the gates to Ereshkigal's domain, she announces herself as "Inanna, of the place where the Sun rises." To which the porter replies: "Why have you come to the place of no return?" The light of consciousness is rarely cast upon the depths of the subconscious; when it is, the shadows often conceal more than is revealed.

And yet creativity springs from those dark, unexplored corners, from the electrically-charged spaces between the ego's psychoatomic nucleus of the thoughts we think and the swirling electron cloud of the feelings we feel.

Predating Inanna and Ereshkigal, but also originating in the Mesopotamian basin, is the creation story involving Apsu and Tiamat, two primordial deities with strong Black Hole affinities relating to chaos and disorder, often a primary manifestation of Black Hole energies. Apsu was the Babylonian lord of the Abyss, the waters which surround and hold up the earth. Originally a female deity, she later changed her sex and divided her watery domain with Tiamat, Goddess of Chaos, who became in some sense his/her consort . Tiamat dwelt in and with Apsu, the primal Abyss, and was envisioned as a great dragoness of immense proportions, jealous guardian of the principles of Life and Order which ensue from the Chaos which is her very being. Tiamat assumed control of Apsu's bitter waters of the sea, reserving the sweet waters for the older god. Ea, Babylonian god of Water, performed various incantations to keep Apsu's tremendous power in check, but he nevertheless broke through the earth in places in the form of springs and streams, lakes and rivers.

From time uncounted Tiamat and Apsu remained alone together, at peace and undisturbed, until Tiamat in a burst of parthenogenic splendor gave birth to the gods of ancient Mesopotamia, beings of Light. Apsu became irritated by the noise and clamor of these recent additions to the Universe, and, upon complaining to their mother Tiamat, persuaded her to discipline them by creating a horde of beings of Darkness, scorpions, serpents, dragons, sphinxes, and all manner of compound species such as goatfish and centaurs, a sort of coterie of Night Nannies to ride roughshod over the willful gods.

Taken aback by the size of the army sent against them, the gods chose from their number Marduk to be their champion. Marduk used magic to call the winds to him, and with their power routed his mother's hordes, after which Marduk slew Tiamat herself, and created Heaven and Earth from the twin halves of her sundered form. Tiamat's end came thus: trapped in a vortex of hurricane winds, Tiamat opened her great and immense jaws to swallow Marduk, who hurled a tornado into her mouth instead; the force of the blast kept her mouth open long enough for Marduk to send an arrow straight down her gullet into her heart, and she expired. This pair's connections to the abyss of nothingness, the chaos before creation, and the creative power to birth a new reality all speak to dominant Black Hole themes.

Other myths which revolve around an Orphean-like descent and return provide appropriate Black Hole metaphors, such as the Greek tales of Kore/Persephone, who divides her time between husband Hades in the Underworld and mother Demeter on Earth. As her Maiden aspect Kore, this goddess was the youthful and innocent daughter of Demeter, mistress of the harvest. Her uncle Hades (who as ruler of the Underworld is himself an apt Black Hole mythic character) saw her walking in the fields and determined to have her. He approached Zeus, Kore's father and his own brother, with an offer of marriage, but the King of the Gods, knowing Demeter's fanatical attachment to her daughter, refused the match.

Not to be outdone, Hades resolved upon deceit. He caused a beautiful and exotic flower to grow in a meadow which Kore frequented. One day, while strolling in the sweet grasses, Kore came upon the blossom, and entranced by its beauty, stooped to pick it. The earth opened before her feet and Hades appeared from the chasm in a great gold coach drawn by coal black horses (remember Hades is the god of wealth as well as death) and carried her off screaming to the Underworld.

Demeter was disconsolate when she found her daughter missing. While she roamed the earth searching for her lost child the crops in the fields withered and died and cold winter descended upon the land. She questioned the gods closely, but could find no one with any information until she stumbled upon Hekate (who is actually the third aspect in this trilogy of goddesses, Maiden, Mother, Crone, and as a chthonic figure associated with the dead is yet another Black Hole representative), who had herself been out walking that day, and had heard Kore's cries of "A rape! A rape!" She had hurried to her rescue, but found no sight of her. Together they resolved to visit the Sun, who sees all things.

Sure enough, Helios the Sun God had indeed seen the abduction, and a tearful and protesting Demeter approached Zeus for justice. Zeus is noted often, not so much for his decisiveness, as his vacillation and inability to avoid complexities involving females. Presented with the rival claims of his brother and sister for "possession" of his niece, Zeus found himself on the horns of a dilemma. At last the ruling came down—Kore would return to the Light World and her Mother, but only if she had not eaten any of the food of the dead.

At first all seemed well, for Kore, in her fright and rage at the abduction, had remained sullen and refused to eat so much as a bite of the choice morsels that were set before her. However, just as the cortege was setting out to return Kore to Olympus, one of Hades' gardener's, Askalaphus, revealed that he had seen the maiden walking in the gardens, pluck a pomegranate from a tree, and eat seven seeds. Exultant, Hades refused to release his bride, but the earth by now had become barren and lifeless, so Zeus, in desperation to save his human worshipers (for what use is a god without anyone to make him sacrifices?), arranged a compromise. Kore would spend six months of the year with her husband Hades in the Underworld, with the title of Persephone (literally, "bringer of destruction"), and the remaining six months of the year with her mother Demeter on earth. Demeter was forced to accept this settlement, but she turned Askalaphus into an owl for his talebearing.

It is as Persephone, Queen of the Underworld, that the maiden Kore reaches her full potential, an apt image of the transformative powers of the Black Hole. Significantly, it is not until the forced separation from her mother, who kept her in a childlike state, that she really comes into her own. Persephone figures in many myths, where she can often be seen in the company of that other underworld goddess, Hekate. At one point she was admitted to the Olympian Pantheon, a specially elevated panel of a dozen gods who held precedence over the others. Her tale was told to explain the seasons to the common people, but the true meaning of the myth was reserved for the initiates of her mystery school, established by Demeter at Eleusis. The so-called Eleusinian Mysteries were held twice yearly, the Greater at the Autumnal Equinox, and the Lesser at Imbolc in early February, to commemorate Persephone's departure for the Underworld and her return in spring, and although the specifics are lost in the mists of time, their themes revolved about death and rebirth, Black Hole metaphors *par excellance*.

There is an echo of her own life journey in the tale of her rivalry with Aphrodite for Adonis, who similarly must split his year between them, and Adonis' story is another which resonates strongly to Black Hole energies. Adonis is a product of incest wrought by the wrath of a goddess. The queen of Cyprus once made so bold as to compare her daughter's beauty to that of the Goddess of Love herself, and Aphrodite was so angered by this insult that she caused the girl to fall in love with her own father, whom she seduced one night when he was in his cups. When he realized what had happened, King Cinyras came at his daughter with a sword; Aphrodite attempted to avert the disaster by changing Smyrna into a myrrh tree, but the sword coming down cleaved her in two, and out of the trunk fell Adonis.

Aphrodite was sorrowed by this turn of events, and also decidedly enamored of the infant Adonis' looks, so she took him into her protection, concealing him in a chest which she entrusted to Persephone in the Underworld.

Apparently, things get pretty dull down there, for before too long Persephone was hunting about for things to do when she spied the chest, and opening it, rescued the now adolescent Adonis. She brought him up in Hades, and eventually made him her lover, before word of the liaison reached Aphrodite, who came to Persephone's palace in Tartarus to reclaim the youth.

Persephone refused to release him, and the dispute was referred to Father Zeus, who was not about to render judgment in so dainty a case. He told the muse Calliope to rule, and she devised a tri-partite splitting of Adonis' year: one third of the time he would remain with Persephone in Hades as her lover, one third would be spent satisfying Aphrodite on Olympus, and the final third was his own, presumably to get some rest.

All might have gone well but for Aphrodite's inability to take "no" for an answer; she wore her magick girdle constantly, which made her irresistible, so that the hapless Adonis not only gave her his third of the year, but refused to leave for Persephone's realm when the time came.

Aphrodite may have been charming, but Persephone had the greater cunning of the two; she went to Ares, Aphrodite's old flame and the father of her children, and so worked upon his jealousy that in a fit of rage he sent a wild boar after Adonis, who was gored and killed before Aphrodite's eyes, his soul descending to Tartarus and Persephone.

Aphrodite fled in tears to Zeus, and begged him to allow the shade of Adonis to return to her for the summer months, to which the Father of the Gods agreed, and Adonis has cycled back and forth between the two rival goddesses ever since.

The image of Adonis pulled this way and that by two of the Olympian pantheon mirrors the gravitational pull of the Black Hole upon the native's psyche, as it tugs and tears in a myriad directions at once.

A classic myth which resonates to the Black Hole's power to captivate us and transport us to other realities or alternate states of being is the tale of Dionysos, Greek god of spiritual transformation, resurrection and ecstatic communion with the universe, a vegetative god honored in the traditions of wine and the harvest. Libations of the fermented juice of the grape were poured on Dionysos' altars, then sopped up in bread and eaten by the celebrants. In this ritual the God himself was deemed to be physically present in these tokens of the bread and wine, an early image of the Christian Mass. Dionysos also has several resurrection myths surrounding his character; before birth his mother was destroyed when Hera tricked her into forcing her lover Zeus (Hera's philandering husband) to reveal himself to her in all his glory. Zeus took the fetus of Dionysos from the charred ashes that were all that remained of Semele and sewed him within his own thigh, from which he was born several months later (hence the young god's appellation, "Twice-Born"). Hera's anger was unappeased, and she caused the child to be flayed alive, after which he was resurrected in a magic cauldron by his grandmother Rhea, Mother of the Gods.

The cult of Dionysos revolves around freedom, role reversal, and ecstatic connection to the life force. Role reversal in particular has ties to Black Hole functioning, but so does Dionysos' connection with the transformations which occur within the wine casket, which mirror the spiritual "ageing" brought on by maturity. Dionysos' followers, the Maenads, wild women of Greek society who cast off their roles with their robes and wandered for periods of time in the wilderness, were given to periodic overindulgence followed by excursions into the wildwood complete with frenzied dancing, ecstatic trance, and occasional bloodletting of any wild beasts encountered. This was not a religion for the squeamish, but the total immersion of Dionysos' followers into the emotion of the moment well portrays the Black Hole's capacity for focus, separation from everyday reality, and self-abandonment.

Another Greek myth with Black Hole connotations is that of Nemesis, perhaps the most fittingly named, considering the connotation the term has acquired over centuries of use. Originally the word meant something more like "due enactment," according to Robert Graves in *The Greek Myths*, but through the years it has come to signify the concept of divine vengeance with which we are more familiar, and thus of sudden reversal which typifies Black Hole action.

Nemesis' ancestry is an impeccable one for a Black Hole mythic figure. According to the cosmology of the ancient Greeks, first there was Darkness, which gave birth to Chaos. Chaos in turn birthed Night, Day, Air, and Erebus, which means "the covered pit" (singularity?). It was Night and Erebus who conceived Nemesis and her sisters, the Three Fates.

Nemesis' history is a chequered one. Originally depicted as a local pastoral goddess, the spirit of the rain-bringing ash tree, Nemesis became identified with the nymph goddess of Death-in-Life, doubtless due to the ash tree's connections with mourning.

Eventually Nemesis developed into the rather vengeful creature we are familiar with today. In part this was devised so that she could become a moral control on Tyche. Tyche (literally "fortune") was a daughter of Zeus to whom he had entrusted the fortunes of mortal men. The only problem with Tyche was that she was the original Air-head; she couldn't decide the thing on merits, so she simply juggled everyone's fortunes and let the chips fall where they may.

Nemesis' role was to step in and exact punishment when some favored mortal had boasted of his good fortune without giving due thanks, and properly giving of his largesse to the coffers of public charity. At this point it was Nemesis' task to intervene and humiliate the offender, sometimes depriving him of all he had to make her point.

Nemesis was portrayed carrying an apple bough and a Sun Wheel, emblem of the turning year, crowned with silver stag horns, and with a scourge hanging from her girdle. She had a large part to play in the early death dramas enacted by the sacrificial kings when, at the midpoint of their seasonal cycle, the Summer Solstice, they were fated to die, only to return to supplant their rivals at their Winter Solstice rebirth. This connection with the Black Hole themes of destruction and renewal assigns her a role in the pantheon of divinities associated with these deep space anomalies

From Asia Minor the story of the dying and resurrected god Attis fits the Black Hole profile also. Mythically Attis is closely aligned with Kybele, his Mother and the Great Goddess whose Anatolian homeland birthed their story. According to one popular version of their myth, Kybele became so enamored of her beautiful son that she begged him never to marry, and to remain faithful to her forever. In utter loyalty and devotion, Attis castrated himself, and expired beneath a pine tree, which has since become sacred to him. Kybele decreed that he would forever be reborn, only to die once more and continue the cycle for eternity. Worshiped by the Phrygians as a vegetation god, Attis' cult grew in popularity, with its eunuch priesthood of temple prostitutes, and it heavily influenced early Christian doctrinal decisions coming out of Asia Minor. In fact, the Council of Ephesus, which finally decided to officially designate the Virgin Mary as "Mother of God," was held within a stone's throw of one of Attis' principal temples, and his followers were among the ecstatic throngs which greeted this pronouncement with fevered excitement. The Great Mother had been reborn in the new cult.

In some bizarre twist of custom and fate, even the tradition among his followers of carrying a decorated pine tree in procession for Attis became translated, centuries after the Christian decimation of their pagan rivals, into the practice of trimming a fir tree at Christmas. The wheel comes round full circle.

Attis' sacrifice reminds us of the ways in which we cut ourselves off from our (pro-)creative source. At times detachment is necessary to bring forth the creative impulses which struggle to erupt from within us. Attis' continuing message is to allow that detachment to come, and more—to embrace it willingly.

Attis teaches us the importance of complete detachment and self-sacrifice, two themes which Black Hole natives are often forced to grapple. Only through dis-identification with the physical vehicle the Self has chosen can we hope to surmount our difficulties on this material plane and progress to a level of spiritual maturity. The emphasis on destruction and rebirth in this myth conforms to these same Black Hole archetypal energies, where natives with strong Black Hole contacts are continually forced to re-image and "rebirth" themselves, creating a new persona from the ashes of the old.

Of course one of the earliest and most emphatic of these myths which resonates with Black Hole energies involves Osiris and Isis, which contains two separate deaths and resurrections by the God of the Dead. Osiris, Isis and their son Horus formed the primary Trinity of ancient Egypt's pantheon, a basic model of Father, Mother and Divine Child archetypes later made popular in the Christian God, Mary and Jesus.

Osiris and Isis were brother and sister as well as husband and wife, and were, like that other sibling union of Set and Nephythys, all children of Geb and Nut, primal Egyptian Earth Father and Sky Mother. Just as the Greek Pantheon developed from Grandfather Ouranos to father Cronos and son Zeus, so in Egypt the succession proceeded from Geb to Osiris to his son Horus.

It was during the rule of Osiris that the royal pair civilized their human subjects, Osiris teaching the arts of baking grain into bread, transforming grapes into wine, and music, as well as codifying laws and setting up religious rituals; while Isis conveyed the arts of spinning and weaving and curing disease, and introduced the custom of marriage. At last when Egypt had been civilized, Osiris grew restless and took his act on the road, so to speak, accompanied in his journeys by Thoth and Anubis, his jackal-headed son by an adulterous (and incestuous) fling with sister/sister-in-law Nephythys.

In his absence Isis governed Egypt as his regent, and Set, who had become increasingly jealous of his brother's success and popularity, plotted his demise. Upon Osiris' triumphal return, Set hosted a huge banquet in his honor. At one point during the evening, Set caused a beautiful sarcophagus to be brought into the banquet hall, and declared that whoever fit the coffin perfectly could have it. Of course, the piece had been made to Osiris' exact measurements, and when the god stepped into the box, Set clapped the lid shut immediately and the sarcophagus was tightly sealed with molten lead. Trapped, Osiris in his box was thrown into the Nile and drifted out to sea, eventually to wash ashore in Phoenicia, where a magical tamarisk tree by the seaside grew to encompass the sarcophagus completely.

When the local king heard of the size of this wondrous tree, and the sweet smells it exuded, he had it cut for the main pillar of his hall, never knowing that Osiris in his sarcophagus lay concealed within it.

Meanwhile Isis, in mourning in Egypt, heard of this wonder; she immediately knew what it was, and traveled incognito to the court of the Phoenician king, where she took service as a nursemaid for his children. To one she became particularly attached, and spent the nights burning off his mortality in the dying embers of the fire, while she, in the form of a luminous white dove, sang mournful songs as she flitted about the column containing her dead husband. One night the queen of Phoenicia happened upon this scene and was understandably disturbed. Isis revealed herself to the king, who listened to her story, gave her the column with Osiris inside, and sent her back to Egypt, where Isis hid in the Nile swamps while she tried to revive the dead god. Changing into the form of a hawk, Isis rested upon Osiris and warmed him enough to conceive a child, the hawk-headed solar deity Horus.

At this juncture Set came upon the body of Osiris while he was out hunting in the swamp. Enraged, he tore the body into fourteen parts and threw them in the Nile. Isis began yet another journey to retrieve the sundered bits of Osiris, but she succeeded in collecting only thirteen; the fourteenth part, the phallus, was never found. Her sister Nephythys, Set's wife, was so disgusted by his behavior that she left him, and helped Isis to embalm Osiris and revive him to eternal life, this time as the Lord of the Dead, supreme judge of men's souls. Osiris retired to the Underworld, while Nephythys and Isis changed themselves into kites, fierce birds of prey, to mourn him (which is why they are depicted with winged arms), and later became protectresses of the dead. Green-skinned Osiris is shown as a mummy with human head, wearing the tall white cap of Upper Egypt, the royal flail and hook in his crossed arms.

Horus, protected from Set by Isis' magical arts, was raised in the swamp regions of Lower Egypt until he grew old enough to challenge his uncle for the kingship. The battles for revenge of Osiris' murder were numerous and long, as well as inconclusive. At last judgement was rendered in favor of Horus by Neith, an ancient war goddess who predated the dynastic struggle and whom the younger generation of deities turned to for advice when accommodation was impossible. Horus ascended to the throne of Upper and Lower Egypt, uniting the two lands; all subsequent Pharaohs claimed descent from him, calling themselves "the living Horus." Osiris' several "remakings" and resurrections typify the Black Hole's power to redirect and realign the psyche, often in dramatically differing ways from what had pertained previously.

From the north of old Europe comes the myth of Hel, another Black Hole deity, the Norse Goddess of Death and the Underworld, and the root word of the English "hell." One of three demoniacal children of the god Loki, himself God of Mischief, Hel ruled Niflheim, the land of mists, with an iron fist. One of several Norse afterworlds, Hel was in particular charge of those who had died of old age or disease, reserving for them especially unpleasant eternities in respect of the fact that they had expired so dishonorably (the warlike Norse reserved space for heros in battle at Valhalla, the preferred destination of Norse souls). Hel's siblings included Midgardsormen, a huge globe-encircling serpent, the Norse version of the tail-biting Ouroboros, and Fenrisulven, a huge and rapacious wolf whom the gods tried to keep chained, to little avail (he was such a kindly creature that only Tyr, the Norse Mars, dared to feed him, and Fenrisulven showed his gratitude by biting off Tyr's arm).

Odin, King of the Gods, consigned Hel to hell and gave her power over nine worlds; she became immensely wealthy, with great tracts of land surrounded by high fences and a high, strong gate (Norse "Helgrind"). Much like Nemesis, who appears with telltale ornamentation, Hel can be discerned by reference to the accouterments she carries. Her knife is Hunger (Norse "Sult") and her plate is Starvation (Norse "Hunger"). The threshold of her home has been translated as Pitfall (Norse "Faldenefare"); her resting place is called Sickbed (Norse "Kor") and the curtain surrounding it is "Awkard Disaster.

And the Lady herself? Her color is blue-black, alternating with pale flesh, like a rotting corpse, which adds to her recognition factor. Like Sumerian Underworld Goddess Ereshkigal, she does not have a pleasant aspect, appearing rather grumpy, rough and rude.

Hel appears in the background of many Norse myths, but there was at least one occasion on which she took center stage, defying the all-powerful Odin himself. The god Balder, son of Odin and Frigg, had been rendered immortal by his mother's clever demand that every living being swear an oath never to harm him. There was one plant, however, which Frigg had not forced the oath upon, namely mistletoe, which she felt was too young to understand.

Enter Loki, the mischievous Trickster. The gods had great fun with Balder, bouncing spears, axes and knives off his invincible hide, until one day Loki (who you will remember was also Hel's father) gave a great spike of mistletoe to the blind god Hoder, and guided his hand; the projectile killed Balder, who, having died dishonorably at play, ended up in Hel's realm. Odin sent his other son, Balder's brother Hermod, to plead for his return. Hel was at first defiant, agreeing at last that Balder should be released upon one condition—that every being on Earth, and the Earth herself, should cry and mourn for Balder, thus assuring Hel that he really was missed.

And so every being did cry—gods, men, rocks, trees, birds and animals, even the Earth herself, all except one old woman (really Loki in disguise) who refused to shed a tear, and therefore, Balder remains Hel's most famous tenant to this day. This myth depicts the insatiable greed of the Black Hole, which is loathe to relinquish that which it has once subsumed.

Celtic myth and legend also provides us Black Hole candidates. Cernunnos was the Horned One of the Celts, a god of death and rebirth, dwelling in the shadows of the forests long before the Roman legions came to "civilize" Gaul. Often depicted as a tall, dark man with stag's horns amid a shock of wild hair, Cernunnos is actually an older, more mature facet of the Green Man, the Lover of the Goddess in the spring, who with her ensures the renewed fertility of the land.

A popular icon of the God shows his duties as Lord of Beasts, ruler of the cold winter season when the Celtic tribes survived by hunting, as opposed to the summer, the Lady's domain as Mistress of the Harvest, when the fruits of the land were theirs to enjoy. Cernunnos the Horned One reclaims his hegemony over the land from the Lady at Samhain (our modern Halloween), the old Celtic New Year, about the time when the Blood Moon signals the slaughter of domestic animals in preparation for the harsh season to come. He will be her steward of the Earth until her return in the spring, when he is again her lover. This cyclic death and renewal aspect is common to Black Hole functioning, where natives commonly adapt and renew themselves on a regular basis, each time adopting another facet of their personas.

Later Celtic tradition includes the story of Merlin, that reverend sage and mage of Arthurian legend, an archetype of pagan knowing which erupts into the Christianized saga like a breath of fresh air or a spring bubbling up in a cavern. Although there most probably was an Arthur, though not exactly of the Camelot variety, Merlin's origin in fact is markedly less certain, making him a semi-mythic character who straddles the doorway between historical fact and fable. Such guardianship makes Merlin, who according to legend has not died but remains immured in walls of crystal until he returns once more with Arthur at the End of the World, a perfect mediator between our own and alternate realities, and thus a typical Black Hole interlocutor.

From Hindu tradition come myths of their divine female trinity of Durga, Parvati and Kali, who roughly approximate pagan European triune goddess aspects. Since Black Holes govern the transformative maturation processes which evolve one goddess form from another, these aspects of divinity also act as appropriate mythic markers of Black Hole energies. Durga, the warrior goddess, is equivalent to the Maiden aspect, while Parvati is the benign Mother aspect of Shiva's triune goddess-wife, and Kali, the death goddess, equates to the Crone aspect.

Durga, whose appellation is "the Inaccessible," is the first of the Hindu Goddess Triad, the warrior maiden, eventual mother of Ganesha. In one of her aspects she is depicted with sharp, vampire-like teeth and a hat wreathed in flames; in her four arms she carries the trident, sword, drum and bowl of blood. Inaccessible, indeed.

But Durga has her protective side, and if you are in her good graces, she is an ally to be grateful for. She is a radiant goddess, her appearance blindingly bright, her brilliant clothes emanating powerful rays, all of which has affinities with the super-heated, glowing accretion disk of infalling matter which accompanies active Black Holes. Often shown mounted on a lion to depict her incredible strength and valor, Durga is a powerful patroness and one of the most popular goddesses in India, her cult celebrated annually in the four-day-long Durga Puja, the largest festival in the Bengal region.

Mythically, Parvati was the daughter of King Himalaya, and her beauty reflected that of the pristine landscape which gave her birth. Although she was the mother aspect of Shiva's consort, most of her children were fosterlings. The story of one of these, Karttikeya, bears an eerie resemblance to the crushing supergravity of the Black Hole. Once Shiva turned his fiery Third Eye on a clear mountain lake; the result was six divine children, created from the waters, which he gave to Parvati to rear. Parvati's loving embrace was perhaps too much of a good thing, for when she had clutched them to her bosom she looked again, and found that she had squeezed the six tiny bodies into one, though all six heads remained—such is Karttikeya. This sense of all things coming together to form a new creation, whether positive or negative, is one with which many Black Hole natives have to learn to cope.

Kali is the final aspect of the Hindu Triune Goddess; all three are the brides of Shiva, Lord of the Dance of Creation and Destruction, and are his shakti, or active force (as one of the supreme Hindu male triad, along with Vishnu and Brahma, Shiva spends much of his time in ecstatic trance from where he dreams the world). In Hindu myth Kali is pictured as wearing a necklace of skulls and serpents, corpses form her earrings and her only clothing is a girdle made of severed human hands. Kali's face is blood-smeared, her eyes red and fierce, and the balsamic moon, symbol of the death of cycles, emerges from her hair. Kali's bloodthirstiness spawned the cult of thuggee, the Thugs, otherwise respected members of society who led double lives and waylaid and killed unsuspecting travelers by strangling them with knotted cloths to prove their devotion to the Black Goddess. This all-is-not-as-it-appears existence resonates strongly with Black Hole energies, which often mimic reality or create false impressions or illusions to deceive.

From the New World we glean the myth of Quetzalcoatl, the Meso-American Plumed Serpent god. Worshiped as early as 300 C.E., Quetzalcoatl, originally a God of Wind and the Dawn, came to exemplify all that was noble and fine in Aztec culture—a patron of the arts, principal deity of the learned caste and the priesthood, symbol of wisdom and knowledge, and originator of the calendar. Quetzalcoatl's worship, though not bloodless, was considerably less sanguine than most of his contemporaries, and in fact, his chief polar opposite in the Aztec pantheon was Tezcatlipoca, God of War.

Quetzalcoatl was identified with Venus, and here we can see the connection with Black Hole symbology. Venus' cycle was crucially important to Meso-American cultures, and great significance was given to the period of her retrogradation, when as the Evening Star she disappeared behind the Sun, only to re-emerge weeks later as the Morning Star. During this time the Aztec envisioned Quetzalcoatl as traveling to the Underworld, a favorite Black Hole haunt, and a mythology surrounding descent and return emerged.

The confusion over this situation grew once folklore and history blended with myth; one of Quetzalcoatl's most important High Priests became so identified with him that he was commonly called by the God's name. This real-life priest was fair of complexion and bearded, and when the proponents of his chief rival deity Tezcatlipoca drove him into exile, he sailed away eastward, and prophesied his return in the year One Reed (which recurred in the Aztec calendar once every 52 years).

Oddly enough, during one of these expectant periods there did indeed emerge a fair-skinned, bearded stranger from the East; unfortunately for the Aztec Empire, it was Hernan Cortes. Welcomed and honored as the reincarnation of Quetzalcoatl, within months Cortes had imprisoned the Emperor Montezuma and effectively wrested control of all of Mexico from his grasp, with just a handful of followers. Such is the power of myth, and this historic incident serves as a potent example of the status quo reversal qualities which are so famous with Black Holes, which can dramatically shift realities in the twinkling of an eye.

Pacific Island cultures provide us with the tale of Pele, the ancient Hawaiian goddess of volcanic fire, an import from Tahiti who personified the female power of destruction and had her residence in a vast burrow beneath Mount Kilauea, Hawaii's most active and long-lived volcano. Altars were erected to her beside lava streams, but her only worshipers were those who claimed descent from the goddess, as she had a reputation for badly treating even her most loyal followers.

Partly this derived from several fractious encounters with would-be suitors, and an ongoing rivalry with her sister, the goddess Ha'iaka, whom Pele brought with her from Tahiti, carried in the crook of her arm. Pele was a restless goddess and on one of her wanderings she encountered a handsome young chieftain of a neighboring island. The two remained in passionate embrace for three days until Pele determined it was time to be back about her goddess work, and left her lover, promising to send a messenger for him. For this thankless task, the goddess chose her sister Ha'iaka, whom she endowed with several magical arts and sent to retrieve the young chieftain. Ha'iaka was delayed *en route* by several monsters who felt it was an insult to their class for Pele to have a mortal consort, and when she finally arrived, alas! the young lover had expired of a broken heart, thinking his beloved had forgotten him.

This presented no difficulty for Ha'iaka, however, who found his spirit in the form of a butterfly and reanimated him with it. The return journey was again fraught with delays caused by irrate divines, and as she waited, Pele grew jealous, thinking that her sister had betrayed her with her lover. She literally blew her top in one of Kilauea's famous volcanic eruptions, devastating Ha'iaka's gardens and killing her friends. When at last Ha'iaka arrived with her charge at the brink of the volcano, she looked behind her to the destruction in the valley below, and, overcome with grief, turned to embrace the young man. Pele stumbled onto this scene, and, without waiting for explanations, her suspicions apparently confirmed, caused the volcano to erupt again, engulfing the pair in furious fires. Ha'iaka's powers, however, enabled her to survive, and she once again revived the young chieftain, who had by now had enough of his first love; he and Ha'iaka retired to exile on his island, leaving Pele the mistress of fiery Kilauea.

Certainly Pele's fiery, destructive nature says much about the Black Hole's astrophysical dynamics, where temperatures of infalling matter reach superheated levels of tens of thousands of degrees Fahrenheit before taking the final plunge into the crushing supergravity of the singularity.

This whirlwind tour of global myths which resonate to the energies of Black Hole interaction shows them to be a common theme in human development. Although any myth involving metaphors for transformation, the primary image for which is death, will suit the Plutonian descent-into-the-maelstrom aspects of Black Holes, those which also speak of a return to the Light World are best suited to depict the entire process of interaction by progression (or transit). And the myth with which we began our journey, that of Orpheus and Eurydice, stands alone in detailing that return process, which can provide vital clues on how best to negotiate our way out of the depths.

The basic archetypal steps involved in the process of the Black Hole interaction are as follows: descent, which is to say, loss of existing conditions, a change in the status quo; transformation, the trip down into the pit of the singularity, which usually involves literal, outward changes in environment and circumstance; resolution, the turning point where the singularity has been reached; transmutation, the journey out, usually involving inner, psychological processes which evoke true and lasting lifestyle changes in the individual; and emergence, which is the point where the native re-crosses the event horizon and returns to life in the Light World.

Although Orpheus' descent is to be feared, his progress downward runs smoothly, as he masters each and every challenge to be faced. The resolution works in his favor as well; restitution of his former estate, wedded bliss with Eurydice, is agreed to by the powers that be.

It is on the return trip that Orpheus encounters difficulties. For, try as he might, Orpheus' mind is clouded with torments of doubt. He dare not look behind, yet there is neither sight nor sound of Eurydice following. He must trust; trust the Lord of Transformation himself that the proffered boon will be delivered. In the end, he fails. Within sight of the Light World and the re-attainment of his cherished former lifestyle, he succumbs to doubt and turns for reassurance, thus losing what he most wants forever.

But could it have been otherwise? In crafting these stories of the interaction of the archetypes of the human psyche, mythmakers were not merely attempting to relate actual events of prehistory, nor to craft pleasant fireside tales; these images are designed to promote understanding of the human condition, when viewed in that light.

Is it possible for humanity to be so trusting, so confident of the beneficence of providence, that we are not always looking over our shoulders? More than that, is it ever possible, after an event of trauma or severe transformation of existing conditions, to return to what had been before? To a semblance, perhaps, though often this existence is hollow and lifeless now that new experience has been accrued, new knowledge attained, perspective shifted.

With Black Hole interaction, the old world no longer exists to be returned to; the Light World into which we reemerge has shifted its spectrum; perspective is forever altered, and what went before, and what transpired during the descent and return, are all vanished, like Shakespeare's "insubstantial pageant faded, leaving not a wrack behind" (*The Tempest*).

To attempt to hang on to existing conditions during this passage through purgatory, or to reconstitute them after the storm has passed, is useless where Black Hole interaction is involved. Life circumstances have a tendency to implode into a pinpoint of nothingness when they interact with these energies of Deep Space, only to explode back into full material manifestation in totally unrecognizable forms, sometimes in the blink of an eye. Like Orpheus, we are left, following the rigors of our journey, with noting but a fleeting glimpse of the life we have left behind before it fades forever into the Underworld of the Past.

# PSYCHOLOGICAL ANATOMY OF A BLACK HOLE

*"People like us, who believe in physics, know that the distinction between past, present and future is only a stubbornly persistent illusion."*

–Albert Einstein

The depths of the psyche. Thought. Memory. Trauma.

Black Hole theory might account for much of what passes today for psychosis. Beyond the simple fact that everything we perceive as objectively real and happening "now" is in fact an interpretation of available data created by our brain, we are mired in universes of thought, dream and memory, some of which have a power over us equal to if not greater than the circumstances of our daily lives in this physical universe which only part of us inhabits.

Take, for example, something irreducible by language, a so-called "concept word." The color orange is a perfect metaphor for this. "Orange" is a concept word which the sighted among us experience regularly, and which from habit we consider as objectively real. We all know "orange" when we see it, and we communicate its presence to others and agree that things such as pumpkins, road construction signs and even oranges, are all "orange."

But there is no way to determine that you and I each perceive "orange" in the same way. If I could put myself into your psyche, into your synaptic structure, and look out at the world about me, I might see pumpkins that I would identify as "blue" from my old perspective. All we can say for sure is that at some point in early childhood we were each confronted with a hue and told, however we may have perceived it individually, that this is "orange." There is no way to confirm that we each see the same hue, only

that we can agree to classify all subsequent hues which match the
original by the agreed-upon term.

Add to this the fact that, in actuality, things we perceive of as
"orange," in fact only reflect that portion of the light spectrum back
to us, absorbing all the others. In actual fact, things are not the color
they seem to be; they are the opposite. Oranges look orange because
they reflect that light; in order to do so, they must actually be blue.
So the next time you see a perfect October sky, remember: blue skies
are really the most lovely shade of orange.

If there can be such confusion and distortion about things as
common and irreducible as color, imagine the range of interpretation available when we are dealing with things as subjective as
individual experience, even shared experience.

Black Holes are the ultimate reality shifters, both spatially and
temporally. The perspective alteration which can result from the
transit, especially of the Sun, Moon or Ascendant, over a Black Hole
could account for much of the psychological dissociation and dys-
function which accompanies such things as mental breakdowns
and psychotic episodes. It is even possible that the seemingly infinite tide of current disclosures of previously unremembered childhood traumatic events such as sexual, extraterrestrial or satanic
abuse may be correlated to the emergence of Black Holes and parallel reality theory into the collective unconscious.

What psychologists have attributed to a re-membering of past
events which have been suppressed may in fact have more to do
with windows into parallel realities which have been opened into
memory via progressions to Black Holes. These "memories" could
be of incidents occurring in nonphysical universes, in lives which
are parallel to this incarnation, or in past or future incarnations of
the subjects involved. Although there certainly are actual cases of
sexual abuse, perhaps even extraterrestrial abduction or satanic
sacrifice, in many cases the factual basis of these events comes
down to one person's word over another's. In such instances, the
possibility of memory alteration is high. What may appear to be
an actual, recently remembered event from a distant childhood
past may in fact be a view into an alternate event scenario, one
which never manifested in the physical past of this incarnation.

These memories may be more like metaphors for a sense of alienation or neglect which most of us experience growing up, much in the way a dream image points to an actual event other than the one symbolically portrayed.

The scientifically postulated temporal effects of Black Holes would seem to support such a view. According to one parallel universe theory currently gaining scientific support, free will and choice causes the universe to split, or "bifurcate," each chosen path creating a myriad of paths not taken in this reality but reflected in others. The net result is a dizzying infinity of universes, some physical, most probably nonphysical, which interpenetrate and connect, fork and divide with mind-boggling complexity. A sudden interaction by progression with a Black Hole, which by its very nature acts as a connector or bridge between universes/realities, could transfer an individual from one temporal path to another, with no visible effects in the physical universe, but landing the subject in an alternate reality where child abuse was a fact of his or her history, a fact which is now remembered as part of the subject's actual past but which did not exist in the temporal universe to which the rest of their family and friends are still connected.

It is as if the non-physical parts of ourselves, such as memory, which may interact more freely with deep space points than our physical selves could ever hope to do, have taken the plunge into a Black Hole's singularity, and re-emerged in a universe wherein the facts of our past have been wholly or partly changed, reworked to suit the ends of who knows what purpose of the individual's essence.

Again, this is not to suggest that cases of child abuse or even alien abduction do not occur, only that in instances where there is no confirmatory evidence and where memory of the incidents was previously suppressed, a keen eye might be brought to bear upon the galactically-sensitive progressions in effect at the time the memories surfaced.

The phenomenal increase in the disclosure of such events during the mid-1990s correlated nicely with the quantum leaps which Black Holes contemporaneously made into the public consciousness. More than with most current scientific theories, Black Holes, with their connections to the consistently fascinating themes of parallel universes and time travel, have made tremendous inroads into mainstream thought. The imaging of several prime Black Hole candidates by NASA early in 1993 coincided with a peak of "suppressed memory" disclosures, with talk shows, magazine articles and books rife with the subject of remembered childhood traumas.

Just as planetary energies become more and more visible and apparent once that planet has been identified and becomes part of humanity's collective daily knowledge, energies molded by deep space forces such as Black Holes will doubtless find greater and greater expression in the collective as they begin to permeate the consciousness of the masses.

In a more positive sense, the connections Black Holes can provide between alternate realities and alternate periods of this physical universe could make them very valuable tools for counselors working with past life regression therapy and depth psychologies which attempt to mediate between forces personal and archetypal. If Black Holes can afford access to past lives, much information could be gleaned regarding the skandahs, a type of karmic residue which accretes from lifetime to lifetime and which often becomes the focus of unresolved conflicts impinging dramatically upon current life circumstances.

We can see potential here as well for better understanding the mechanism behind channeling or more common psychic phenomenon. Both the means of connection with nonphysical entities as well as the means of collecting and transmitting vital, factual information about total strangers could be explained via natal or progressed contacts with Black Holes and their easy access to other paths along time's bifurcating structure.

As an illustration of this, the only channel with whom I am acquainted, and who has always proved a remarkably accurate source, has exactly the sort of Black Hole contacts one would expect to find, based on the theory developed above. Born 23 January 1956, Robin's nativity shows the Sun at 2 Aquarius, exactly opposed the natal degree of the Black Hole at 2/3 Leo, with an Ascendant of 29 Aquarius, within two degrees of BH 27/28 Aquarius, and the Moon at 6 Gemini, conjoined a Maser there and squared BH 6/7 Virgo while opposed to BH 5 Sagittarius, and inconjunct BH 6/7 Scorpio. Obviously she is not the only individual with such contacts, and not all of these are channels, but I believe these dramatic aspects to the three key chart points strongly influenced her susceptibility and receptivity to nonphysical entities.

On a less esoteric level, Black Holes often have dramatic effects upon matter and time in ways which may seem improbable. My Sun progressed through the singularity of BH 6/7 Virgo, 1993-95, and there were some unusual manifestations to report. This passage began five years earlier, when the progressed Sun entered the event horizon just before I had my first astrological reading. Needless to say, at that time I was completely unaware of Black Holes and their significance, as was the astrologer who read me, but never have I experienced a period of more growth and transformation than over the ensuing five years.

During the summer of 1993 I spent a great deal of time in my garden, and the growth there has reflected a compression of time typical of a Black Hole's influence. One of the birch clumps on the property, a sapling four years old which that spring was about seven feet high with a trunk diameter of perhaps an inch and a half, had, in one season, shot up to nearly thirty feet and increased its trunk girth by at least three inches. It is as if three or perhaps four years of growth were compressed into that one year (and the solar-ruled birch had acted as a referent for this solar-ruled Leo, undergoing just such expedited change). Philip Sedgwick, in *The Astrology of Deep Space*, writes: "The experiences of consciousness created within the Black Hole change the perception of one's physical reality, and obvious changes in one's material sphere of influence begin to manifest in undeniable ways."

When I came across that passage again late that summer while reviewing his work, I was able to heartily confirm that this is, in fact, the case.

The birch tree incident brought home to me very clearly how nonphysical energies can and do influence the material realm; when we are dealing exclusively with the interaction of nonphysical components, such as memory and cosmic consciousness, the results might be even more distorted or pronounced.

Black Holes and their manipulation of matter, energy and time could be the key not only to identifying psychological trauma, but also to curing it. With a better understanding of how deep space points interact with the human synaptic structure, it may only be a matter of time before we unlock the mysteries of the psyche.

# BLACK HOLES: MECHANICS OF PROGRESSION

*"When a seed—or an animal—or a man is ripe, it must mature to its next phase. Or rot."*

–Stewart Edward White

While natal contacts to Black Holes provide important avenues of experience into the parallel dimensions they evoke, it is by progression that we experience the journey through the Underworld in its entirety. Whereas natal conjunctions remain static, with the planetary body in question held in place at the point along the journey where it was at birth, interaction by progression yields the richness of seeing the entire journey, not dwelling eternally at one stage.

Progressed conjunctions with Black Holes are particularly useful in dramatizing, highlighting, and therefore helping to identify the patterns already in existence which are reflective of natal contacts. The years of a progression over the event horizon and singularity of a Black Hole are ones in which a sharper focus can be brought to bear on the life scripts and behavioral patterns which affect us constantly, but which may be so deeply ingrained in our subconscious that we are unaware of their influence in our daily lives. It is contact by progression which can signal their silent, subterranean gravitational pull, which warps our interactions in the Light World of which we are a part.

Progression by one of the inner planets is the most likely to yield fruitful information, as this process will take a relatively short period of time. Progression requires an average of 6-7 years for Mercury, 8-9 years for Venus, 10 years for the Sun, and 13-15 years for Mars. In contrast, Jupiter can take up to fifty years to complete such a progression, and it would take several lifetimes for Pluto to do so. The angles and the Moon are other factors which will progress quickly, but for purposes of illustration we will concentrate on a solar progression.

In considering this progress, unlike that of a progression over a "typical" natal point, the distance the Black Hole has moved since birth is an important factor. The native is both most vulnerable and most powerful during the period between the conjunction with the degree and minute of the natal singularity, and that of the transit singularity, which creates a sort of astrological no man's land, or psychic eye of the storm, if you will, between them. During this time the native is asked to remember and reprocess everything he or she has experienced relative to the planet in question during the course of the incarnation thus far. Careful attention to patterns revealed and manifestations elicited during this time can yield vital insights into the native's developmental stage and growth to date.

As an illustration of this process, consider the progression of my Sun over the Black Hole at 6/7 Virgo. For purposes of simplification, let us estimate solar progression at a rate of exactly one degree per year, or 1.25 minutes per week, and galactic progression at the rate of one minute per year.

In 1960, and thus in the birthchart, this Black Hole was to be found at 6 degrees 31 minutes of Virgo. The Sun of this chart is at 4 Leo, thus we can see that 32+ years would elapse before the solar progression would reach the natal singularity. However, by this time, the transit singularity has moved as well, approximately 32 minutes, showing a current position of 7 degrees Virgo 03 minutes. During the period of the Sun's progression from 6 Virgo 31 to 7 Virgo 03, a period of approximately six months, ten days, the native will have the opportunity to re-experience and reevaluate the totality of his psychic lessons during the first 32 years of the incarnation; in fact, the incarnation is actually relived, in the form of spontaneous release of body memory often processed in dream images, at a rate proportional to the intervening span of time. That is to say, the first week of the progression between the singularities, the native will relive the first 15 months of life, and will attract to himself experiences which mirror the lessons accrued during this time. This process continues until the Sun has progressed to conjoin the transit singularity, when time has caught up with itself and the native emerges from the time warp in present day, ready to begin the slow ascent from the pit.

The descent from the Light World of flat spacetime into the infinite curvature of the Black Hole can be envisioned as a downward spiral, resolving itself in the pit of the natal singularity, from whence the wormhole of warped time translates the native to the singularity of the transit anomaly, whereupon the Sun reemerges from the pit and begins the spiral upwards, in reverse direction to the descent. There is almost a feeling of cosmic pinball as the Sun revolves more swiftly downward in ever-decreasing spirals, disappearing into a blind alley only to be ejected upward once again when it has contacted the buzzer.

As stated above, this interim period of transit between the two singularities has the potential of yielding the richest observations concerning the native's current life circumstances, and can also provide an effective window for enacting change. Often the critical mass point of the native's life will be reached during this stage, with life circumstances imploding into a pinpoint of infinity, only to explode back into physical manifestation in wholly or partially unrecognizable forms.

And what of the earlier and later stages of the progression? Five years before the progressed Sun reaches the singularity, it will have crossed the event horizon, the outer boundary delimiting the Black Hole's gravitational grasp. At this time, very often, the native will experience an event of symbolic importance which relates to the upcoming passage.

In my own case, the year that my Sun crossed the event horizon into BH 6/7 Virgo's jurisdiction, I shifted my employment to a very lucrative part-time job which paid me enough for my needs while freeing up vast portions of my time for contemplation and study (this is the job I subsequently lost after my Sun had progressed onto the natal singularity, thus freeing up all my time), I met and formed a relationship with my partner, who has been an important catalyst in my spiritual journey, and I first found astrology, which has since become my life's work. None of these incidents in themselves seemed particularly significant at the time, but they set the tone for the next five year period, which continued to resolve and refine itself during the progression up and out. [As an aside here, it may be of interest to note that it was during the progression over the information-evoking Pulsar at 3 Virgo, within the Black Hole's

event horizon, that I first became aware of galactics. Also, my partner's Sun was at that time progressing through the pit of the anomaly, while I gingerly peered over the lip; that progression was all but
complete as I reached the singularity.]

If you're looking for more verifiable life histories, consider the
cases of Madonna and Roseanne Barr.

Both these doyens of the American penchant for vulgarity
and tastelessness (not to take anything away from their respective
talents, which are considerable) were facing their own passages
through the Underworld at about the time I dealt with my own.

Madonna, who by her thirty-sixth birthday the summer of 1994
had her progressed Sun within three degrees of the singularity of
BH 1 Libra, the biggest Black Hole of them all, had been particularly
hasty in her descent. Her Sun crossed the Black Hole's event horizon just before the release of her show-all book, *Sex* and the accompanying album "Erotica" in the fall of 1992. After which she continued to shock, and sometimes repulse, even her loyal fans, with
such bizarre escapades as her 1993 "Girlie Show" Tour, which featured nude dancers and was broadcast on HBO from Australia, and
her March 31st 1994 appearance on David Letterman, during Holy
Week, no less, when she looked tough in coal black locks pulled
back scalp tight, smoking a huge cigar, refusing to leave the set
when her time ran out and using the F-word 18 times. Her descent
had seen her transformation from Material Girl to Millennial Bitch,
with a harsh brittleness the likes of which we have rarely seen in
pop icons.

Roseanne's tales of woe are perhaps more bizarre. With her Sun
in 1994 less than three degrees from the singularity of the Galactic
Center, the two years prior (just after her crossing of the event
horizon) saw a dizzying spate of "confessions," everything from
being sexually abused by her father as a child and turning tricks
in cars between sets when she was a rising young standup comic,
to assertions that she suffers from Associative Personality Disorder,
to allegations of physical abuse by her husband Tom Arnold, from
whom she twice filed for divorce in 1994. There is a serious question
here whether these wee actual events, publicity stunts, or fantasies
enacted by the Black Hole descent. In time both women navigated
the singularities and returned to a semblance of normalcy, though

never again to the prominence in their careers which their Black Hole progressions also elicited.

Although each of the degrees encompassed by the event horizon shows the progressed planet, and thus that aspect of the native, to be more than usually susceptible to galactic influences, the degree delimiting the event horizon has a particular "trip wire" effect which can make the aspects to it from other galactics particularly stimulating, and show especially potent or significant moments to watch in the progression.

By progression, we experience the full range of Black Hole interaction, and can gain vital insights into how our natal contacts are affected by the stage at which they became concretized in our psyches. So take the time to check your Black Hole progressions: they may prove to be the time of your life!

# BLACK HOLES AND PARALLEL UNIVERSES

*"Listen, there's a hell of a universe next door: let's go!"*
                                                    −e. e. cummings

One of the most intriguing areas of theoretical research regarding the effects of Black Holes involves parallel universes and higher dimensions. Physicists are currently speculating upon the mathematical feasibility of higher dimensions beyond the three of space and one of time with which we are familiar. The possible function of Black Holes as connectors between these parallel realities is being investigated in much of today's cutting edge physics theory in these areas.

One current physics model of the Universe includes a "hyperspace" of ten dimensions. It is impossible for our 3D brains to picture a ten-dimensional universe, and yet the properties of matter become more simple and elegant the higher one goes dimensionally. On paper, a simple 2D surface, it is comparatively easy to work out the mathematics of such a universe, but we cannot visualize this degree of complexity mentally.

Higher dimensions have been sought as a way of uniting all known forces in the Universe, principally those of gravity, electromagnetism, and the strong and weak nuclear forces. In 3D, physicists since Einstein have been struggling in vain the past century to find some Grand Unifying Theory, or the GUTs of the cosmos, which would combine all the known laws of physics and nature into one simple equation. With ten dimensions, this is easy.

But how do we visualize them? Physics experts tell us that after the fourth dimension, the barrier of time, matter becomes "crumpled"; everything that exists in 3D has a reference in higher dimensions from which it has unfolded. Although we cannot visualize what these dimensions might be, we can perhaps get an idea of them by imagining how a race of beings in 2D might conceptualize and experience 3D, and use this as a model of how we might extrapolate from the fifth dimension.

Imagine a place called Flatland, which exists in a two-dimensional universe. The beings which inhabit this paper-sheet-like world have no concept of depth, only height and width. One day a sphere enters their Universe. The Flatlanders are shocked by the apparently nonphysical properties this strange object displays. As they are incapable of visualizing 3D, all the Flatlanders can see of the sphere is its changing cross section as it passes through their Universe, appearing magically from nowhere as a pinpoint, becoming an ever larger circle, then suddenly beginning to decrease in radius and disappearing again without a trace. So would a being from the Fifth Dimension enter our world in bits and pieces at a time; at least that is how it would look to our senses.

There is one obvious metaphysical analogy to this process which we could use to image 5D beings: that is the reincarnational model. According to one popular conception of reincarnation, we are born again and again in different physical forms, but retain a connection to a higher form of spirit or soul which is unchanging, and present in each of the incarnations. On this model we can easily visualize the soul as a 5D being, different "segments" of which are manifesting as 3D individuals sundered by the fourth dimension of time. In the same way as the Flatlanders saw the different cross sections of the 3D sphere in their 2D Universe, we can view the subsequent incarnations of the 5D soul in our 3D world, thanks to our uniquely human 4D perspective which includes an understanding of time.

And time may well be the key here. Apparently the ultimate barrier to the higher dimensions, time may prove to be the bridge to them as well. Is it possible that beyond 3D, physical matter becomes the subtle matter of things such as thoughts and ideas? After the first nonphysical dimension of time has been conquered, that barrier shattered and its now understood building blocks reconstructed into a bridge, will we see the higher dimensions as the answers to states which mystics have expounded upon for millennia? Perhaps the quantum realm, where physical matter first proceeds from the nonphysical, Flesh from Spirit, is in fact that liminal twilight world of magick which has formed such a great part of the studies of ancient man. Might the magical realm be the fifth dimension, enfolded within the spatial voids in our atomic structure, and giving rise to the smallest 3D particles, the subatomic quantum world of quarks? From this point, extrapolating backwards along traditional lines describing the descent of matter, we may define the sixth dimension as the Imaginal realm, that aboriginal dreamtime world from which we emerge as co-creators of our reality, and beyond that, the seventh dimension of the Mythic/Archetypal realm, providing the blueprints for what we enact in 3D. Beyond that, who can say? Our existence in 3D might, indeed, in some presently inconceivable fashion, be merely a thought in the Mind of God, All-that-Is.

The second promising field of theory in regards to a Black Hole's usefulness involves parallel universes. This is another concept that is difficult to represent visually. Most people find it difficult to conceive of a Universe at all (that is, an infinite yet constantly expanding, boundary-less realm which constitutes all that is), let alone an infinity of such structures. Yet quantum theory provides for the possibility that there are in fact numberless numbers of alternate universes, some which interpenetrate our own, some which are connected via the wormhole passage through a Black Hole, some which are completely sundered but may be reached by traveling through intervening universes. Some of these are physical, obeying laws similar to our own, some are physical but obey completely different sets of laws, many are most probably not physical. A dizzying infinity of universes, indeed.

Again, part of the problem lies in conceptualization. With our finite and limited individual experience of this one world, it is hard to conceive of the effects of an infinite number of alternate ones. But, just as with the world of the Flatlanders, we can perhaps draw models which will allow us to imagine what such a situation might be like.

One way to conceptualize this complex web of parallel realities is to look with a new perspective upon the common permutations of our existence which we perform in our daily lives. Imagine the following scenario: you awake in the morning, shower, dress, and prepare to meet your day. You are in a relatively safe, stable, controlled environment, or, Universe A. You emerge from the front door and step smack into Universe B, that of the outside world, where you are much less in control of what happens to you. You proceed without incident to work, only to find that the company has made some layoffs and you are no longer employed. In that moment you have shifted from Universe B, where you are employed in the outside world, to Universe C, where you are not. Distraught, you leave the office, walking for hours in the cold, rainy city streets, until, worn down by stress, you carelessly step into the path of an oncoming taxi, which strikes you, breaking both your legs. You have now left Universe C, where you are healthy, and entered Universe D, where you are hospitalized. In one short day you have shifted from Universe A, the at-home Universe, where you had total freedom, safety, and control, to Universe D, the in-hospital Universe, where, unemployed, injured and in traction, you are now completely at the mercy of others.

This may seem an oversimplification, and surely, actual parallel universes generally play out on a much bigger scale than that recorded above, but the theory is in essence much the same. Consider the ways we effect transformation and initiate change: at any given moment one set of circumstances pertains, then the kaleidoscope shifts, we perform an action or have one performed upon us, and the net result is a complete reversal of the former status quo. It may be that Black Hole interaction in the chart is the driving mechanism behind how we attract experience to ourselves, how we learn and process that information, and what we do with it to enact change and growth.

Galactic study provides for astrology what quantum mechanics provides for physics: a way of relating ourselves to the border region between the manifest and unmanifest, between physical and nonphysical reality, between order and chaos.

There is a new emerging science termed complexity which deals with just such a region, and it is appropriately named, for it is in fact the complexity of the psyche which creates order from the apparent chaos generated by man's emergence at a new level of consciousness, the humanoid referent of the planetary initiation spoken of by many as the Earth struggles to evolve its light body.

The use of galactic points provides a deeper understanding of these deep space levels of higher human understanding. The gravity well (another name for a Black Hole, but in a metaphysical sense this applies to any object having mass, including humans) is the perfect metaphor for precisely this state of inward turning taken literally ad infinitum, to the furthest extreme, which creates in the individual a control over environment and ability to manifest vital essence exemplified by the nature of the Quasar.

This is in fact the Ascension process of which many traditions speak; it is a literal Ascent to a higher level of reality, one which, like hyperspace theory's fifth dimension, is curled in upon itself in a ball so tight and tiny that no one can see it. This state of knowing was once the common state of man, and it has happened occasionally to humanity after the Fall, but what is described in the Bible, for example, as the literal Ascension to Heaven of Elijah, Jesus and the Virgin Mary, must be understood in the context of the psychological transformation that awakened these individuals. As Joseph Campbell has said, even at the speed of light Jesus would not yet be out of the galaxy, so we have to redefine the term Ascension, and understand that "...he didn't go out there [gesturing away and up]; he went in here [gesturing inward to the heart center]." This is a vital psychological transformation which in turn yields a new relationship to matter and the way we express through it in the physical.

Understanding Deep Space is the way you can begin to understand your personal connection to this new level. Our connection to Deep Space is our connection to infinity and timelessness. Think of the ways in which having Pluto in a certain sign unites large portions of humanity across the globe; there is an urge to fulfillment of this archetype in the psyches of up to thirty years of humanity at a time. Imagine the great number of souls with which that gives you a direct link in today's world. Now realize that galactics are like having dozens of Plutos, always in the same basic geometric relation to each other, and in the same signs for 1800 years at a clip. Understanding of this level is a truly unitive experience.

Galactics further describe and relate to, or "govern," the psychological processes which regulate our interface with physical reality and our ability to create, transform and recreate that reality.

# BLACK HOLES AND
# TIME REFRACTION

*"Time is what keeps the light from reaching us."*

–Meister Eckhart

Time and Light are inextricably linked in the human condition. The three major indicators of the passage of time which would have been obvious even to prehistoric societies are all based on the changing relationship of Light with the Earth. Primary, of course, is the daily cycle of daylight and darkness; it is the break in the Sun's illumination of the Earth, caused by our planet's rotation upon its axis once every 24 hours, which provides our basic sense of change from one day to the next. Periods of light, warmth and activity naturally alternate with periods darker, cooler, and relatively less active, encouraging a sense of the passage of time. If we lived on a planet which did not rotate, half would always be in light, and half always in darkness, with no temporal spur for the inhabitants of either half.

The second most obvious feature is the monthly cycle of the Moon, again a temporal reference derived from Light, based on our view of relatively more or less of her Sun-illuminated surface. By comparing how many light/dark daily periods encompass a full cycle of the Moon from Light to Dark, the concept of the Month (literally, "'moon'th") was originated. This changing pattern of light and dark is caused by the Moon's 28+ day revolution period about the Earth.

Finally there is the cycle of the year, based on daylight periods which range in temperate regions from little more than 9 hours at the Winter Solstice to almost 15 at the Summer Solstice. The lengthening light brings warmer temperatures, more favorable conditions for plant growth, etc., and provides an obvious pattern of changing seasons which goes to formulate a concept of the Year, which can be subdivided into a certain number of lunar cycles (13) and daily cycles (365). This effect is caused by the fact that the Earth is tilted on its axis, and thus the light from the Sun reaches different parts of the globe more intensely at certain times during its yearly revolution about the Sun. If we lived on a planet whose polar axis was at right angles to its orbital plane, then seasons as we know them would not exist; one would always experience summer at the equator, winter at the poles, and spring or fall-like weather somewhere in between.

It is too much to say that Time does not exist without Light, but, at least in this system, it is fairly certain that the recognition of Time would have been much delayed had it not been for the changing patterns of the Light. In considering, therefore, the effects which Black Holes may have upon Time, which still lies in the realm of theory, we might begin by examining what effect they have upon Light, which is more completely understood.

Stephen Hawking's *A Brief History of Time* (Bantam, 1988) is still probably the best, most accessible source on this subject for the lay person. Hawking (whose fascination with Black Holes has now progressed to considering the fate of information which collides with one) lays out very plainly the ways in which Einstein's understanding of the effects of gravity upon light predetermines its performance when subjected to a Black Hole's supergravity. Confirmed years after its postulation by measurements taken of stars visible during an eclipse, Einstein's principles of General Relativity show that light is warped by gravity. Eventually, in the case of the supermassive collapsing stars which create Black Holes, the gravity becomes so overpowering that the star's radiated energy is warped, or curved, back in upon itself, and the collapsed star ceases to emit even light, giving rise to the anomaly for which physicist John Wheeler coined the term "Black Hole" in the late 60's. [For a fuller understanding of how gravity and light interact, see *Black Holes and Time Warps* (W.W. Norton, 1994), by Kip Thorne, a contemporary of Hawking.]

"Gravity," which is based upon an object's mass or weight, is the force which attracts all bodies towards their centers, and determines "gravitation," which is the tendency of all objects to be attracted to one another. "Tidal gravity" is the term for "gravitational accelerations which squeeze objects along some directions and stretch them along others" (Thorne, p. 558). It is such interactions between the gravitational fields of the Sun and Moon which cause the phenomenon of the oceans' tides (hence the term's derivation), the rising and falling of the water level as the aquatic medium is squeezed and stretched between these two forces.

"Tidal Gravity" is possessed by all stellar bodies; "quantum gravity" is the force which "takes over when the oscillating tidal gravity (AKA the spacetime curvature) becomes so large that it completely deforms all objects" (Thorne, p. 476). This is the famed "spaghetti-stringer" of the Black Hole, which crushes anything which falls into its grasp by stretching and squeezing it until all individual character is lost. Quantum gravity does not stop with the merely material as we know it, it extends to the very fabric of spacetime itself, whose character it "radically changes....It ruptures the unity of space and time [as] spacetime. It unglues space and time from each other, and then destroys time as a concept and destroys the definiteness of space. Time ceases to exist;...Space, the sole remaining remnant of what was once a unified spacetime, becomes a random froth, like soap suds," which "is the thing of which the [Black Hole's] singularity [(its center)] is made..." (Thorne, pp. 476-7).

This destruction of Time as a concept is crucial to an understanding of the native who is linked astrologically to a Black Hole. Exact contacts to a Black Hole's singularity, or center, whether natally or by progression, promote a sense of timelessness which may prove very disorienting to the native.

In an astronomic sense, Black Holes create an effect termed "time dilation," which is specifically a slowing of time. As the event horizon is approached, the astronaut would not notice a change in the passage of time, but to an observer he or she would appear to move more and more slowly, until finally, as the event horizon was crossed, all movement would cease from the observer's perspective, due to the cessation of Time. Kip Thorne illustrates the awesome power of this time dilation by stating that for a Black Hole of 10 solar masses, Time flows 6 million times more slowly at 1 centimeter above the surface of the event horizon than it does for us in "normal" conditions. At the event horizon, Time stops completely.

Clearly, time dilation is a force for NASA to reckon with should they attempt interaction with a Black Hole in future. In the birth chart, however, a more appropriate term for this temporal disruption would seem to be "time refraction," for the normal laws of the passage of time which we experience in this plane are simply altered, not necessarily delayed. Time is bent, twisted, turned in upon itself, leaving scars or slashes in the even fabric of Time's passing which is recorded by our clocks. At times the passage of Time is apparently slowed, while at other times it is dramatically accelerated, and in yet other periods there is no sense of Time whatsoever; it has completely stopped, and may even seem to have reversed itself to a slight degree. Philip Sedgwick in *The Astrology of Deep Space* (Seek-It Publications, 1984) specifically states that among the properties of the Black Hole native is "the ability to warp time" (page 117). However, the degree to which this is brought under conscious control remains very definitely subject to each individual case.

In my own experience of the passage of my progressed Sun through the double Black Hole section of early Virgo, from 1989 when I crossed the event horizon of BH 6/7 Virgo, through my contact with its singularity 1993-95, there was definitely a sense of the breakdown and evaporation of my former sense of the temporal. This was doubtless enhanced by successive stations of transit Saturn, Uranus and Neptune on my natal Saturn (the traditional time-keeper of the cosmos) at 13 Capricorn, contemporaneous with my progressed Sun's crossing of the event horizon and the first few years of the descent into the pit. Events in my personal life conspired to aid this process. I acquired a cooking job at a university which gave me nearly five months of free time every summer, and without having to conform to a rigid daily schedule, the fluid aspects of Time more naturally asserted themselves. My sense of Time's structure became, in the words of Kip Thorne, "unglued" from any sense of ordinary temporal reality; hours passed like days, days like minutes, and weeks and months were wholly interchangeable. This may sound inconsistent, but in the moment itself, it was quite possible to have a minute that seemed endless incorporated into a day which seemed fleeting.

We have all experienced a sense of time passing at a different rate depending upon the way we occupy ourselves, and, indeed, we all have Black Hole contacts of some type, and every day has its moments of peak Black Hole activity as anomalies become angular or are conjoined or aspected by transit planets. These commonplace effects are dramatically enhanced by direct contact with a Black Hole's singularity.

Time Refraction is an intriguing, disconcerting, and powerful effect of a Black Hole's interaction in the life of the native who contacts one. Having once experienced it, the rigid, Saturnian elements of Time are destroyed, affording a glimpse into the freedom to be gained when Time's restraints are loosed. Interaction with Time on the galactic level is creative, illuminative, and, though disorienting when one returns to interactions in the Light World, the experience is ultimately growth-producing and powerfully transformative.

# AFTERWORD

Perhaps this should have been read first as a warning, or disclaimer. With the reading of this book, you have traversed a Galactic Gateway. Your Universe, whether large or small, will never be the same. For consciousness is itself a Black Hole process, and your conscious understanding and acknowledgment of these Deep Space behemoths has granted them new and revitalized powers in your life. As with any increase in knowledge, the seeker has been transformed by the attainment of his or her goal, and it is impossible to unlearn what one has learned. Having crossed the event horizon of this knowledge, you are now firmly in their grasp. May your galactic journeys be filled with love, hope, and peace...

# APPENDIX: NEW TOOLS

# ADDITIONAL BLACK HOLES

BH 3 Taurus
BH 6 Taurus
BH 7 Taurus
BH 13 Taurus
BH 9 Gemini
BH 13 Gemini
BH 6 Cancer
BH 9 Cancer
BH 28 Leo
BH 8 Virgo
BH 14 Virgo
BH 25 Virgo
BH 22 Libra
BH 11 Scorpio
BH 26 Scorpio
BH 8 Sagittarius
BH 11 Sagittarius
BH 3 Capricorn
BH 16 Capricorn
BH 22 Capricorn
BH 4 Aquarius
BH 17 Aquarius
BH 2 Pisces
BH 16 Pisces
BH 24 Pisces

# ASTEROIDS & MINOR PLANETS

The more we explore, the more we know. And the more we know, the more astrology needs to integrate into its repertoire. The first asteroid was discovered in 1801, and at first erroneously identified as a planet. Pluto, also, was identified as a planet upon its discovery in 1930, but once astronomers began to realize that it was but one among a host of similar objects in the vast Kuiper Belt region which stretches beyond Neptune, it was demoted to "minor planet" status, which it shares with its neighbors. There are also asteroid-like bodies which fill in the gaps between the orbits of Jupiter and Neptune, known as Centaurs, Trojans, and Damocloids, all of which can give vital clues to character and the unfolding of mundane events when strongly placed in charts.

Since the discovery of Ceres in 1801, we have found more than 300,000 of these minor planets, of which barely 13,000 have names, out of an estimated number perhaps as high as 1.9 million. That's a huge battery of information to incorporate, and obviously, no one can do so fully. Complicating the issue is the nomenclature. It's relatively easy, from its mythic context, to determine what asteroid Polyhymnia (#33), named for the Greek Muse of Song, might represent, and finding that asteroid exactly conjunct Michael Jackson's Sun is therefore no great shock. And Ixion, a Trans-Neptunian Object named for the first murderer in Greek mythology, lies exactly opposed to Venus in the chart of Aileen Wuornos, America's most famous female (Venus) serial killer, a Florida prostitute accused of murdering six of her "lovers" (Venus again). But what are we to do with an asteroid named "Richard" (#3972) or "Monica" (#833)?

Well, you'd be surprised. When Captain Richard Phillips of the cargo ship Maersk Alabama was taken captive by Somali pirates on 9 April 2009, asteroid Richard at 24 Leo was tightly opposed

Neptune, ruler of the seas, at 25 Aquarius (itself exactly conjunct a spotlighting Quasar, bringing the incident to public notice and prominence). When we check Phillips' natal chart (born 16 May 1955) we see no less than seven major planets all within 24-26 degrees of various Signs, and thus all currently aspected by that same Neptune, which indicates the personalization of this energy to Richard Phillips specifically. Asteroid Monica's celestial footprints are all over Bill Clinton's birth chart (she squares Clinton's 26 Leo Sun from 29 Scorpio) as well as key moments from their memorable affair, from its inception (11/15/95, when it conjoined Clinton's natal Uranus, squared transit Saturn and opposed a transit Mars/Jupiter conjunction) to its public revelation (1/17/98, when transit Monica conjoined transit Chiron and Nemesis and squared asteroid Hillary conjoined Clinton's natal Pluto).

To look at today's world, we can see a stunning example of the relevance of these minor planets in the chart of Barack Obama (born 8/4/61), which sports an exact Grand Cross composed of Sun at 12 Leo squared asteroid Nancy (#2056, for House Speaker Nancy Pelosi) at 12 Scorpio and Reid (#3422, for Senate Majority Leader Harry Reid) at 12 Taurus, and opposed Damocles (#5335, representing impending doom) at 12 Aquarius. Obviously, these two congressional leaders are among those having the greatest impact upon the success or failure of the Obama administration, and that this should be so is clearly prefigured in Obama's nativity. So, yes, we can even track highly personal celestial names and correlate them to terrestrial events.

These few brief examples are just to say that the importance of all named bodies in the solar system cannot be underestimated, and these often provide useful clarifying information which aids in refining interpretations and understanding events as they unfold. So I have used them liberally in the examples given in this book, hoping the reader will begin to appreciate their impact. Asteroids, Centaurs, TNOs (Trans-Neptunian Objects), KBOs (Kuiper Belt Objects), and SDOs (Scattered Disk Objects); all these minor planets potentially have a tale to tell, if we will but listen.

# THE NOVEM SERIES

The Novem (Latin for "nine") is a series of aspects of primarily esoteric significance, comprising forty segments of nine degrees apiece. I term them "essential" aspects because the degree of consciousness required to fully appreciate and integrate each of them on a daily conscious basis would be commensurate with a level of functioning normally reserved to the essence of pure spirit itself.

This series adapts itself particularly well to Galactics, perhaps because of their extremely slow movement. Since they activate one degree for such extensive periods, the aspects they make from that degree to others in the zodiac remain stable long enough for these minor aspects to assert themselves and make their influences felt. Moreover, even for our normal level of functioning, when viewing the artificially static elements of the nativity, frozen in time at the moment of birth, these aspects can provide much useful information regarding growth potential and karmic inheritance. Ohio astrologer Robert "Buz" Meyers asserts that as our consciousness grows and expands, so too can we expand the orbs of influence for aspects. I would agree with that position, and contend further that as consciousness expands, we can see more and more of the "minor" aspects playing lead roles in our lives.

The novem series, superimposed over the more usual 30-degree increments and the nine 40-degree segments of the novile series, creates a flexible framework of interpretation, providing as it does the maximum number of potential interaspects while still retaining individual character for each one. Many of the aspects included in the novem series, such as the traditional square, opposition, and "phase" aspects such as the semisquare and sesquiquadrate, as well as the quintile, biquintile, and tredecile (a 108-degree aspect popularized by astrologer Dusty Bunker) will already be familiar to the experienced astrologer. Others, like the 99-degree crucinovem or the 162 degree quadnovem, will be less apparent.

Obviously, when one is subdividing the circle into such small segments, the question of orbs becomes of more than ususal importance. I generally use a nine degree orb for a conjunction, which is not really an aspect at all in traditional astrology. An aspect shows a way of relating. A particular "face," if you will, of these planets is turned towards each other, but you can always turn your face away; with a conjunction there is nowhere else to look, the two are inextricably bound together with no hope of escape. For the more traditional aspects I use an orb of anywhere from five to seven degrees, and my feeling is that aspects of the novem could receive up to a two degree orb. However, for purposes of clarifying and cataloging their effects, I prefer to restrict examples in this book to exact aspects or at most a one degree orb.

In both the natal chart and mundane events charts, the use of the novem series provides a window onto a level of underlying interaction between points normally left unintegrated, an important linking function they have in common with Galactic Points. If planets connected by traditional aspects can be envisioned as talking to one another, then those linked by the novem series "whisper." There is a communication nonetheless, and if the astrologer is sensitive enough to attune his/her hearing to their conversational level, these essential aspects have quite a tale to tell.

# THE WEB

Everything is energy. All radiant energy interpenetrates. Everything that is, results from the interaction of one type of energy with another.

In a psychic sense, we *are* the cosmos. The energies we reference with outward manifestations such as the planets and asteroids of our own system are really just anthropomorphisms, or personifications, of the energies we perceive within us. This may seem more or less obvious when we consider the inner, personal planets, but a lot of people would have difficulty at first understanding this for the more inaccessible, outer planets. And yet, we can see that we are constantly immersed in elements of these radically transpersonal energies as well. Without Neptune, for example, we would not dream, could never fantasize or have any imagination with which to create. Pluto is there in the constant immersion of death within life, whether it be walking down the street and stepping on an ant, enduring the loss of a loved one, or simply the death and regeneration of our cellular structures, which is constant.

The energies which flow from these points within the psyche are truly wavelike, emanating like a great cloud of light from the center. Yet, within this underlying wave, we can perceive particle beams, avenues of access to other centers representing different energies. These streams of energy exchange become well-worn and rutted into the psyche from constant use, drawing more and more energy to them with time and usage. It is from these first tentative thickenings of the wavelike energy that we can perceive the web forming, like Avalon rising from the mists.

The chart can be seen as a great white orb, white because of the constant interaction of each varying shade of color, since for light, thus radiant energy, the color white is the presence of all colors of the spectrum. Once we differentiate the orb, divide the psyche and classify it into its component parts, we can see the underlying spheres of each celestial, colored with its particular shade of light. If we chose to depict Neptune as violet light, we can, when we image Neptune's effects in the chart, envision these as an orb colored purple, with the most intense version of that color coinciding with Neptune's position in the nativity, increasingly paler variants of the base tone emanating from that central point. As we look closer, the aspects resolve themselves into the standing beams of light: major aspects perhaps thicker, darker; minor aspects paler, less thickly drawn.

If we use the Novem series plus noviles and semisextiles, we can see a hairline fracture-like pattern emerging which extends from Neptune's zodiacal degree to no less than 53 other degrees. Any of these which are occupied by angles, planets, asteroids or galactics show a constant, almost opaque glow of free-flowing energy. Those unoccupied glimmer faintly in the twilight world of energetic potential, shot through with brilliant color when a transiting celestial contacts that degree and activates the latent particle beam.

This concept, of each point permeating the chart, and giving rise to its own web of etheric energy, is essential in understanding the prime Philosophy of Wholeness which Galactic Astrology evokes from the chart. In that philosophy, the Principle of Interconnectedness is essential, a principle aptly illustrated by the use of the Novem series of aspects. Interconnectedness provides the realization of the underlying unity and wholeness in a depiction of the psyche which is otherwise apparently fragmented and disparate.

# NEW PATTERNS AND MAJOR CONFIGURATIONS

The use of the Novem series of aspects, as well as the inclusion of additional power points with Galactics, creates a new visual feel for the chart. Patterns emerge which were undreamt of before. Although we will detail these in later chapters, for now there are two basic patterns which should be mentioned.

The first is a class of yod-like structures, called Mirror Configurations, which, like yods, are formed from symmetrical patterns and carry a "fated" quality to them. Principal among these is the Configuration formed from two planets in square to each other, each sesquiquadrate a third planet; this is a particularly dynamic structure as all of the planets are in the process of changing phase relationship with one another.

Another notable example is that of two planets in quintile, each biquintile to a third, but the process in varied and the permutations frequent when the Novem series is used. One illustration of this would be a Mirror Configuration formed by two planets in tredecile (108 degrees), each transinovem (126 degrees) to a third.

The second class of structures I call "Asterisms," after the astronomical appellation for a grouping of stars forming a constellation, which is similar to a Planetary Picture in a chart. Asterisms are themselves divided into several classes, depending on the degree of exactness of the aspects involved, but their basic structure is composed of at least five chart points which all interaspect. Asterisms containing all aspects which are exact are termed Supernovae, those with at least one aspect having a one degree orb are Blue Giants. Two degree orbs involved in the pattern create Red Giants, while orbs of three degrees are found in Yellow Stars, and the weakest class, White Dwarf, is composed of aspects with up to a four degree orb of exactness.

Asterisms often contain Galactics (which may also form one of the points in a Mirror Configuration) and are formative structures which tie varying elements of the psyche to each other in patterns previously unsuspected. Again, the use of the Novem series here brings together elements of the chart/psyche which formerly had no apparent linkage, but which can now be seen to provide vital clues to the native's development and personality.

# SELECTED BIBLIOGRAPHY

Combs, Allan and Mark Holland. *Synchronicity: Science, Myth and the Trickster.* St. Paul, MN: Paragon House, 1990.

Halpern, Paul. *Cosmic Wormholes.* New York: Dutton, 1992.

Hawking, Stephen. *A Brief History of Time.* New York: Bantam Books, 1988.

Kaku, Michio. *Hyperspace.* New York: Oxford University Press, 1994.

Kaufmann, William J. III. *Black Holes and Warped Spacetime.* New York: W.H. Freeman and Company, 1979.

Sedwick, Philip. *The Astrology of Deep Space.* Famington Hills, MI: Seek-It Publications, 1984.

Thorne, Kip S. *Black Holes & Time Warps.* New York: W.W. Norton & Company, 1994.

Wolf, Fred Alan. *Parallel Universes: The Search for Other Worlds* New York: Simon & Schuster, 1988.

# BLACK HOLE QUOTATIONS

*"There's a black hole  in the L.A. P.D."*

—F. Lee Bailey, attorney
Simpson Defense Team
August 1995

*"How your money is  disappearing into the black hole where the military hides its secrets..."*

—Peter Jennings, anchor
*ABC World News Tonight*
July 1995

*"The next thing he [comedian Jim Carrey] knew, he was broke and in a hell of a black hole."*

—Jeff Giles, reporter
*Newsweek*
June 1995

*"For years, North Korea was a black hole; we had no idea what was going on there. Now it's more of a  dark grey."*

—anonymous Senior Gov't official
quoted on *CNN*
December 1994

*"Philadelphia, the black hole of cyberspace"*

—Cover Story Headline
*The Welcomat*
November 1994

*"You do good work down here, notwithstanding the FYI black hole where staples and little boxes of grape juice disappear at twice the rate of my other shows."*

—Gary Marshall, as TV network executive on *Murphy Brown*
October 1994

*"...if the rest of Congress is swallowed up by the black hole of debate on Haiti."*

—George Will, columnist
Commenting on Congressional Gridlock
September 1994

*"You think there's some big black hole you're going to fall into and that all of a sudden people who have loved you all your life aren't going to love you anymore."*

—Melissa Etheridge, musician
interview response to her greatest fear
about coming out
*Advocate*
July 1994

# ABOUT THE AUTHOR

A lex Miller is a professional writer and astrologer, past president of Philadelphia Astrological Society and editor of "The Galactic Calendar." His pioneering work with Black Holes in astrological interpretation began in 1991, when his progressed Sun unwittingly fell into one. A frequent contributor to *Daykeeper Journal*, The *Mountain Astrologer*, and *Planet Waves*, Alex's work focuses on deep space points and minor bodies of our solar system.

Curious about other Crossroad Press books?
Stop by our site:
http://store.crossroadpress.com
We offer quality writing
in digital, audio, and print formats.

Enter the code FIRSTBOOK
to get 20% off your first order from our store!
Stop by today!

Made in the USA
Las Vegas, NV
19 September 2023

77838709R00155